Stories in Perspective

HAYDEN SERIES IN LITERATURE

Robert W. Boynton, Consulting Editor

*Former Principal, Senior High School
and Chairman, English Department
Germantown Friends School*

Stories in Perspective

ERIC W. JOHNSON

Germantown Friends School

HAYDEN BOOK COMPANY, INC.

Rochelle Park, New Jersey

Library of Congress Catalog Card Number 76-188519

          3   4   5   6   7   8   9   PRINTING
——
                   76 77 78   YEAR

To Students and Teachers

Among the stories in this book, you'll meet a trapeze artist with a truly unique talent, a young woman who cannot escape her past, and a sniper who makes a horrifying discovery. You'll also follow a famous detective puzzling through a bizarre crime, relive a young boy's first meeting with death, share an old couple's numbness of despair, and watch a skilled hunter tracking a most unusual prey. There's plenty here for everyone.

All of the stories included here should give pleasure, but tastes differ. Some of the stories that grabbed me may not grab you. My one guarantee is that they are all stories that many students and many adults have liked and remembered.

I don't want to go into any great detail about the form of the short story, but a few things should be said. Basically, a story centers on what happens to a person (occasionally more than one person) who faces a problem. In a good story the people seem real and the problems they face seem real—*real*, that is, in some way, even though what happens may be quite fantastic.

A story also has a point to it. Somehow the person "solves" his problem. I put *solves* in quotation marks because sometimes the point of the story is that the main character can't solve his problem and that he learns something about himself or about other people through that experience.

A story does not always have a happy ending, but a good story does have an ending, a "solving," a *resolution*. At the beginning our curiosity about human behavior is aroused, and then that curiosity is satisfied in some way.

As you read a story, it's most important to know *who* is telling it —through whose eyes and ears and understanding are the events being revealed? Different people see and understand things differently in the real world, as we all know, and the same applies to the story world. Is the main character telling his own story? Or is a minor character telling it as an onlooker? Is the author speaking through one of the characters or through several of them? Or is he reporting what only a total outsider could possibly know? It makes a difference.

Since a good story is an *interpretation* of what happens to people, not just a catalogue of events, it is obviously carefully put together. No reader gets everything out of a good story on one reading. As with all art, the short story writer asks his reader to put some of the effort into reading the story that went into writing it.

At the beginning of each story I've written a brief lead-in. Sometimes this explains something that will help you understand the story. Sometimes it simply sets the stage and suggests what the players are up to. The lead-in usually ends with a question for you to keep in mind while reading.

After each story there are a few *Questions for Discussion and Writing*. They can be used as a basis for class or small group discussion. Sometimes you may want to respond to one or two of them in writing. Some of the questions will simply help you understand better what happens in the story. Others will help you dig more meaning out of the story and thus enjoy it more. To many of the questions there is no "right" answer. You and your classmates and your teacher may disagree about what the story means, about whether it is "true" in any sense or whether it seems fake, and about what the author is trying to say about life. Through the give-and-take of classroom discussion you will come to see truth and interest in the story that you didn't see when you first read it.

Most good stories come in some way out of the experiences of the writer, even though they probably never "really" happened to him. For example, Evan Hunter, the author of "The Fallen Angel," the first story in the book, must have been to circuses and felt that some people in circus audiences secretly hope that a trapeze artist will fall. He builds this idea into a story about a man who has learned to do something to capitalize on this unpleasant expectation.

After the *Questions*, I have suggested some experiences of your own or ideas that you might like to write about or discuss. Certainly no one will want to deal with them all, and occasionally not with any. These further suggestions usually ask you to go from the story into your own experience, or they propose an idea to be considered in relation to the story. It would be good if members of the class— the teacher too—wrote enough stories, or bits of stories and experiences, to put together into a class collection which might be mimeographed and shared with friends, parents, and others in the school or community.

The stories have been arranged in groupings, because it's often helpful to see one story in relation to another—for contrast, for comparison. Of course, they don't have to be read that way, and there's nothing logical about going methodically from front to back. This is a book full of good stories, no matter where you start or finish.

Contents

Four Stories, Four Problems

A circus manager interviews a unique trapeze artist.
A boy tries to be a man before he is ready.
An old couple struggle to save their crop.
A successful, but unhappy, diplomat possesses a magic charm.

THE FALLEN ANGEL

by Evan Hunter

Anthony Mullins is the overworked manager of a small circus. The last thing he needs is another trapeze artist. What is it about Sam Angeli that gets him a job?

He first came in one morning while I was making out the payroll for my small circus. We were pulling up stakes, ready to roll on to the next town, and I was bent over the books, writing down what I was paying everybody, and maybe that is why I did not hear the door open. When I looked up, this long, lanky fellow was standing there, and the door was shut tight behind him.

I looked at the door, and then I looked at him. He had a thin face with a narrow moustache, and black hair on his head that was sort of wild and sticking up in spots. He had brown eyes and a funny, twisted sort of mouth, with very white teeth which he was showing me at the moment.

"Mr. Mullins?" he asked.

"Yes," I said, because that is my name. Not Moon Mullins,[1] which a lot of fellows jokingly call me, but Anthony Mullins. And that is my real name, with no attempt to sound showman-like; a good name, you will admit. "I am busy."

"I won't take much time," he said very softly. He walked over to the desk with a smooth, sideward step, as if he were on greased ball bearings.

"No matter how much time you will take," I said, "I am still busy."

"My name is Sam Angeli," he said.

"Pleased to meet you, Mr. Angeli," I told him. "My name is Anthony Mullins, and I am sorry you must be running along so quickly, but . . ."

"I'm a trapeze artist," he said.

"We already have three trapeze artists," I informed him, "and they are all excellent performers and the budget does not call for . . ."

1. Moon Mullins: a comic strip character.

"They are not Sam Angeli," he said, smiling and touching his chest with his thumb.

"That is true," I answered. "They are, in alphabetical order: Sue Ellen Bradley, Edward the Great, and Arthur Farnings."

"But not Sam Angeli," he repeated softly.

"No," I said. "It would be difficult to call them all Sam Angeli since they are not even related, and even if they were related, it is unlikely they would all have the same name—even if they were triplets, which they are not."

"*I* am Sam Angeli," he repeated softly.

"So I have gathered. But I already have three. . . ."

"I'm better," he said flatly.

"I have never met a trapeze artist who was not better than any other trapeze artist in the world," I said.

"In my case it happens to be true," he said.

I nodded and said nothing. I chewed my cigar awhile and went back to my books, and when I looked up he was still standing there, smiling.

"Look, my friend," I said, "I am earnestly sorry there is no opening for you, but . . ."

"Why not watch me a little?"

"I am too busy."

"It'll take five minutes. Your big top is still standing. Just watch me up there for a few minutes, that's all."

"My friend, what would be the point? I already have. . ."

"You can take your books with you, Mr. Mullins; you won't be sorry."

I looked at him again, and he stared at me levelly, and he had a deep, almost blazing, way of staring that made me believe I would really not be sorry if I watched him perform. Besides, I could take the books with me.

"All right," I said, "but we're only wasting each other's time."

"I've got all the time in the world," he answered.

We went outside, and sure enough the big top was still standing, so I bawled out Warren for being so slow to get a show on the road, and then this Angeli and I went inside, and he looked up at the trapeze, and I very sarcastically said, "Is that high enough for you?"

He shrugged and looked up and said, "I've been higher, my friend. Much higher." He dropped his eyes to the ground then, and I saw that the net had already been taken up.

"This exhibition will have to be postponed," I informed him. "There is no net."

"I don't need a net," he answered.

"No?"

"No."

"Do you plan on breaking your neck under one of my tops?
I am warning you that my insurance doesn't cover. . . ."

"I won't break my neck," Angeli said. "Sit down."

I shrugged and sat down, thinking it was his neck and not
mine, and hoping Dr. Lipsky was not drunk as usual. I opened
the books on my lap and got to work, and he walked across
the tent and started climbing up the trapeze. I got involved with
the figures, and finally he yelled, "Okay, you ready?"

"I'm ready," I said.

I looked up to where he was sitting on one trapeze, holding
the bar of the other trapeze in his big hands.

"Here's the idea," he yelled down. He had to yell because
he was a good hundred feet in the air. "I'll set the second trapeze
swinging, and then I'll put the one I'm on in motion. Then I'll
jump from one trapeze to the other one. Understand?"

"I understand," I yelled back. I'm a quiet man by nature,
and I have never liked yelling. Besides, he was about to do a
very elementary trapeze routine, so there was nothing to get excited and yelling about.

He pushed out the second trapeze, and it swung away out
in a nice clean arc, and then it came back and he shoved it
out again, and it went out farther and higher this time. He set
his own trapeze in motion then, and both trapezes went swinging
up there, back and forth, back and forth, higher and higher.
He stood up on the bar and watched the second trapeze, timing
himself, and then he shouted down, "I'll do a somersault to make
it interesting."

"Go ahead," I said.

"Here I go," he said.

His trapeze came back and started forward, and the second
trapeze reached the end of its arc and started back, and I saw
him bend a little from the knees, calculating his timing, and
then he leaped off, and his head ducked under, and he went
into the somersault.

He did a nice clean roll, and then he stretched out his hands
for the bar of the second trapeze, but the bar was nowhere near
him. His fingers closed on air, and my eyes popped wide open
as he sailed past the trapeze and then started a nose dive for
the ground.

I jumped to my feet with my mouth open, remembering
there was no net under him and thinking of the mess he was

going to make all over my tent. I watched him falling like a stone, and then I closed my eyes as he came closer to the ground. I clenched my fists and waited for the crash, and then the crash came, and there was a deathly silence in the tent afterward. I sighed and opened my eyes.

Sam Angeli got up and casually brushed the sawdust from his clothes. "How'd you like it?" he asked.

I stood stiff as a board and stared at him.

"How'd you like it?" he repeated.

"Dr. Lipsky!" I shouted. "Doc, come quick!"

"No need for a doctor," Angeli said, smiling and walking over to me. "How'd you like the fall?"

"The . . . the fall?"

"The fall," Angeli said smiling. "Looked like the real McCoy, didn't it?"

"What do you mean?"

"Well, you don't think I missed that bar accidentally, do you? I mean, after all, that's a kid stunt."

"You fell on purpose?" I kept staring at him, but all his bones seemed to be in the right places, and there was no blood on him anywhere.

"Sure," he said. "My specialty. I figured it all out, Mr. Mullins. So you know why people like to watch trapeze acts? Not because there's any skill or art attached. Oh, no." He smiled, and his eyes glowed, and I watched him, still amazed. "They like to watch because they are inherently evil, Mr. Mullins. They watch because they think that fool up there is going to fall and break his neck, and they want to be around when he does it." Angeli nodded. "So I figured it all out."

"You did?"

"I did. I figured if the customers wanted to see me fall, then I would fall. So I practiced falling."

"You did?"

"I did. First I fell out of bed, and then I fell from a first-story window, and then I fell off the roof. And then I took my biggest fall, the fall that . . . But I'm boring you. The point is, I can fall from any place now. In fact, that trapeze of yours is rather low."

"Rather low," I repeated softly.

"Yes."

"What's up?" Dr. Lipsky shouted, rushing into the tent, his shirttails trailing. "What happened, Moon?"

"Nothing," I said, wagging my head. "Nothing, Doc."

"Then why'd you . . . ?"

"I wanted to tell you," I said slowly, "that I've just hired a new trapeze artist."

"Huh?" Dr. Lipsky said, drunk as usual.

QUESTIONS FOR DISCUSSION AND WRITING

1. The story is told from the point of view of Anthony Mullins, but it is mainly about "the fallen angel," Sam Angeli. Angeli is very self-confident. Which remark of his first shows us this? How are we made increasingly aware of how self-confident he is? How does he, step by step, break down Mullins's resistance to watching him perform?
2. Anthony Mullins is quietly humorous and not unkind. How does he show this in his conversation with Sam Angeli?
3. What are Angeli's problems with Anthony Mullins? What are Mullins's problems with Angeli? How does each deal with the other?
4. When Angeli starts to fall, Mullins tells us that he was "thinking of the mess he was going to make all over my tent." How do we know that he is not really as cold-blooded as all that?
5. After the fall, what is Sam Angeli's state of mind? How does it contrast with that of Mullins?
6. Why did Angeli choose falling as his specialty? What does he say about the motives of those who like to watch trapeze artists? Do you think he is right? Does it matter to the story?
7. The story is fiction. It never happened. Does it seem realistic? Do you think a man could really develop his ability so that he could safely "fall from any place"? Go back over the story, making note of all the clues to what sort of man Sam Angeli is. Taking what you find into consideration, how would you explain the title of the story?

SUGGESTIONS FOR FURTHER WRITING OR DISCUSSION

1. Do you know anyone, perhaps yourself, who has developed an unusual skill, probably less spectacular than Sam Angeli's? If so, describe the person, the skill, and how he developed it. If you prefer, work up a story about such a person. If you do the story, don't forget that to make a story you will need to tell it from someone's point of view, you will need

to develop a main character, you will need to present some problem that the character faces, and you will need to resolve the story in some way.

2. Describe some performance you saw that amazed you. It may be a performance in real life, on TV, at the movies, anywhere. Make it part of a story if you wish.

THE CHRISTMAS HUNT

by Borden Deal

*"I'm old enough to go on the Christmas hunt," Tom
said to his father, and his father laughed. Tom made
a terrible mistake in trying to prove his father wrong.
How did he and his father make something good come
out of it?*

It should have been the best Christmas of them all, that
year at Dog Run. It started out to be, anyway. I was so excited,
watching my father talking on the telephone, that I couldn't
stand still. For I was thirteen years old and I had never been
on a quail shoot in my whole life. I wanted to go on the big
Christmas Day hunt even more than I wanted that bicycle I was
supposed to get. And I really needed the bicycle to cover with
speed and ease the two miles I had to walk to school.

The Christmas Day hunt was always the biggest and best
of the season. It was almost like a field trial; only the best hunters and the finest dogs were invited by my father. All my life
I had been hearing great tales of past Christmas Day hunts. And
now I knew with a great thirteen-year-old certainty that I was
old enough to go. My father hung up the phone and turned
around, grinning. "That was Walter," he said. "There'll be ten
of them this year. And Walter is bringing his new dog. If all
he claims for that dog is true—"

"Papa," I said.

"Goodness," my mother said. "That'll be a houseful to feed."

My father put his arm around her shoulders, hugging her.
"Oh, you know you like it," he said. "They come as much for
your cooking as they do for the hunting, I think."

My mother pursed her lips in the way she had, and then
smiled. "Wild turkey," she said. "You think you could shoot me
four or five nice fat wild turkeys?"

I wanted to jump up and down to attract attention. But
that was kid stuff, all right for the five-year-olds, though I had
to admit it was effective. But I was thirteen.

So I said, "Papa."

My father laughed. "I think I can," he said. "I'll put in a couple of mornings trying."

"Papa," I said desperately.

"Wild turkey stuffed with wild rice," my mother said quickly, thoughtfully, in her planning voice. "Giblet gravy, mashed potatoes, maybe a nice potato salad."

"If I don't fail on the turkeys," my father said.

"Papa!" I said.

My father turned to me. "Come on, Tom," he said. "We got to feed those dogs."

That's the way parents are, even when you're thirteen years old. They can talk right on and never hear a word you say. I ran after my father as he left the kitchen, hoping for a chance to get my words in edgewise. But my father was walking fast, and already the clamor of the bird dogs was rising up to cover any speech I might want to make.

The dogs were standing on the wire fence in long dappled rows, their voices lifted in greeting. Even in my great need I had to stop and admire them. There's nothing prettier in the whole world than a good bird dog. There's a nobleness to its head, an intelligence in its eyes that no other animal has. Just looking at them sent a shiver down my backbone, and the thought of shooting birds over them—well, the shiver wasn't just in my backbone now, I was shaking all over.

All of the dogs except one were in the same big run. But my father kept Calypso Baby in her own regal pen. I went to her and looked into her soft brown eyes. She stood up tall on the fence, her strong, lithe body stretched to its full height, as tall as I was.

"Hello, Baby," I whispered, and she wagged her tail. "You gonna find me some birds this Christmas, Baby? You gonna hunt for me like you do for Papa?"

She lolled her tongue, laughing at me. We were old friends. Calypso Baby was the finest bird dog in that part of the country. My father owned a number of dogs and kept and trained others for his town friends. But Calypso Baby was his personal dog, the one that he took to the field trials, the one he shot over in the big Christmas Day hunt held at Dog Run.

My father was bringing the sack of feed from the shed. I put out my hand, holding it against the wire so Calypso Baby could lick my fingers.

"This year," I whispered to her. "This year I'm going." I

left Calypso Baby, went with determination toward my father.

"Papa," I said, in a voice not to be denied this time.

My father was busy opening the sack of dog food.

"Papa," I said firmly. "I want to talk to you."

It was the tone and the words my father used often toward me, so much so that my father looked down at me in surprise, at last giving me his attention.

"What is it?" he said. "What do you want?"

"Papa, I'm thirteen years old," I said.

My father laughed. "Well, what of it?" he said. "Next year you'll be fourteen. And the next year fifteen."

"I'm old enough to go on the Christmas hunt," I said.

My father laughed. "At thirteen?" he said. "I'm afraid not."

I stood, stricken. "But—" I said.

"No," my father said, in the voice that meant No, and no more talking about it. He hoisted the sack of feed and took it into the wire dogpen, the bird dogs crowding around him rearing up on him in their eagerness.

"Well, come on and help me," my father said impatiently. "I've got a lot of things to do."

Usually I enjoyed the daily feeding of the dogs. But not to-day; I went through the motions dumbly, silently, not paying any attention to the fine bird dogs crowding around me. I cleaned the watering troughs with my usual care, but my heart was not in it.

After the feeding was over, I scuffed stubbornly about my other tasks and then went up to my room, not even coming down when my father came home at dusk excited with the two wild turkeys he had shot. I could hear him talking to my mother in the kitchen, and the ring of their voices had already the feel of Christmas, a hunting cheer that made them brighter, livelier than usual. But none of the cheer and the pleasure came into me, even though Christmas was almost upon us and yesterday had been the last day of school.

That night I hunted. In my dreams I was out ahead of all the other men and dogs, Calypso Baby quartering the field in her busy way, doing it so beautifully I ached inside to watch her. All the men and dogs stopped their own hunting to watch us, as though it were a field trial. When Calypso Baby pointed, I raised the twelve-gauge shotgun, moved in on her on the ready, and Calypso Baby flushed the birds in her fine, steady way. They came up in an explosive whir, and I had the gun to my shoulder, squeezing off the shot just the way I'd been told to do. Three quail dropped like stones out of the covey and I swung the gun, following a single. I brought down the single with the second barrel, and Calypso Baby was already bringing the first bird to me in her soft, unbruising mouth. I knelt to pat her for a moment, and Baby whipped her tail to tell me how fine a shot I was, how much she liked my being the one shooting over her today.

Soon there was another covey, and I did even better on this one, and then another and another, and nobody was hunting at all, not even my father, who was laughing and grinning at the other men, knowing this was his boy, Tom, and his dog, Calypso Baby, and just full of pride with it all. When it was over, the men crowded around and patted me on the shoulder, hefting the full game bag in admiration, and then there was my father's face close before me, saying, "I was wrong, son, when I said a thirteen-year-old boy isn't old enough to go bird hunting with the best of us."

Then I was awake and my father, dressed in his hunting clothes, was shaking me, and it was morning. I looked up dazedly into his face, unable to shake off the dream, and I knew what it was I had to do. I had to show my father. Only then would he believe.

"Are you awake?" my father said. "You'll have to change the water for the dogs. I'm going to see if I can get some more turkeys this morning."

"All right," I said. "I'm awake now."

My father left. I got up and ate breakfast in the kitchen, close to the warm stove. I didn't say anything to my mother about my plans. I went out and watered the dogs as soon as the sun was up, but I didn't take the time, as I usually did, to play with them.

"Me and you are going hunting," I told Calypso Baby as I changed her water. She jumped and quivered all over, knowing the word as well as I did.

I went back into the house, listening for my mother. She was upstairs, making the beds. I went into the spare room where my father kept all the hunting gear. I was trembling, remembering the dream, as I went to the gun rack and touched the cold steel of the double-barreled twelve-gauge. But I knew it would be very heavy for me. I took the single-barreled gun instead, though I knew that pretty near ruined my chances for a second shot unless I could reload very quickly.

I picked up a full shell bag and hung it under my left arm. I found a game bag and hung it under my right arm. The strap was too long and the bag dangled emptily to my knees, banging against me as I walked. I tied a knot in the strap so the bag would rest comfortably on my right hip. The gun was heavy in my hands as I walked into the hallway, listening for my mother. She was still upstairs.

"Mamma, I'm gone," I shouted up to her. "I'll be back in a little while." That was so she wouldn't be looking for me.

"All right," she called. "Don't wander far off. Your father will be back in an hour or two and might have something for you to do."

I hurried out of the house, straight to Calypso Baby's pen. I did not look up, afraid that my mother might be watching out of the window. That was a danger I could do nothing about, so I just ignored it. I opened the gate to Baby's pen and she came out, circling and cavorting.

"Come on, Baby," I whispered. "Find me some birds now. Find me a whole lot of birds."

We started off, circling the barn so we would not be seen from the house, and going straight away in its shadow as far as we could. Beyond the pasture we crossed a cornfield, Calypso Baby arrowing straight for the patch of sedgegrass beyond. Her tail was whiplike in its thrash, her head high as she plunged toward her work, and I had to hurry to keep up. The gun was clumsy in my hands and the two bags banged against my hips. But I remembered not to run with the gun, remembered to keep the breech open until I was ready to shoot. I knew all about hunting: I just hadn't had a chance to practice what I knew. When I came home with a bag full of fine birds my father would have to admit that I knew how to hunt, that I was old enough for the big Christmas Day hunt when all the great hunters came out from town for the biggest day of the season.

When I ducked through the barbed-wire fence Calypso Baby was waiting for me, standing a few steps into the sedgegrass, her head up watching me alertly. Her whole body quivered with her eagerness to be off. I swept my arm in the gesture I had seen my father use so many times, and Calypso Baby plunged instantly into the grass. She was a fast worker, quartering back and forth with an economical use of her energy. She could cover a field in half the time it took any other dog. The first field was empty, and we passed on to the second one. Somehow Calypso Baby knew that birds were here. She steadied down, hunting slowly, more thoroughly.

Then, startling me though I had been expecting it, she froze into a point, one foot up, her tail straight back, her head flat with the line of her backbone. I froze too. I couldn't move. I couldn't even remember to breech the gun and raise it to my shoulder. I stood as still as the dog, all of my knowledge flown out of my head, and yet far back under the panic I knew that the birds weren't going to hold, they were going to rise in just a moment. Calypso Baby, surprised at my inaction, broke her point to look at me in inquiry. Her head turned toward me and she asked the question as plain as my father's voice: *Well, what are you going to do about these fine birds I found for you?*

I could move then. I took a step or two, fumblingly breeched the gun, raised it to my shoulder. The birds rose of their own accord in a sudden wild drum of sound. I yanked at the trigger, unconsciously bracing myself against the blast and the recoil. Nothing happened. Nothing at all happened. I tugged at the trigger wildly, furiously, but it was too late and the birds were gone.

I lowered the gun, looking down at it in bewilderment. I had forgotten to release the safety. I wanted to cry at my own stupidity. This was not at all like my dream of last night, when I and the dog and the birds had all been so perfect.

Calypso Baby walked back to me and looked up into my face. I could read the puzzled contempt in her eyes. She lay down at my feet, putting her muzzle on her paws. I looked down at her, ashamed of myself and knowing that she was ashamed. She demanded perfection, just as my father did.

"It was my fault, Baby," I told her. I leaned over and patted her on the head. "You didn't do anything wrong. It was me."

I started off then, looking back at the bird dog. She did not follow me. "Come on," I told her. "Hunt."

She got up slowly and went out ahead of me again. But she worked in a puzzled manner, checking back to me frequently. She no longer had the joy, the confidence, with which she had started out.

"Come on, Baby," I coaxed her. "Hunt, Baby. Hunt."

We crossed into another field, low grass this time, and when we found the covey there was very little time for setting myself. Calypso Baby pointed suddenly; I jerked the gun to my shoulder, remembering the safety this time, and then Calypso Baby flushed the birds. They rose up before me and I pulled the trigger, hearing the blast of the gun, feeling the shock of it into my shoulder knocking me back a step.

But not even one bird dropped like a fateful stone out of the covey. The covey had gone off low and hard on an angle to the left, and I had completely missed the shot, aiming straight ahead instead of swinging with the birds. Calypso Baby did not even attempt to point singles. She dropped her head and her tail and started away from me, going back toward the house.

I ran after her, calling her. Baby would never like me again. She would hold me in the indifference she felt toward any person who was not a bird hunter. She would tolerate me as she tolerated my mother, and the men who came out with shiny new hunting clothes and walked all over the land talking about how the dogs didn't hold the birds properly so you could get a decent shot.

I couldn't be one of those! I ran after the dog, calling her, until at last she allowed me to come near. I knelt, fondling her head, talking to her, begging her for another chance.

"I'll get some birds next time," I told her. "You just watch. You hear?"

At last, reluctantly, she consented to hunt again. I followed her, my hands gripping the heavy gun, determined this time. I knew it was my last chance; she would not give me another. I could not miss this time.

We hunted for an hour before we found another covey of birds. I was tired; the gun was heavier with every step. But, holding only last night's dream in my mind, I refused to quit. At last Calypso Baby froze into a beautiful point. I could feel myself sweating, my teeth gritted hard. I had to bring down a bird this time.

It seemed to be perfect. I had plenty of time but I hurried anyway, just to be sure. Then the birds were rising in a tight cluster and I was pulling the trigger before I had the heavy gun lined up—and in the midst of the thundering blast I heard Calypso Baby yell with pain as the random shot tore into her hip.

I threw down the gun and ran toward her, seeing the blood streaking down her leg as she staggered away from me, whimpering. I knelt, trying to coax her to me, but she was afraid. I was crying, feeling the full weight of the disaster. I had committed the worst crime of any bird hunter; I had shot my own dog.

Calypso Baby was trying to hide in a clump of bushes. She snapped at me in her fear when I reached in after her, but I did not feel the pain in my hand. I knelt over her, looking at

the shredded hip. It was a terrible wound. I could see only blood
and raw flesh. I snatched off the empty hunting bag I had put
on so optimistically, the shell bag, and took off my coat. I
wrapped her in the coat and picked her up in my arms. She
was very heavy, hurting, whining with each jolting step as I
ran toward the house.

I came into the yard doubled over with the catch in my
side from the running, and my legs were trembling. My father
was sitting on the back porch with three wild turkeys beside him.
cleaning his gun. He jumped to his feet when he saw the
wounded dog.

"What happened?" he said. "Did some fool hunter shoot
her?"

I stopped, standing before my father and holding the
wounded dog; I looked into his angry face. They were the most
terrible words I ever had to say. "I shot her, Papa," I said.

My father stood very still. I did not know what would happen. I had never done anything so bad in my whole life and
I could not even guess how my father would react. The only
thing right would be to wipe me off the face of the earth with
one angry gesture of his hand.

I gulped, trying to move the pain in my throat out of the
way of the words. "I took her out bird hunting," I said. "I wanted
to show you—if I got a full bag of birds, I thought you'd let
me go on the Christmas Day hunt—"

"I'll talk to you later," my father said grimly, taking the dog
from me and starting into the kitchen. "I've got to try to save
this dog's life now."

I started into the kitchen behind my father. He turned.
"Where's the gun you shot her with?" he said.

"I—left it."

"Don't leave it lying out there in the field," my father said
in a stern voice.

I wanted very badly to go into the kitchen, find out that
Calypso Baby would live. But I turned, instead, and went back
the way I had come, walking with my head down, feeling shrunken
inside myself. I had overreached; I had risen up today full of
pride beyond my ability, and in the stubbornness of the pride
I had been blind until the terrible accident had opened my eyes
so that I could see myself clearly—too clearly. I found the gun,
the two bags, where I had dropped them. I picked them up without looking at the smear of blood where Calypso had lain. I went
back to the house slowly, not wanting to face it, reluctant to
see the damage I had wrought.

When I came into the kitchen, my father had the dog stretched out on the kitchen table. My mother stood by his side with bandages and ointment in her hands. The wound was cleaned of the bird shot and dirt and blood. Calypso Baby whined when she saw me and I felt my heart cringe with the rejection.

My father looked at me across the dog. The anger was gone out of him, his voice was slow and searching and not to be denied.

"Now I want to know why you took my gun and my dog without permission," he said.

"David," my mother said to him.

My father ignored her, kept his eyes hard on my face. I knew it wouldn't do any good to look toward my mother. This was between me and my father, and there was no refuge for me anywhere in the world. I didn't want a refuge; I knew I had to face not only my father, but myself.

"I—I wanted to go on the Christmas Day hunt," I said again. "I thought if I . . ." I stopped. It was all that I had to say; it seemed pretty flimsy to me now.

My father looked down at the dog. I was surprised at the lack of anger in him. I could read only sadness in his voice. "She may be ruined for hunting," he said. "Even if the wound heals good, if she doesn't lose the use of her leg, she may be gun-shy for the rest of her life. At best, I'll never be able to show her in field trials again. You understand what you've done?"

"Yes, sir," I said. I wanted to cry. But that would not help, any more than anger from my father would help.

"You see now why I said you weren't old enough?" my father said. "You've got to be trained for hunting, just as a dog is trained. Suppose other men had been out there, suppose you had shot a human being?"

"David!" my mother said.

My father turned angrily toward her. "He's got to learn!" he said. "There are too many people in this world trying to do things without learning how to do them first. I don't want my boy to be one of them."

"Papa," I said. "I'm—I'm sorry. I wouldn't have hurt Calypso Baby for anything in the world."

"I'm not going to punish you," my father said. He looked down at the dog. "This is too bad for a whipping to settle. But I want you to think about today. I don't want you to put it out of your mind. You knew that when the time came ripe for it, I intended to teach you, take you out like I'd take a puppy, and hunt with you. After a while, you could hunt by yourself. Then

if you were good enough—and *only* if you were good enough—
you could go on the Christmas Day hunt. The Christmas Day
hunt is the place you come to, not the place you start out from.
Do you understand?"

"Yes, sir," I said. I would have been glad to settle for a
whipping.

"You've got to take special care of Calypso Baby," my father
said. "Maybe if you take care of her yourself while she's hurt,
she'll decide to be your friend again."

I looked at the dog and I could feel the need of her confidence and trust. "Yes, sir," I said. Then I said humbly. "I hope
she will be friends with me again."

I went toward the hall, needing to be alone in my room.
I stopped at the kitchen doorway, looked back at my father and
mother watching me. I had to say it in a hurry if I was going
to say it at all.

"Papa," I said, the words rushing softly in my throat, threat-
ening to gag there before I could get them out. "I—I don't think
I deserve that bicycle this Christmas. I don't deserve it at all."

My father nodded his head. "All right, son," he said gravely.
"This is your own punishment for yourself."

"Yes," I said, forcing the word, the loss making me empty
inside and yet feeling better too. I turned and ran out of the
room and up the stairs.

Christmas came, but without any help from me at all. I
went to bed on Christmas Eve heavy with the knowledge that
tomorrow morning there would be no shiny new bicycle under
the tree, there would be no Christmas Day hunt for me. I couldn't
prevent myself from waking up at the usual excited time, but
I made myself turn over and go back to sleep. When I did, reluctantly, go downstairs, the Christmas tree did not excite me, nor
the usual gifts I received every year: the heavy sweater, the
gloves, the scarf, the two new pairs of blue jeans. I just wouldn't
let myself think about the bicycle.

After my father had gone outside, my mother hugged me
to her in a sudden rush of affection. "He would have given you
the bicycle anyway," she said. "If you hadn't told him you didn't
want it."

I looked up at her. "I didn't deserve it," I said. "Maybe next
year I will."

She surprised me then by holding me and crying. I heard
the first car arrive outside, the voices of the men excited with
the promise of hunting. My mother stood up and said briskly,
"Well, this is not getting that big dinner cooked," and went into

the kitchen without looking back.

I went out on the front porch. It was perfect quail-hunting weather, cold but not too cold, with a smoky haze lying over the earth. The dogs knew that today was for hunting; I could hear them from around behind the house, standing on the wire fence in broad-shouldered rows, their voices yelping and calling. All except Calypso Baby. All except me.

I stood aside, watching the men arrive in their cars, my father greeting them. Their breaths hung cloudy in the air and they moved with a sharp movement to their bodies. These were the best hunters in the whole countryside, and today would be a great comradeship and competition. Any man invited on this hunt could be proud of the invitation alone.

I felt almost remote as I watched, as I went with them around the side of the house to the dogs. They all went to examine Calypso Baby, and I felt a freezing inside; but my father only said, "She got shot by accident," and did not tell the whole terrible story.

Then my father looked at his watch and said, "Let's wait a few more minutes. Walter ought to be here soon. Hate to start without him."

One of the men called, "Here he comes now," and Walter drove up in his battered car.

"Come here, son," my father said, speaking to me for the first time this morning, and I went reluctantly to his side. I was afraid it was coming now, the whole story, and all the men would look at me in the same way that Calypso Baby had after I had shot her.

My father drew me to the side of Walter's car, reached in, and brought out a basket. "You wanted a bicycle," he said. "Then you decided yourself you should wait. Because you made the decision yourself, I decided you were old enough for this."

I looked at the bird-dog puppy in the basket. All of a sudden Christmas burst inside me like a skyrocket, out of the place where I had kept it suppressed all this time.

"Papa," I said. "Papa—"

"Take him," my father said.

I reached into the basket and took out the puppy. The puppy licked my chin with his harsh warm tongue. He was long, gangly—his feet and head too big for his body—but absolutely beautiful.

My father knelt beside me, one hand on the puppy. "I told Walter to bring me the finest bird-dog puppy he could find," he said. "He's kin to Calypso Baby; he's got good blood."

"Thank you, Papa," I said in a choking voice. "I—I'd rather have him than the bicycle. I'll name him Calypso Boy. I'll—"

"When this puppy is ready for birds, we'll train him," my father said. "While we train the puppy, we'll train you too. When the time comes, you can both go on the Christmas Day hunt—if you're good enough."

"We'll be good enough," I said. "*Both* of us will be good enough."

"I hope so," my father said. He stood up and looked at the men standing around us, all of them smiling down at me and Calypso Boy.

"Let's go," he said. "Those birds are going to get tired of waiting on us."

They laughed and hollered, and the dogs moiled and sounded in the excitement as they were let out of the pen. They fanned out across the pasture, each man or two men taking a dog. I stood watching, holding the puppy warm in my arms. I looked at Calypso Baby, standing crippled in her pen looking longingly after the hunters. I went over and spoke to her. She whined; then for the first time since the accident she wagged her tail at me.

I looked down at the puppy in my arms. "We'll be going," I told him, as he licked at my chin. "One of these days when you're a dog and I'm a man, we'll be right out there with the best of them."

It was three years more before I went on my first Christmas hunt. Papa had been right, of course. In the time between, I had learned a great deal myself while training Calypso Boy to hunt. With the good blood in him he turned out to be a great bird dog—second only, I guess, to Calypso Baby, who recovered well from her wound and was Papa's dog the day Calypso Boy and I made our first Christmas Day hunt.

But of all the Christmases, before and since, I guess I remember best the one when Calypso Baby was hurt—and Calypso Boy first came to me.

QUESTIONS FOR DISCUSSION AND WRITING

1. How do you know that Tom is telling the story years after the events happened? What does he mean when he says, on page 8, "I knew with a great thirteen-year-old certainty

that I was old enough to go"? How is the certainty of a
   thirteen-year-old different from that of an adult?
2. In the first section of the story, before the dream, how does
   Tom's father treat him? How does the father's conversation
   with his wife and with Tom reveal this? How does Tom react
   to his father's laughter as he says, "I'm afraid not"?
3. Why do you think Borden Deal tells us about Tom's dream?
4. As Tom tells about his effort at hunting with Calypso Baby,
   he says, "She demanded perfection just as my father did"
   and, later, after he missed the birds, "She would never like
   me again . . . She would tolerate me as she tolerated my
   mother." What do these comments show about Tom's relationship with his father? with his mother?
5. Think about how Tom's father dealt with him at different
   points in the story. Do you think he handled him well? Give
   examples to explain your opinion. Did he make any mistakes? Suppose that, after the hunting disaster, the father
   had turned the job of dealing with Tom over to the mother.
   Might the results have been different? Explain.
6. After Tom's father sternly orders him to go and get the gun
   he left in the field, Tom tells us: "I had been blind until
   the terrible accident had opened my eyes so that I could see
   myself clearly—too clearly." What did he see? How is this
   the beginning of the resolution of the story?
7. Why does Tom's father think it is right to give him the
   puppy? Tom thinks that Calypso Boy is a better present than
   the bicycle would have been? Why?

SUGGESTIONS FOR FURTHER WRITING OR DISCUSSION

1. Tell about some privilege you had to earn and how you
   earned it, or that you tried to take before you were really
   prepared for it.
2. Tell about a terrible mistake you or someone else made and
   the results that came from it.
3. Describe a situation in which your father and your mother
   treated you differently. Show us what it was like by using
   their real words and actions, and yours.
4. Use any of the three suggestions above as the basis for a
   story.

THE WHISTLE

by Eudora Welty

Jason and Sara Morton, old too early, lie in bed trembling in the cold night, when a whistle blows. What did the whistle mean for them?

Night fell. The darkness was thin, like some sleazy[1] dress that has been worn and worn for many winters and always lets the cold through to the bones. Then the moon rose. A farm lay quite visible, like a white stone in water, among the stretches of deep woods in their colorless dead leaf. By a closer and more searching eye than the moon's, everything belonging to the Morton's might have been seen—even to the tiny tomato plants in their neat rows closest to the house, gray and feather-like, appalling in their exposed fragility. The moonlight covered everything, and lay upon the darkest shape of all, the farmhouse where the lamp had just been blown out.

Inside, Jason and Sara Morton were lying between the quilts of a pallet which had been made up close to the fireplace. A fire still fluttered in the grate, making a drowsy sound now and then, and its exhausted light beat up and down the wall, across the rafters, and over the dark pallet where the old people lay, like a bird trying to find its way out of the room.

The long-spaced, tired breathing of Jason was the only noise besides the flutter of the fire. He lay under the quilt in a long shape like a bean, turned on his side to face the door. His lips opened in the dark, and in and out he breathed, in and out, slowly and with a rise and fall, over and over, like a conversation or a tale—a question and a sigh.

Sara lay on her back with her mouth agape, silent, but not asleep. She was staring at the dark and indistinguishable places among the rafters. Her eyes seemed opened too wide, the lids strained and limp, like openings which have been stretched shapeless and made of no more use. Once a hissing yellow flame stood erect in the old log, and her small face and pale hair, and one hand holding to the edge of the cover, were illuminated for

1. sleazy: thin and easily torn.

a moment, with shadows bright blue. Then she pulled the quilt clear over her head.

Every night they lay trembling with cold, but no more communicative in their misery than a pair of window shutters beaten by a storm. Sometimes many days, weeks went by without words. They were not really old—they were only fifty; still, their lives were filled with tiredness, with a great lack of necessity to speak, with poverty which may have bound them like a disaster too great for any discussion but left them still separate and undesirous of sympathy. Perhaps, years ago, the long habit of silence may have been started in anger or passion. Who could tell now?

As the fire grew lower and lower, Jason's breathing grew heavy and solemn, and he was even beyond dreams. Completely hidden, Sara's body was as weightless as a strip of cane, there was hardly a shape to the quilt under which she was lying. Sometimes it seemed to Sara herself that it was her lack of weight which kept her from ever getting warm.

She was so tired of the cold! That was all it could do any more—make her tired. Year after year, she felt sure that she would die before the cold was over. Now, according to the Almanac, it was spring . . . . But year after year it was always the same. The plants would be set out in their frames, transplanted always too soon, and there was a freeze. . . . When was the last time they had grown tall and full, that the cold had held off and there was a crop?

Like a vain dream, Sara began to have thoughts of the spring and summer. At first she thought only simply, of the colors of green and red, the smell of the sun on the ground, the touch of leaves and of warm ripening tomatoes. Then, all hidden as she was under the quilt, she began to imagine and remember the town of Dexter in the shipping season. There in her mind, dusty little Dexter became a theater for almost legendary festivity, a place of pleasure. On every road leading in, smiling farmers were bringing in wagonloads of the most beautiful tomatoes. The packing sheds at Dexter Station were all decorated—no, it was simply that the May sun was shining. Mr. Perkins, the tall, gesturing figure, stood in the very center of everything, buying, directing, waving yellow papers that must be telegrams, shouting with grand impatience. And it was he, after all, that owned their farm now. Train after train of empty freight cars stretched away, waiting and then being filled. Was it possible to have saved out of the threat of the cold so many tomatoes in the world? Of course, for here marched in a perfect parade of Florida packers, all the way from Florida, tanned, stockingless, some of them tattooed. The music box was playing in the cafe across the way, and the crippled man that walked like a duck was back taking poses for a dime of the young people with their heads together. With shouts of triumph the men were getting drunk, and now and then a pistol went off somewhere. In the shade the children celebrated in tomato fights. A strong, heady, sweet smell hung over everything. Such excitement! Let the packers rest, if only for a moment, thought Sara. Stretch them out, stained with sweat, under the shade tree, and one can play the guitar. The girl wrappers listen while they work. What small brown hands, red with juice! Their faces are forever sleepy and flushed; when the men speak to them they laugh. . . . And Jason and Sara themselves are standing there, standing under the burning sun near the first shed, giving over their own load, watching their own tomatoes shoved into the process, swallowed away—sorted, wrapped, loaded, dispatched in a freight car—all so fast. . . . Mr. Perkins holds out his hard, quick hand. Shake it fast! How quickly it is all over!

Sara, weightless under the quilt, could think of the celebrations of Dexter and see the vision of ripe tomatoes only in brief snatches, like the flare-up of the little fire. The rest of the time she thought only of cold, of cold going on before and after. She could not help but feel the chill of the here and now, which was not to think at all, but was for her only a trembling in the dark.

She coughed patiently and turned her head to one side. She peered over the quilt just a little and saw that the fire had at last gone out. There was left only a hulk of red log, a still, red, bent shape, like one of Jason's socks thrown down to be darned somehow. With only this to comfort her, Sara closed her eyes and fell asleep.

The husband and wife now lay perfectly still in the dark room, with Jason's hoarse, slow breathing, like the commotion of some clumsy nodding old bear trying to climb a tree, heard by nobody at all.

Every hour it was getting colder and colder. The moon, intense and white as the snow that does not fall here, drew higher in the sky, in the long night, and more distant from the earth. The farm looked as tiny and still as a seashell, with the little knob of a house surrounded by its curved furrows of tomato plants. Cold like a white pressing hand reached down and lay over the shell.

In Dexter there is a great whistle which is blown when a freeze threatens. It is known everywhere as Mr. Perkins' whistle. Now it sounded out in the clear night, blast after blast. Over the countryside lights appeared in the windows of the farms. Men and women ran out into the fields and covered up their plants with whatever they had, while Mr. Perkins' whistle blew and blew.

Jason Morton was not waked up by the great whistle. On he slept, his cavernous breathing like roars coming from a hollow tree. His right hand had been thrown out, from some deepness he must have dreamed, and lay stretched on the cold floor in the very center of a patch of moonlight which had moved across the room.

Sara felt herself waking. She knew that Mr. Perkins' whistle was blowing, what it meant—and that it now remained for her to get Jason and go out to the field. A soft laxity, an illusion of warmth, flowed stubbornly down her body, and for a few moments she continued to lie still.

Then she was sitting up and seizing her husband by the shoulders, without saying a word, rocking him back and forth. It took all her strength to wake him. He coughed, his roaring was over, and he sat up. He said nothing either, and they both sat with bent heads and listened for the whistle. After a silence it blew again, a long, rising blast.

Promptly Sara and Jason got out of bed. They were both fully dressed, because of the cold, and only needed to put on their shoes. Jason lighted the lantern, and Sara gathered the bed-clothes over her arm and followed him out.

Everything was white, and everything looked vast and extensive to them as they walked over the frozen field. White in a shadowed pit, abandoned from summer to summer, the old sorghum mill stood like the machine of a dream, with its long prostrate pole, its blunted axis.

Stooping over the little plants, Jason and Sara touched them and touched the earth. For their own knowledge, by their hands, they found everything to be true—the cold, the rightness of the warning, the need to act. Over the sticks set in among the plants they laid the quilts one by one, spreading them with a slow ingenuity. Jason took off his coat and laid it over the small tender plants by the side of the house. Then he glanced at Sara, and she reached down and pulled her dress off over her head. Her hair fell down out of its pins, and she began at once to tremble violently. The skirt was luckily long and full, and all the rest of the plants were covered by it.

Then Sara and Jason stood for a moment and stared almost idly at the field and up at the sky.

There was no wind. There was only the intense whiteness of moonlight. Why did this calm cold sink into them like the teeth of a trap? They bent their shoulders and walked silently back into the house.

The room was not much warmer. They had forgotten to shut the door behind them when the whistle was blowing so hard. They sat down to wait for morning.

Then Jason did a rare, strange thing. There long before morning he poured kerosene over some kindling and struck a light to it. Squatting, they got near it, quite gradually they drew together, and sat motionless until it all burned down. Still Sara did not move. Then Jason, in his underwear and long blue trousers, went out and brought in another load, and the big cherry log which of course was meant to be saved for the very last of winter.

The extravagant warmth of the room had sent some kind of agitation over Sara, like her memories of Dexter in the shipping season. She sat huddled in a long brown cotton petticoat, holding onto the string which went around the waist. Her mouse-colored hair, paler at the temples, was hanging loose down to her shoulders, like a child's unbound for a party. She held her knees against her numb, pendulant breasts and stared into the fire, her eyes widening.

On his side of the hearth Jason watched the fire burn too. His breath came gently, quickly, noiselessly, as though for a little time he would conceal or defend his tiredness. He lifted his arms and held out his misshapen hands to the fire.

At last every bit of the wood was gone. Now the cherry log was burned to ashes.

And all of a sudden Jason was on his feet again. Of all things, he was bringing the split-bottomed chair over to the hearth. He knocked it to pieces. . . . It burned well and brightly. Sara never said a word. She did not move . . . .

Then the kitchen table. To think that a solid, steady four-legged table like that, that had stood thirty years in one place, should be consumed in such a little while! Sara stared almost greedily at the waving flames.

Then when that was over, Jason and Sara sat in darkness where their bed had been, and it was colder than ever. The fire the kitchen table had made seemed wonderful to them—as if what they had never said, and what could not be, had its life, too, after all.

But Sara trembled, again pressing her hard knees against her breast. In the return of winter, of the night's cold, something strange, like fright, or dependency, a sensation of complete help-lessness, took possession of her. All at once, without turning her head, she spoke.

"Jason . . ."

A silence. But only for a moment.

"Listen," said her husband's uncertain voice. They held very still, as before, with bent heads.

Outside, as though it would exact something further from their lives, the whistle continued to blow.

QUESTIONS FOR DISCUSSION AND WRITING

1. In the first paragraph of the story, Eudora Welty describes the tiny tomato plants as "appalling in their exposed fragil-ity." In what ways are Jason and Sara equally fragile? She describes Jason's body as "a long shape like a bean" and Sara's as a "weightless. . . strip of cane." Why do you think she chooses these comparisons instead of just saying they were both very thin?

2. Why did Jason and Sara feel "a great lack of necessity to speak"?

3. Who is Mr. Perkins? How has he affected the lives of Jason and Sara? Reread her half-dream on pages 22 and 23 be-fore you answer this question.

4. This is a story of poverty and loneliness, of the emptiness and hopelessness of two lives. What did Jason and Sara do when the whistle started blowing? How do their acts show their desperation and hopelessness? Was it foolish of them to put their own clothes and bedclothes on the plants and to burn up all their fuel and furniture in one night? Why do you think they did it?

5. At the end of the story they speak to each other for the first time in weeks. What do they say? What do they mean? What does the whistle mean for them now? How is the story re-solved?

SUGGESTIONS FOR FURTHER WRITING OR DISCUSSION

1. Jason and Sara lived together but "sometimes many days, weeks went by without words." Eudora Welty says: "Perhaps, years ago, the long habit of silence may have been started in anger or passion. Who could tell now?" Try to imagine and then to write a scene that might have led to their silence.
3. Tell a story about a character, not necessarily old, in a situation of total discouragement and hopelessness. Give thought to how you are going to resolve the story.

THE TALISMAN

by Pardo Bazán

The events of this story take place in Madrid, Spain, in the 19th century. It was a time in Europe when men from noble families often held positions of power and when social life among diplomats and their friends was formal and polite. A talisman—a magic charm— brought good fortune and then disaster to Baron Helynagy, the Austrian diplomat. Or did it?

This story, which is a true one, cannot be read in broad daylight. I advise you, reader, to turn on artificial light—not electricity or gas, or even a kerosene lamp, but one of those old-fashioned oil lamps that give only a faint light and leave most of the room in shadows. Or better yet: turn on no light at all; go out into the garden, and near the fountain where magnolias give off their heady fragrance and moonlight floods down in silvery beams, listen to the tale of Baron Helynagy and the mandrake.

I met the foreign gentleman (and I do not say this to lend an aura of truth to the tale, but because I really did meet him) in the simplest, most ordinary way in the world: he was introduced to me at one of the many parties given by the Austrian ambassador. The Baron was First Secretary of the Embassy, but neither his position nor his appearance nor his conversation— much like that of the majority of the people one meets—really called for the tone of mystery and the hesitant phrases with which I was informed that he would be introduced to me. It was as if they were announcing some important event.

My curiosity aroused, I proposed to observe the Baron carefully. He seemed very refined, with the refinement which is characteristic of diplomats, and handsome, with the somewhat stereotyped good looks of a typical well-groomed gentleman. As for the Baron's character and intellectual worth, it was hard for me to make a judgment in such ordinary surroundings. After a half hour's conversation I thought to myself once more, "I simply don't understand why they consider this man so remarkable."

Immediately after my chat with the Baron I began asking questions of everyone, and what I found out increased my lively interest in him. They told me that the Baron carried a talisman, no less. Yes, a real talisman: something that enabled him to carry out all his wishes and to be successful in everything he undertook. They told me about inexplicable strokes of luck attributable only to the magic influence of the talisman.

The Baron was a Hungarian, the last male member of the Helynagy family; and though he took pride in being a descendant of Taksony, the famous Magyar leader, the fact is that he was living in poverty in the old ancestral mansion in the mountains. Suddenly a series of rare coincidences dropped a considerable fortune into his lap: not only did several rich relatives die quite opportunely, leaving him their sole heir, but while repairs were being made in the ancient Helynagy castle a treasure in jewels and coins was discovered.

The Baron then presented himself at Court in Vienna, as befitted his rank, and there new signs were seen that only some mysterious protection could furnish the key to such extraordinary good fortune. If the Baron gambled, he was certain to win everyone's money; if he looked at a lady, it was a foregone conclusion that she would be receptive to his attentions. He fought three duels, and in all three he wounded his adversary; the third man died of his wound, and this was taken as Destiny's warning to the Baron's rivals in future. When he felt like entertaining political ambitions, the doors of Parliament opened wide for him; and his present post as Secretary of the Embassy in Madrid was simply a stepping-stone to higher honors. It was already being said that he would be named Minister Plenipotentiary[1] next month.

Provided all of this was not a hoax, it was certainly worth my while to find out the sort of talisman with which one obtains such enviable results. I determined to investigate, because I have always worked on the principle that one should believe completely in the fantastic and the miraculous. One who does not believe—at least from eleven at night until five o'clock the next morning—is rather foolish.

To achieve my purpose I did exactly the opposite of what is usually done in such cases: I sought out the Baron and took every opportunity to speak to him frankly; but I never mentioned the talisman. Bored, probably, with amorous conquests, the Baron was quite willing to be a friend—nothing more—to a

---

1. Minister Plenipotentiary: official in a diplomatic position with the power to transact *any* business for his country.

woman who treated him with cordial frankness. Nevertheless, for some time my strategy had no effect at all. What I discovered in the Baron was not the devil-may-care cheerfulness of one favored by Fate, but a certain sadness and restlessness, a kind of brooding pessimism. On the other hand, his repeated references to other times—his obscure and humble past—and to the sudden rise in his fortunes, confirmed the stories that were current. The news that the Baron had been recalled to Vienna, and that his departure was imminent, caused me to lose hope of learning anything more.

I was thinking about all this one afternoon, when whom should they announce but the Baron. He was calling to say goodbye to me, no doubt, and was carrying in his hand an object that he placed on the nearest small table. Then he seated himself and looked around as if to make certain that we were alone. I felt deeply stirred, for with feminine intuition I quickly sensed that he was going to speak of the talisman.

"I am here," said the Baron, "to ask you, madam, to do me a favor of inestimable value. You already know that I have been called to my homeland, and I imagine that my absence will be a short one. I have something . . . a kind of relic . . . and I fear that the hazards of the journey . . . . In short, I fear it may be stolen from me, for it is highly coveted and many people attribute astonishing powers to it. My trip has been publicized, and it is even quite possible that some plot may be afoot to rob me of this object. I am entrusting it to you; keep it for me until I return, and I shall be truly grateful to you."

So the precious talisman was right here, two feet from me, on top of a piece of my furniture, and was going to be placed in my hands!

"You may rest assured," I replied vehemently, "that if I keep it for you it will be well protected. But before accepting custody of it, I should like you to inform me what it is that I am going to protect. Although I have never asked you any indiscreet questions, I am aware of what is being said, and I understand that you possess a prodigious talisman that has brought you all kinds of good fortune. I will not keep it without knowing what it is, and if it really merits such great interests."

The Baron hesitated. I saw that he was debating within himself before speaking with complete truth and frankness. Finally sincerity prevailed, and not without some effort he replied:

"You have touched, madam, upon the one great grief in my heart. The constant burden of my life is my doubt as to whether I really possess a treasure with magic properties, or whether I am keeping, through superstition, some worthless fetish. Belief in the supernatural is always, in these modern times, like a tower with no firm foundation: the slightest puff of wind topples it to the ground. People believe I am 'fortunate' when in reality I am just 'lucky'; I would be happy if I were completely certain that what is enclosed in this box is, indeed, a talisman that makes my dreams come true and wards off the blows of fate. But this is precisely the point I am unable to verify.

"What can I possibly tell you? I was poor and unnoticed by anybody, when one afternoon an Israelite on his way from Palestine passed through Helynagy and insisted upon selling me this thing, assuring me that it would bring me all kinds of happiness. I bought it...the way one buys a thousand useless things...and put it into a box. In a short time things began to happen that changed my luck. But all of them have an explanation...without the need of miracles."

Here the Baron smiled, and his smile was contagious. Then his melancholy expression returned, and he continued

"Every day we see men succeeding in fields where they do not deserve it...unskilled duellists quite often defeat famous swordsmen. If I were convinced that talismans really exist, I would enjoy my prosperity in peace. What embitters me is the thought that I may be the victim of some cruel self-deception, and that when I least expect it the sad fate of my race may overtake me. Look how those who envy me are already doing me harm, and how this tormenting fear of the future is clouding my happiness! Even so, I still have enough faith left to beg you to guard the box well for me...because the greatest misfortune a man can have is to be neither a complete skeptic nor a devout believer."

This frank confession explained the sadness I had noted on the Baron's face. His spiritual situation seemed pathetic to me, for amid the greatest good fortune lack of faith was gnawing at his soul. The masterful haughtiness of great men always comes from firm belief in their destiny, and Baron Helynagy, incapable of this belief, was incapable of winning through to success.

The Baron rose, and picking up the object he had brought, he unfolded the black silk cloth in which it was wrapped. I saw a little crystal box with a silver lock. When the cover was raised I beheld upon a linen shroud which the Baron delicately unwound a horrid thing: a blackish, grotesque little figure that looked like the body of a man. My gesture of repugnance did not surprise the Baron.

"But . . . what is it?" I forced myself to ask him.

"This," replied the diplomat, "is one of the marvels of Nature. It is not a carving or an imitation; it is a genuine root of the mandrake plant, exactly as it grows beneath the earth. The superstition that attributes weird powers to the mandrake root is as old as the world itself. They say it grows from the blood of people who have been executed, and that for this reason the mandrake can be heard moaning in the middle of the night as if some soul dwelt captive within it, sunk in deep despair. Ah! Be careful, for the love of Heaven, to keep it wrapped constantly in a silk or linen shroud; only in this way does the mandrake afford its protection."

"And you believe all this?" I exclaimed, eyeing the Baron steadily.

"Would that I did!" he answered in a tone so bitter that at first I could find no words in reply.

In a short while the Baron said good-bye, and he repeated his admonition that I should be very careful of the box and its contents—just in case anything should happen. He stated that he expected to return within a month, and that he would pick up the box at that time.

As soon as the talisman came into my custody, you may be sure that I examined it more closely. I confess that although the whole legend of the mandrake seemed to me a crude hoax and an evil superstition from the Orient, I could not but be impressed by the rare perfection with which that root resembled the human body. I thought it must be some clever imitation, but careful inspection convinced me that the hand of man had no part in the freakish thing; it was a natural phenomenon, the root itself just as it had been pulled from the ground. I asked several people who had lived for a long time in Palestine; they assured me that it is not possible to counterfeit a mandrake, and that it is plucked and sold just that way by shepherds in the hills of Gilead and on the plains of Jericho.

No doubt the strangeness of the object, completely unfamiliar to me, was what excited my imagination. The fact of the matter is that I began to be afraid, or at least to feel an uncontrollable revulsion toward the accursed talisman. I had put it away with my jewels inside the safe in my bedroom. The slightest noise would awaken me trembling, and sometimes the wind rattling the window panes and rustling the curtains made me imagine that the mandrake was sobbing with unearthly cries. . . .

In short, there was no living with the horrid thing, and I decided to take it out of my room and put it into a glass cabinet in the living room where I kept rare coins and medallions. This act was the source of my everlasting sorrow, which will never leave me as long as I live.

Fate so willed it that a new servant, tempted by the coins in the cabinet, broke the glass in order to steal them, and at the same time carried off the little box with the talisman.

It was a terrible blow to me. I notified the police, who moved heaven and earth. The thief was found . . . yes, found; the coins were recovered, along with the little box and the winding cloth . . . but the man confessed that he had thrown the talisman into a sewer. It was nowhere to be found, even at the cost of the most expensive investigations imaginable.

"And Baron Helynagy?" I asked the lady who had told me this singular story.

"He died in a railroad accident on the way back to Spain," she answered, turning away her face, which had grown paler than usual.

"So that was indeed a real talisman . . . ?"

"Good Heavens!" she replied. "Don't you believe at all in coincidences?"

QUESTIONS FOR DISCUSSION AND WRITING

1. Before the real story begins, the reader is advised not to read it in broad daylight, that perhaps it would be best to listen to it in a moonlit garden. Reread the first paragraph and discuss why Pardo Bazán begins his tale in this way.
2. The relationship between the Baron and the lady who tells the story is unusual. How? Why does the baron choose to leave the talisman with her? What is her reaction to his request? What does this show about the sort of person she is?
3. The baron is troubled by the question of whether he is "fortunate" or just "lucky"? Why should this trouble him so? How did the baron obtain the talisman? What facts do we learn about mandrake roots? Reread the section of the story, on page 31, which describes the talisman and its container. How does the lady react to it? Does it seem in keeping with what we know of her character that she should react in this way?
4. At the end the talisman is lost and the baron dies. How does Pardo Bazán indicate that the lady believes that the loss

of the talisman caused the baron's death? But then the story
is resolved in the last sentence. How? Are we sure, then,
that the talisman is "a worthless fetish," as the baron described it earlier? Is there any solid evidence given that the
baron's life was changed by the talisman? Explain.
5. Why do you think Pardo Bazán told the story? Is he just
having fun with his readers or is he saying something
serious? If the latter, what?

SUGGESTIONS FOR FURTHER WRITING OR DISCUSSION

1. Make up a story about some other talisman. Make it seem
as real as you can even though it is fantasy.
2. Tell about an experience, real or made-up, in which some
sort of magic, or seeming magic, played a part.

A Change of Viewpoint

A boy watches a man attempt suicide.
A woman tells of a terrifying girlhood experience.
An old mountain couple get a divorce.

ON SATURDAY AFTERNOON

by Alan Sillitoe

*A young boy is "blackly" depressed by his harsh family
and his poor life. Then he sees a man try to kill himself. How does this experience change his view of his
own life?*

I once saw a bloke[1] try to kill himself. I'll never forget the
day because I was sitting in the house on Saturday afternoon,
feeling black and fed-up because everybody in the family had
gone to the pictures, except me who'd for some reason been left
out of it. 'Course, I didn't know then that I would soon see something you can never see in the same way on the pictures, a real
bloke stringing himself up. I was only a kid at the time, so you
can imagine how much I enjoyed it.

I've never known a family to look as black as our family
when they're fed-up. I've seen the old man with his face so dark
and full of murder because he ain't got no fags[2] or was having
to use saccharine to sweeten his tea, or even for nothing at all,
that I've backed out of the house in case he got up from his
fireside chair and came for me. He just sits, almost on top of
the fire, his oil-stained Sunday-joint maulers[3] opened out in front
of him and facing inwards to each other, his thick shoulders
scrunched forward, and his dark brown eyes staring into the fire.
Now and again he'd say a dirty word, for no reason at all, the
worst word you can think of, and when he starts saying this
you know it's time to clear out. If mam's in it gets worse than
ever, because she says sharp to him: "What are yo' looking so
bleddy[4] black for?" as if it might be because of something she's
done, and before you know what's happening he's tipped up
a tableful of pots and mam's gone out of the house crying. Dad

---

1. bloke: British slang for guy or man.
2. fags: cigarettes.
3. maulers: He means hands. To maul is to handle roughly so as to injure.
4. bleddy: bloody—considered in England to be a crude word, about equivalent
   to "damn".

---

hunches back over the fire and goes on swearing. All because of a packet of fags.

I once saw him broodier than I'd ever seen him, so that I thought he'd gone crackers in a quiet sort of way—until a fly flew to within a yard of him. Then his hand shot out, got it, and slung it crippled into the roaring fire. After that he cheered up a bit and mashed some tea.

Well, that's where the rest of us get our black looks from. It stands to reason we'd have them with a dad who carries on like that, don't it? Black looks run in the family. Some families have them and some don't. Our family has them right enough, and that's certain, so when we're fed-up we're really fed-up. Nobody knows why we get as fed-up as we do or why it gives us these black looks when we are. Some people get fed-up and don't look bad at all: they seem happy in a funny sort of way, as if they've just been set free from clink after being in there for something they didn't do, or come out of the pictures after sitting plugged for eight hours at a bad film, or just missed a bus they ran half a mile for and seen it was the wrong one just after they'd stopped running—but in our family it's murder for the others if one of us is fed-up. I've asked myself lots of times what it is but I never can get any sort of answer even if I sit and think for hours, which I must admit I don't do, though it looks good when I say I do. But I sit and think for long enough, until mam says to me, at seeing me scrunched up over the fire like dad: "What are yo' looking so black for?" So I've just got to stop thinking about it in case I get really black and fed-up and go the same way as dad, tipping up a tableful of pots and all.

Mostly I suppose there's nothing to look so black for: though it's nobody's fault and you can't blame anyone for looking black because I'm sure it's summat[5] in the blood. But on this Saturday afternoon I was looking so black that when dad came in from the bookie's he said to me: "What's up wi' yo'?"

"I feel badly," I fibbed. He'd have had a fit if I'd said I was only black because I hadn't gone to the pictures.

"Well have a wash," he told me.

"I don't want a wash," I said, and that was a fact.

"Well, get outside and get some fresh air then," he shouted.

I did as I was told, double-quick, because if ever dad goes as far as to tell me to get some fresh air I know it's time to get away from him. But outside the air wasn't so fresh, what

5. summat: something.

with that bloody great bike factory bashing away at the yard-end. I didn't know where to go, so I walked up the yard[6] a bit and sat down near somebody's back gate.

Then I saw this bloke who hadn't lived long in our yard. He was tall and thin and had a face like a parson except that he wore a flat cap and had a moustache that drooped, and looked as though he hadn't had a square meal for a year. I didn't think much o' this at the time: but I remember that as he turned in by the yard-end one of the nosy gossiping women who stood there every minute of the day except when she trudged to the pawn-shop with her husband's bike or best suit, shouted to him: "What's that rope for, mate?"

He called back: "It's to 'ang messen[7] wi', missis," and she cackled at his bloody good joke so loud and long you'd think she never heard such a good 'un, though the next day she cackled on the other side of her fat face.

He walked by me puffing a fag and carrying his coil of brand-new rope, and he had to step over me to get past. His boot nearly took my shoulder off, and when I told him to watch where he was going I don't think he heard me because he didn't even look round. Hardly anybody was about. All the kids were still at the pictures, and most of their mams and dads were down-town doing the shopping.

The bloke walked down the yard to his back door, and having nothing better to do because I hadn't gone to the pictures I followed him. You see, he left his back door open a bit, so I gave it a push and went in. I stood there, just watching him, sucking my thumb, the other hand in my pocket. I suppose he knew I was there, because his eyes were moving more natural now, but he didn't seem to mind. "What are yer going to do wi' that rope, mate?" I asked him.

"I'm going ter 'ang messen, lad," he told me, as though he'd done it a time or two already, and people had usually asked him questions like this beforehand.

"What for, mate?" He must have thought I was a nosy young bogger.

"'Cause I want to, that's what for," he said, clearing all the pots off the table and pulling it to the middle of the room. Then he stood on it to fasten the rope to the light-fitting. The table creaked and didn't look very safe, but it did him for what he wanted.

6. yard: a square of houses.
7. 'ang messen: hang myself.

"It wain't hold up, mate," I said to him, thinking how much better it was being here than sitting in the pictures and seeing the Jungle Jim serial.

But he got nettled now and turned on me. "Mind yer own business."

I thought he was going to tell me to scram, but he didn't. He made ever such a fancy knot with that rope, as though he'd been a sailor or sommat, and as he tied it he was whistling a fancy tune to himself. Then he got down from the table and pushed it back to the wall, and put a chair in its place. He wasn't looking black at all, nowhere near as black as anybody in our family when they're feeling fed-up. If ever he'd looked only half as black as our dad looked twice a week he'd have hanged himself years ago, I couldn't help thinking. But he was making a good job of that rope all right, as though he'd thought about it a lot anyway, and as though it was going to be the last thing he'd ever do. But I knew something he didn't know, because he wasn't standing where I was. I knew the rope wouldn't hold up, and I told him so, again.

"Shut yer gob," he said, but quiet like, "or I'll kick yer out."

I didn't want to miss it, so I said nothing. He took his cap off and put it on the dresser, then he took his coat off, and his scarf, and spread them out on the sofa. I wasn't a bit frightened, like I might be now at sixteen, because it was interesting. And being only ten I'd never had a chance to see a bloke hang himself before. We got pally, the two of us, before he slipped the rope around his neck.

"Shut the door," he asked me, and I did as I was told. "Ye're a good lad for your age," he said to me while I sucked my thumb, and he felt in his pockets and pulled out all that was inside, throwing the handful of bits and bobs on the table: fag-packet and peppermints, a pawnticket, an old comb, and a few coppers. He picked out a penny and gave it to me, saying: "Now listen ter me, young 'un. I'm going to 'ang messen, and when I'm swinging I want you to gi' this chair a bloody good kick and push it away. All right?"

I nodded.

He put the rope around his neck, and then took it off like it was a tie that didn't fit. "What are yer going to do it for, mate?" I asked again.

"Because I'm fed-up," he said, looking very unhappy. "And because I want to. My missus left me, and I'm out o' work."

I didn't want to argue, because the way he said it, I knew he couldn't do anything else except hang himself. Also there was

a funny look in his face: even when he talked to me I swear
he couldn't see me. It was different to the black looks my old
man puts on, and I suppose that's why my old man would never
hang himself, worse luck, because he never gets a look into his
clock like this bloke had. My old man's look stares *at* you, so
that you have to back down and fly out of of the house: this
bloke's look looked *through* you, so that you could face it and
know it wouldn't do you any harm. So I saw now that dad would
never hang himself because he could never get the right sort
of look into his face, in spite of the fact that he'd been out of
work often enough. Maybe mam would have to leave him first,
and then he might do it: but no—I shook my head—there wasn't
much chance of that even though he did lead her a dog's life.

"Yer wain't forget to kick that chair away?" he reminded
me, and I swung my head to say I wouldn't. So my eyes were
popping and I watched every move he made. He stood on the
chair and put the rope around his neck so that it fitted this time,
still whistling his fancy tune. I wanted to get a better goz at
the knot, because my pal was in the scouts, and would ask to
know how it was done, and if I told him later, he'd let me know
what happened at the pictures in the Jungle Jim serial, so's I
could have my cake and eat it as well, as mam says, tit for tat.
But I thought I'd better not ask the bloke to tell me, and I stayed
back in my corner. The last thing he did was take the wet dirty
butt-end from his lips and sling it into the empty firegrate, following it with his eyes to the black fireback where it landed—as
if he was then going to mend a fault in the lighting like any
electrician.

Suddenly his long legs wriggled and his feet tried to kick
the chair, so I helped him as I'd promised I would and took
a runner at it as if I was playing centre-forward for Notts Forest,
and the chair went scooting back against the sofa, dragging his
muffler to the floor as it tipped over. He swung for a bit, his
arms chafing like he was a scarecrow flapping birds away, and
he made a noise in his throat as if he'd just took a dose of salts
and was trying to make them stay down.

Then there was another sound, and I looked up and saw
a big crack come in the ceiling, like you see on the pictures
when an earthquake's happening, and the bulb began circling
round and round as though it was a space ship. I was just beginning to get dizzy when, thank Christ, he fell down with such
a horrible thump on the floor that I thought he'd broke every
bone he'd got. He kicked around for a bit, like a dog that's got
colic bad. Then he lay still.

I didn't stay to look at him. "I told him that rope wouldn't hold up," I kept saying to myself as I went out of the house, tut-tutting because he hadn't done the job right, hands stuffed deep into my pockets and nearly crying at the balls-up[8] he'd made of everything. I slammed his gate so hard with disappointment that it nearly dropped off its hinges.

Just as I was going back up the yard to get my tea at home, hoping the others had come back from the pictures so's I wouldn't have anything to keep on being black about, a copper passed me and headed for the bloke's door. He was striding quickly with his head bent forward, and I knew that somebody had narked.[9] They must have seen him buy the rope and then tipped-off the cop. Or happen the old hen at the yard-end had finally caught on. Or perhaps he'd even told somebody himself, because I supposed that the bloke who'd strung himself up hadn't much known what he was doing, especially with the look I'd seen in his eyes. But that's how it is, I said to myself, as I followed the copper back to the bloke's house, a poor bloke can't even hang himself these days.

When I got back the copper was slitting the rope from his neck with a pen-knife, then he gave him a drink of water, and the bloke opened his peepers. I didn't like the copper because he'd got a couple of my mates sent to approved school[10] for pinching lead piping from lavatories.

"What did you want to hang yourself for?" he asked the bloke, trying to make him sit up. He could hardly talk, and one of his hands was bleeding from where the light-bulb had smashed. I knew that rope wouldn't hold up, but he hadn't listened to me. I'll never hang myself anyway, but if I want to I'll make sure I do it from a tree or something like that, not a light fitting. "Well, what did you do it for?"

"Because I wanted to," the bloke croaked.

"You'll get five years for this," the copper told him. I'd crept back into the house and was sucking my thumb in the same corner.

"That's what yo' think," the bloke said, a normal frightened look in his eyes now. "I only wanted to hang myself."

"Well," the copper said, taking out his book, "it's against the law, you know."

"Nay," the bloke said, "it can't be. It's my life, aint' it?"

"You might think so," the copper said, "but it ain't."

8. balls-up: mess.
9. narked: told, tattled.
10. approved school: reform school.

He began to suck the blood from his hand. It was such a little scratch though that you couldn't see it. "That's the first thing I knew," he said.

"Well I'm telling you," the copper told him.

'Course, I didn't let on to the copper that I'd helped the bloke to hang himself. I wasn't born yesterday, nor the day before yesterday either.

"It's a fine thing if a bloke can't tek his own life," the bloke said, seeing he was in for it.

"Well he can't," the copper said, as if reading out of his book and enjoying it, "It ain't your life. And it's a crime to take your own life. It's killing yourself. It's suicide."

The bloke looked hard, as if every one of the copper's words meant six-months cold. I felt sorry for him, and that's a fact, but if only he'd listened to what I'd said and not depended on that light-fitting. He should have done it from a tree, or something like that.

He went up the yard with the copper like a peaceful lamb, and we all thought that that was the end of that.

But a couple of days later the news was flashed through to us—even before it got to the *Post* because a woman in our yard worked at the hospital of an evening dishing grub out and tidying up. I heard her spilling it to somebody at the yard-end. "I'd never 'ave thought it. I thought he'd got that daft idea out of his head when they took him away. But no. Wonders'll never cease. Chucked 'issen[11] from the hospital window when the copper who sat near his bed went off for a pee. Would you believe it? Dead? Not much 'e ain't."[12]

He'd heaved himself at the glass, and fallen like a stone on to the road. In one way I was sorry he'd done it, but in another I was glad, because he'd proved to the coppers and everybody whether it was his life or not all right. It was marvellous though, the way the brainless bastards had put him in a ward six floors up, which finished him off, proper, even better than a tree.

All of which will make me think twice about how black I sometimes feel. The black coal-bag locked inside you, and the black look it puts on your face, doesn't mean you're going to string yourself up or sling yourself under a double-decker or chuck yourself out of a window or cut your throat with a sardine-tin or put your head in the gas-oven or drop your rotten sack-bag

11. 'issen: himself.
12. Not much 'e ain't: She means he *is*.

of a body on to a railway line, because when you're feeling that black you can't even move from your chair. Anyhow, I know I'll never get so black as to hang myself, because hanging don't look very nice to me, and never will, the more I remember old what's-his-name swinging from the light-fitting.

More than anything else, I'm glad now I didn't go to the pictures that Saturday afternoon when I was feeling black and ready to do myself in. Because you know, I shan't ever kill myself. Trust me. I'll stay alive half-barmy[13] till I'm a hundred and five, and then go out screaming blue murder because I want to stay where I am.

13. half-barmy: half crazy.

QUESTIONS FOR DISCUSSION AND WRITING

1. The kid who tells the story lives in a harsh, cruel, "fed-up" family. "Black looks run in the family," he says. Why does the family feel so "black"? What does he mean when he says, "it's sommat in the blood"? How do the father and mother get along with each other? What examples of the father's brutality are given?
2. When the ten-year-old boy sees the tall, thin man and asks him, "What's the rope for?" what is surprising about the man's answer? What is the boy's reaction to the answer? What is his attitude towards the suicide he expects to see? Why do you think he "wasn't a bit frightened, like I might be now at sixteen"?
3. The man tells why he's going to hang himself. What reasons does he give? What does this make the boy think about his own father?
4. What is the boy's reaction just after the suicide attempt fails? What is the reaction of the "copper"? The man and the cop get into an argument about it after the policeman says, "You'll get five years for this." Read the argument aloud. What is the point of view of each man? Why does he hold that point of view?
5. The man finally succeeds in killing himself. How? How does the boy react to this? Read the last two paragraphs of the story aloud. How has the boy's point of view toward his own life changed? Why has he come to feel that he wants to hold onto life no matter how bad it is?

6. The boy saw the suicide attempt when he was ten years old, but he tells the story six years later when he's sixteen. How is the tone of his telling different from what it would have been if he'd told it at age ten? What does his "cool" way of telling show he has learned about surviving in his world? What has the boy learned about "black looks" and "black feelings"? Also, what does it tell us that he remembers the suicide details so vividly six years later even though he casually refers to the suicide as "old-what's-his-name"?

SUGGESTIONS FOR FURTHER WRITING OR DISCUSSION

1. The boy's father was cruel, mean and hopeless. Describe a cruel, mean person that you know (or one that you make up) and how he got the way he (or she) is, or how you try to deal with him.
2. The man and the cop argue about the man's right to take his own life. Write a statement of your own position on this question. Is your life really "your life" and should you have the right to do what you want with it?
3. Write a story about a person who is driven to the point of suicide. Concentrate on making the reader understand how the person feels and why he feels that way.

THE DAY THE WORLD ALMOST CAME TO AN END

by Pearl Crayton

This story takes place in rural Louisiana in 1936. The woman who tells it, long afterwards, remembers how ignorant and superstitious she was then—and how childish for a twelve-year-old. She had never before even heard an airplane fly over. She lived "close to the earth and God, and all wrapped up in religion," and the people around her believed in the Bible, a real Hell, the dangers of sin, and the importance of being saved. Why does her terrifying experience suddenly revolutionize her view of the world?

If you haven't had the world coming to an end on you when you're twelve years old and a sinner, you don't know how lucky you are! When it happened to me it scared the living daylights and some of the joy of sinning out of me and, in a lot of other ways, messed up my life altogether. But if I am to believe Ralph Waldo Emerson's "Compensation,"[1] I guess I got some good out of it too.

The calamity befell me back in 1936. We were living on a plantation in Louisiana at the time, close to the earth and God, and all wrapped up in religion. The church was the axis around which plantation life revolved, the Mother to whom the folks took their problems, the Teacher who taught them how the Lord wanted them to live, the Chastiser[2] who threatened the sinful with Hell.

In spite of the fact that my parents were churchgoing Christians, I was still holding on to being a sinner. Not that I had anything against religion, it was just a matter of integrity. There was an old plantation custom that in order to be baptized into the church a sinner had to "get religion," a mystical experience

1. Emerson's "Compensation": an essay of a famous American philosopher in which he says that when something bad happens to us, we receive, as compensation, something good.
2. Chastiser: punisher.

in which the soul of the sinner was converted into Christian. A Christian had to live upright, and I knew I couldn't come up to that on account of there were too many delicious sins around to get into. But a world coming to an end can be pretty hard on a sinner.

The trouble began when my cousin Rena came upon me playing in the watermelon patch, running like the devil was behind her. I was making a whole quarter of mud cabins by packing dirt over my foot in the shape of a cabin, putting a chimney on top, then pulling my foot out. The space left by my foot formed the room of the cabin. I'd broken some twigs off chinaberry and sycamore trees which I planted in the ground around the cabins to make "trees." Some blooming wild flowers that I had picked made up a flower yard in front of each cabin. It was as pretty a sight as you ever want to see before she came stepping all over everything. I let her know I didn't like it real loud, but she didn't pay what I said any attention, she just blurted out, "The end of the world is coming Saturday; you'd better go get you some religion in a hurry!"

That was on a Friday afternoon, getting late.

A picture of Hell flashed across my mind but I pushed it back into the subconscious. "The world's not coming to an end!" The confidence I tried to put in my voice failed; it quaked a little. "Who told you the world is coming to an end?"

"I heard Mama and Miss Daya talking about it just now. There's going to be an eclipse Sunday. You know what an eclipse is, don't you?"

I didn't know but I nodded anyhow.

"That's when the sun has a fight with the moon. If the sun whips, the world goes on; if the moon whips, then the world comes to an end. Well, they say that Sunday the moon is going to whip the sun!"

I wasn't going to be scared into giving up my sinning that easily. "How do they know the moon is going to whip?" I asked.

"They read it in the almanac. And it's in the Bible too, in Revelation. It says in Revelation that the world is supposed to end this year. Miss Daya is a missionary sister and she knows all about things like that."

"Nobody knows anything about Revelation, my daddy says so," I rebutted. "Ain't never been nobody born smart enough to figure out Revelation since that Mister John wrote it. He's just going to have to come back and explain it himself."

She acted like she didn't hear that. "And Reverend Davis said in church last Sunday that time is winding up," she said.

"He's been saying that for years now, and time hasn't wound up yet."

"That's what I know, he's been saying it for years, and all the while he's been saying it time's been winding right along, and now it's just about all wound up!"

That made sense to me and I began to consider that maybe she could be right. Then that Miss Daya happened by.

"Lord bless you down there on your knees, baby! Pray to the Lord 'cause it's praying time!"

I hadn't gotten up from where I'd been making mud cabins, but I jumped up quick to let her know I wasn't praying.

"Both of you girls got religion?" she asked, and without waiting for an answer, "That's good. You're both big girls, big enough to go to Hell. You all be glad you all got religion 'cause the Lord is coming soon! He said he was coming and he's coming soon!" And she went on towards our cabin before I could ask her about the world ending Sunday.

Rena just stood there and looked at me awhile, shaking her head in an "I told you so," and advised me again to get some religion in a hurry. Then she ran off to warn someone else.

Although I was a sinner, I was a regular churchgoing sinner and at our church we had a hellfire-preaching pastor. He could paint pictures of Hell and the Devil in his sermons horrible enough to give a sinner a whole week of nightmares. Nobody with a dime's worth of sense wanted to go to a hot, burning Hell where a red, horned Devil tormented folks with a pitchfork, but I'd been taking a chance on enjoying life another thirty years or so before getting some religion—getting just enough to keep me out of Hell. I hadn't figured on time running out on me soon, and I still wasn't taking anybody's word before asking my daddy about it first. But it was plowing time and Daddy was way back in the cornfield where I'd already run across a rattlesnake, so I figured even the world coming to an end could wait until suppertime.

I went around the rest of that day with my mind loaded down. Now I didn't exactly believe that the world was coming to an end, but I didn't exactly believe it wasn't either. About two years before, I'd went and read the worst part of Revelation and it had taken my daddy two weeks to convince me that I didn't understand what I had read, which still didn't keep me from having bad dreams about the moon dripping away in blood and a lot of other distressing visions aroused from misunderstood words.

Those dreams were only a vague and frightening memory

the Friday I'm talking about, and Revelation an accepted mystery. Yet things like that have a way of sneaking back on you when you need it the least. I got to "supposing" the world did come to an end with earthquakes and hail and fire raining down from the sky and stars falling, exactly like it read in Revelation, and "supposing" the Devil got after me and took me to Hell like folks on the plantation said he would, and "supposing" Hell really and truly was as horrible as the preacher said it was. The way the preacher told it, in Hell a person got burned and burned up and never died, he just kept on burning, burning, burning. With "supposing" like that going through it, my mind was really loaded down! I figured there was no use talking to Mama about what was bothering me because that Miss Daya had stayed at our cabin for over an hour, and I was sure she had convinced Mama that the moon was going to whip the sun.

It seemed to me like it took Daddy longer than ever to come home. It was the Friday of Council Meeting at the church, and Daddy, a deacon, had to be there. I knew he wouldn't have much time to talk to me before he'd have to leave out for the church, so I started walking up the turnrow through the fields to meet him. When I finally saw him riding towards home on his slide I ran to meet him.

Daddy always hitched a plank under his plow to keep the plow blades from cutting up the turnrow when he came home from plowing the fields. The plank, which we called a slide, was long enough behind the plow for him to stand on and ride home, pulled by his plow horse. Whenever I ran to meet him he'd let me ride home with him on the slide.

"Daddy," I said as soon as he'd put me on the slide in front of him and "gee'd" the horse to go on, "is the world going to come to an end Sunday?"

"I don't know, honey," he replied. "Why do you want to know?"

I told him about Rena's prophecy. That really tickled him! He laughed and laughed like that was the funniest thing he'd ever heard! I laughed a little too, though I didn't get the joke in it.

"There's always somebody coming around prophesying that the world's coming to an end," he said after he'd laughed himself out. "Folks been doing that ever since I was a boy, they were doing it when my daddy was boy, aw, they've been doing that for hundreds of years and the world is still here. Don't you ever pay any attention to anybody that comes around telling you the world is going to end, baby."

"But ain't the world *ever* going to end?" I wanted to know.

"Yeah, but don't anybody know when. Only the Lord knows that. Why, the world might not end for another thousand years, then again it might end tonight, we just don't know. . . ."

"TONIGHT! You mean the world might end TONIGHT!"

"Sure. I'm not saying it will but it could. A person never can tell about a thing like that. But if you let that bother you, why you'll be scared to death every day of your life looking for the world to end. You're not going to be that silly, are you?"

"Aw, shucks no," I lied. I was that silly. Right then and there I got to looking for the world to end, right there on the *spot!*

Like anybody expecting a calamity, I decided to sit up all night that night but Mama made me go to bed. My room was full of the plantation, the darkest of darkness. Before Daddy returned from church Mama put out the coal oil lamp and went to bed.

The lazy old moon was on its vacation again; there was no light anywhere, not a speck. Although my eyes couldn't see anything in that awful dark, my mind had always been very good at seeing things in the dark that weren't there. I got to "seeing" how it was going to be when the world ended, the whole drama of it paraded right before my mind. Then my imagination marched me up before the judgment seat to give account for my past sins and I tried to figure out how much burning I'd get for each offense. Counting up all the ripe plums and peaches I'd saved from going to waste on the neighbors' trees, neglecting to get the owners' permission, the fights I'd had with that sassy little Catherine who lived across the river, the domino games I'd played for penny stakes with my sinner-cousin, Sam, the times I'd handled the truth careless enough to save myself from a whipping, and other not so holy acts, I figured I'd be in for some real hot burning.

While I lay there in that pitch-black darkness worrying myself sick about burning in Hell, a distant rumbling disturbed the stillness of the night, so faint that at first I wasn't sure I'd heard it. I sat up in the bed, straining my ears listening. Sure enough there was a rumbling, far away. The rumbling wasn't thunder. I was sure of that because thunder rumbled, then died away, but this rumbling grew louder and louder and LOUDER. A slow-moving, terrible, loud rumbling that was to my scared mind the earth quaking, the sky caving in, the world ending!

I got out of there, I got out of there *fast!* I didn't even think about being dressed only in my nightgown or the awful dark outside being full of ghosts and bogeymen and other horrors, I just ran!

"The world is ending! The world is ending! Run! Run for your life!" I shouted a warning to Mama, and I just kept on hollering as I ran down the road past the other plantation cabins. "The world is ending! The world is ending! Run! Run for your life!"

Doors opened and folks came out on the cabin porches, some holding coal oil lamps in their hands. They'd look at me in my white nightgown running down the road as fast as a scared rabbit, then look up at the sky, rumbling like it was caving in, and a few of them hollered something at me as I passed by, but I couldn't make out what any of them said.

I might have run myself plumb to the ocean or death if Daddy and some other deacons hadn't been coming up the road on their way from church. Daddy caught me. He had a hard time holding me though. The fear of the Devil and Hell was stronger in me than reason. I was dead set on escaping them.

Daddy had heard my hollering about the world ending as I ran down the road towards them, so he kept telling me, "That's just an old airplane, honey, the world's not ending. That's just an old airplane making all that racket!"

When his words got through the fear that fogged my mind I calmed down a bit. "Airplane?" I'd only heard about airplanes, never had I seen one or heard one passing by.

Daddy laughed. "You were just about outrunning that old airplane and keeping up almost as much racket!" He pointed toward the sky. "Look up there, you see, it's gone now. See that light moving towards town? That's it. Those old airplanes sure have scared a lot of folks with all that racket they make."

I looked up. Sure enough there was a light that looked like a star moving across the sky. The rumbling was way off in the distance, going away slowly like it had come. And the sky was whole, not a piece of it had caved in! I broke down and cried because I was so relieved that the world wasn't coming to an end, because I'd been so scared for so long, because I'd made such a fool of myself, and just because.

Daddy pulled off his suit coat and wrapped it around me to hide the shame of my nightgown from the deacons. After I'd had a real good cry we walked home.

As he walked up the ribbon of road bordering the plantation

on our way home I felt a new kind of happiness inside of me.
The yellow squares of light shining from the black shapes of
the plantation cabins outlined against the night made a picture
that looked beautiful to me for the first time. Even the chirping
of the crickets sounded beautiful, like a new song I'd never heard
before. Even the darkness was beautiful, everything was beautiful. And I was alive, I felt the life within me warming me from
the inside, a happy feeling I'd never had before. And the world
was there all around me, I was aware of it, aware of all of it,
full of beauty, full of happy things to do. Right then and there
I was overwhelmed with a desire to *live*, really live in the world
and enjoy as much of it as I could before it came to an end.
And I've been doing so ever since.

QUESTIONS FOR DISCUSSION AND WRITING

1. How do you know on the first page of the story that it is
   being told by a mature, well-educated woman?
2. The girl's view of the local religion is interesting. What does
   she mean when she describes the church as the Mother, the
   Leader, and the Chastiser? She says she was "holding on
   to being a sinner . . . as a matter of integrity." What does
   she mean by this?
3. When Cousin Rena comes running by blurting out, "You'd
   better get some religion in a hurry!" how do we know that
   the girl really is scared, but that she's thinking about it too
   and is a bit skeptical? What was her plan to have some fun
   and yet to avoid Hell?
4. Then she remembers the "worst part of Revelation" in the
   Bible, in which there are some very gory passages about what
   will happen to sinners. How does her father try to ease her
   fears, and what is her reaction to what he says?
5. When she lies in bed fearfully imagining Hell and the end
   of the world, what sins does she remember? What does this
   show us about her? Then the airplane sets her off, running
   and shouting in terror. How does her father deal with her
   terror?
6. How does she then, rather suddenly, come to see the world?
   How is she a different person at the end of the story from
   the child she was at the beginning?

SUGGESTIONS FOR FURTHER WRITING OR DISCUSSION

1. Have you ever had an experience that made you have bad dreams, or have you had fears that kept you from going to sleep? Describe your dreams and feelings, or make up a story based on them.
2. Describe the "sins" of the twelve-year-old girl and compare them with some of your "sins" as a younger person—or now.
3. Tell or write a story about an experience where you or the main character mistook something ordinary for something terrifying and terrible.

THE WHIRLIGIG OF LIFE

by O. Henry

*Ransie Bilbro, and Ariela, his wife, who live in the back
country of the Cumberland Mountains of Tennessee,
have agreed to get a divorce. They come to town to
get one from Justice-of-the-peace Benaja Widdup. Why
does O. Henry call his story "The Whirligig (merry-go-
round) of Life"?*

Justice-of-the-peace Benaja Widdup sat in the door of his
office smoking his elder-stem pipe. Halfway to the Zenith the
Cumberland range rose blue-gray in the afternoon haze. A
speckled hen swaggered down the main street of the "settlement," cackling foolishly.

Up the road came a sound of creaking axles, and then a
slow cloud of dust, and then a bull-cart bearing Ransie Bilbro
and his wife. The cart stopped at the Justice's door, and the two
climbed down. Ransie was a narrow six feet of sallow brown
skin and yellow hair. The imperturbability of the mountains
hung upon him like a suit of armor. The woman was calicoed,
angled, snuff-brushed, and weary with unknown desires.
Through it all gleamed a faint protest of cheated youth unconscious of its loss.

The Justice of the Peace slipped his feet into his shoes, for
the sake of dignity, and moved to let them enter.

"We-all," said the woman, in a voice like the wind blowing
through pine boughs, "wants a divo'ce." She looked at Ransie
to see if he noted any flaw or ambiguity or evasion or partiality
or self-partisanship in her statment of their business.

"A divo'ce," repeated Ransie, with a solemn nod. "We-all
can't git along together nohow. It's lonesome enough fur to live
in the mount'ins when a man and a woman keers fur one another. But when she's a-spittin' like a wildcat or a-sullenin' like a
hoot-owl in the cabin, a man ain't got no call to live with her."

"When he's a no'count varmint," said the woman, without
any especial warmth, "a-traipsin' along of scalawags and moonshiners[1] and a-layin' on his back pizen[2] 'ith co'n[3] whiskey, and

1. moonshiners: people who make illegal whiskey.
2. pizen: poisoned.
3. co'n: corn.

a-pesterin' folks with a pack o'hungry, triflin' houn's to feed!"

"When she keeps a-throwin' skillet lids," came Ransie's anti-phony, "and slings b'ilin' water on the best coon-dog in the Cumberlands, and sets herself again' cookin' a man's victuals, and keeps him awake o'nights accusin' him of a sight of doin's!"

"When he's al'ays a-fightin' the revenues,[4] and gits a hard name in the mount'ins fur a mean man, who's gwine to be able fur to sleep o' nights?"

The Justice of the Peace stirred deliberately to his duties. He placed his one chair and a wooden stool for his petitioners. He opened his book of statutes on the table and scanned the index. Presently he wiped his spectacles and shifted his inkstand.

"The law and the statutes," said he, "air[5] silent on the subject of divo'ce as fur as the jurisdiction of this co't[6] air concerned. But, accordin' to equity and the Constitution and the golden rule, it's a bad barg'in that can't run both ways. If a justice of the peace can marry a couple, it's plain that he is bound to be able to divo'ce 'em. This here office will issue a decree of divo'ce and abide by the decision of the Supreme Co't to hold it good."

Ransie Bilbro drew a small tobacco-bag from his trousers pocket. Out of this he shook upon the table a five-dollar note. "Sold a b'arskin and two foxes fur that," he remarked. "It's all the money we got."

"The regular price of a divo'ce in this co't," said the Justice, "air five dollars." He stuffed the bill into the pocket of his homespun vest with a deceptive air of indifference. With much bodily toil and mental travail he wrote the decree upon half a sheet of foolscap, and then copied it upon the other. Ransie Bilbro and his wife listened to his reading of the document that was to give them freedom:

Know all men by these presents that Ransie Bilbro and his wife, Ariela Bilbro, this day personally appeared before me and promises that hereinafter they will neither love, honor, nor obey each other, neither for better nor worse, being of sound mind and body, and accept summons for divorce according to the peace and dignity of the State. Herein fail not, so help you God. Benaja Widdup, justice of the peace in and for the county of Piedmont, State of Tennessee.

4. revenues: tax collectors.
5. air: are.
6. co't: court.

The Justice was about to hand one of the documents to Ransie. The voice of Ariela delayed the transfer. Both men looked at her. Their dull masculinity was confronted by something sudden and unexpected in the woman.

"Judge, don't you give him that air paper yit. 'Tain't all settled, nohow. I got to have my rights first. I got to have my ali-money.[7] 'Tain't no kind of a way to do fur a man to divo'ce his wife 'thout her havin' a cent fur to do with. I'm alayin' off to be a-goin' up to brother Ed's up on Hogback Mount'in. I'm bound fur to hev a pa'r of shoes and some snuff and things besides. Ef Ranse kin affo'd a divo'ce, let him pay me ali-money."

Ransie Bilbro was stricken to dumb perplexity. There had been no previous hint of alimony. Women were always bringing up startling and unlooked-for issues.

Justice Benaja Widdup felt that the point demanded judicial decision. The authorities were also silent on the subject of alimony. But the woman's feet were bare. The trail to Hogback Mountain was steep and flinty.

"Ariela Bilbro," he asked, in official tones, "how much did you 'low would be good and sufficient ali-money in the case befo' the co't?"

"I 'lowed," she answered, "fur the shoes and all, to say five dollars. That ain't much fur ali-money, but I reckon that'll git me up to brother Ed's."

"The amount," said the Justice, "air not onreasonable. Ransie Bilbro, you air ordered by the co't to pay the plaintiff the sum of five dollars befo' the decree of divo'ce air issued."

"I hain't no mo' money," breathed Ransie, heavily. "I done paid you all I had."

"Otherwise," said the Justice, looking severely over his spectacles, "you air in contempt of co't."

"I reckon if you gimme till to-morrow," pleaded the husband, "I mout[8] be able to rake or scrape it up somewhars. I never looked for to be a-payin' no ali-money."

"The case air adjourned," said Benaja Widdup, "til tomorrow, when you-all will present yo-selves and obey the order of the co't. Followin' of which the decrees of divo'ce will be delivered." He sat down in the door and began to loosen a shoestring.

"We mout as well go down to Uncle Ziah's," decided Ransie, "and spend the night." He climbed into the cart on one side,

7. ali-money: alimony; money paid by a divorced husband to his ex-wife.
8. mout: might.

and Ariela climbed in on the other. Obeying the flap of his rope, the little red bull slowly came around on a tack, and the cart crawled away in the nimbus[9] arising from its wheels.

Justice-of-the-peace Benaja Widdup smoked his elder-stem pipe. Late in the afternoon he got his weekly paper, and read it until the twilight dimmed its lines. Then he lit the tallow candle on his table, and read until the moon rose, marking the time for supper. He lived in the double log cabin on the slope near the girdled poplar. Going home to supper he crossed a little branch darkened by a laurel thicket. The dark figure of a man stepped from the laurels and pointed a rifle at his breast. His hat was pulled down low, and something covered most of his face.

"I want yo' money," said the figure, " 'thout any talk. I'm gettin' nervous, and my finger's a-wabblin' on this here trigger."

"I've only got f-f-five dollars," said the Justice, producing it from his vest pocket.

"Roll it up," came the order, "and stick it in the end of this here gun-bar'l."

The bill was crisp and new. Even fingers that were clumsy and trembling found little difficulty in making a spill of it and inserting it (this with less ease) into the muzzle of the rifle.

"Now I reckon you kin be goin' along," said the robber.

The Justice lingered not on his way.

The next day came the little red bull, drawing the cart to the office door. Justice Benaja Widdup had his shoes on, for he was expecting the visit. In his presence Ransie Bilbro handed to his wife a five-dollar bill. The official's eye sharply viewed it. It seemed to curl up as though it had been rolled and inserted into the end of a gun-barrel. But the Justice refrained from comment. It is true that other bills might be inclined to curl. He handed each one a decree of divorce. Each stood awkwardly silent, slowly folding the guarantee of freedom. The woman cast a shy glance full of constraint at Ransie.

"I reckon you'll be goin' back up to the cabin," she said, "along 'ith the bull-cart. There's bread in the tin box settin' on the shelf. I put the bacon in the b'ilin'-pot to keep the hounds from gettin' it. Don't forget to wind the clock tonight."

"You air a-goin' to your brother Ed's?" asked Ransie, with fine unconcern.

9. nimbus: low, gray cloud.

"I was 'lowin' to get along up thar afore night. I ain't sayin' as they'll pester theyselves any to make me welcome, but I hain't nowhar else fur to go. It's a right smart ways, and I reckon I better be goin'. I'll be a-sayin' good-bye, Ranse—that is, if you keer fur to say so."

"I don't know as anybody's a hound dog," said Ransie, in a martyr's voice, "fur to not want to say good-bye—'less you air so anxious to git away that you don't want me to say it."

Ariela was silent. She folded the five-dollar bill and her decree carefully, and placed them in the bosom of her dress. Benaja Widdup watched the money disappear with mournful eyes behind his spectacles.

And then with his next words he achieved rank (as his thoughts ran) with either the great crowd of the world's sympathizers or the little crowd of its great financiers.

"Be kind o' lonesome in the old cabin to night, Ransie," he said.

Ransie Bilbro stared out at the Cumberlands, clear blue now in the sunlight. He did not look at Ariela.

"I 'low it might be lonesome," he said, "but when folks gits mad and wants a divo'ce, you can't make folks stay."

"There's others wanted a divo'ce," said Ariela, speaking to the wooden stool. "Besides, nobody don't want nobody to stay."

"Nobody never said they didn't."

"Nobody never said they did. I reckon I better start on now to brother Ed's."

"Nobody can't wind that old clock."

"Want me to go along 'ith you in the cart and wind it fur you, Ranse?"

The mountaineer's countenance was proof against emotion. But he reached out a big hand and enclosed Ariela's thin brown one. Her soul peeped out once through her impassive face, hallowing it.

"Them hounds sha'n't pester you no more," said Ransie. "I reckon I been mean and low down. You wind that clock, Ariela."

"My heart hit's in that cabin, Ranse," she whispered, "along 'ith you. I ain't a-goin' to git mad no more. Le's be startin', Ranse, so's we kin git home by sundown."

Justice-of-the-peace Benaja Widdup interposed as they started for the door, forgetting his presence.

"In the name of the State of Tennessee," he said, "I forbid you-all to be a-defyin' of its laws and statutes. This co't is mo' than willin' and full of joy to see the clouds of discord and misunderstandin' rollin' away from two lovin' hearts, but it air the duty of the co't to p'eserve the morals and integrity of the State. The co't reminds you that you air no longer man and wife, but air divo'ced by regular decree, and as such air not entitled to the benefits and 'purtenances of the mattermonal estate."

Ariela caught Ransie's arm. Did those words mean that she must lose him now when they had just learned the lesson of life?

"But the co't air prepared," went the Justice, "fur to remove the disabilities set up by the decree of divo'ce. The co't air on hand to perform the solemn ceremony of marri'ge, thus fixin' things up and enablin' the parties in the case to resume the honor'ble and elevatin' state of mattermony which they desires. The fee fur performin' said ceremony will be, in this case, to wit, five dollars."

Ariela caught the gleam of promise in his words. Swiftly her hand went to her bosom. Freely as an alighting dove the bill fluttered to the Justice's table. Her sallow cheek colored as she stood hand in hand with Ransie and listened to the reuniting words.

Ransie helped her into the cart, and climbed in beside her. The little red bull turned once more, and they set out, hand-clasped, for the mountains.

Justice-of-the-peace Benaja Widdup sat in his door and took off his shoes. Once again he fingered the bill tucked down in his vest pocket. Once again he smoked his elder-stem pipe. Once again the speckled hen swaggered down the main street of the "settlement," cackling foolishly.

QUESTIONS FOR DISCUSSION AND WRITING

1. You find out very early in the story that, although it is about two unhappy people, O. Henry means it to be humorous. Find and read aloud passages from the first two or three pages that show this.
2. How does Benaja Widdup explain that he has the right to grant a divorce? What do his explanation and his decision about the price of a divorce show you about the sort of person he is?
3. The next day Ransie pays the alimony to his ex-wife Ariela. How did he get the money to do it? How does Justice Widdup start Ransie and Ariela thinking about coming together

again? What does O. Henry mean when he says of Widdup (on page 57) "he achieved rank. . .with the great crowd of the world's sympathizers or the little crowd of its great financiers"? How was he a sympathizer? How was he a financier? Explain whether you think he was more sympathizer or financier.

4. How does it come about that Ransie and Ariela decide to undo the divorce? What have they learned from the experience?
5. Who "wins" in the story? How? The whirligig has gone around. How are things different at the end of the story from what they were at the beginning? How are they the same?

SUGGESTIONS FOR FURTHER WRITING OR DISCUSSION

1. Think of a married couple that you know or of one that you make up. Describe their lives, showing what forces hold them together and what forces pull them apart.
2. For fun, try to write an account of the scene as it might have been when Ransie and Ariela got back to the cabin. If you want to have a try at O. Henry's version of Mountain dialect, go ahead, but if not, write the dialogue in ordinary English.

Recovering Lost Power

In the South, a young black boy and his principal display courage.

A technician of the future discovers a surprising source of power.

THE BOY WHO PAINTED CHRIST BLACK

by John Henrik Clarke

*A lot has changed in race relations in Georgia since
the 1930's when the events of this story took place.
But the act of a black boy who paints some "sacrilegious nonsense" might still cause a crisis between a
black principal and a white superintendent. What examples of courage can you find in this story?*

He was the smartest boy in the Muskogee County School—
for colored children. Everybody even remotely connected with
the school knew this. The teacher always pronounced his name
with profound gusto as she pointed him out as the ideal student.
Once I heard her say: "If he were white he might, some day,
become President." Only Aaron Crawford wasn't white; quite the
contrary. His skin was so solid black that it glowed, reflecting
an inner virtue that was strange, and beyond my comprehension.

In many ways he looked like something that was awkwardly
put together. Both his nose and his lips seemed a trifle too large
for his face. To say he was ugly would be unjust and to say
he was handsome would be gross exaggeration. Truthfully, I
could never make up my mind about him. Sometimes he looked
like something out of a book of ancient history . . . looked as
if he was left over from that magnificent era before the machine
age came and marred the earth's natural beauty.

His great variety of talent often startled the teachers. This
caused his classmates to look upon him with a mixed feeling
of awe and envy.

Before Thanksgiving, he always drew turkeys and pumpkins
on the blackboard. On George Washington's birthday, he drew
large American flags surrounded by little hatchets. It was these
small masterpieces that made him the most talked-about colored
boy in Columbus, Georgia. The Negro principal of the Muskogee
County School said he would some day be a great painter, like
Henry O. Tanner.[1]

1. Henry O. Tanner: black American painter (1859-1939).

For the teacher's birthday, which fell on a day about a week before commencement, Aaron Crawford painted the picture that caused an uproar, and a turning point, at the Muskogee County School. The moment he entered the room that morning, all eyes fell on him. Besides his torn book holder, he was carrying a large-framed concern wrapped in old newspapers. As he went to his seat, the teacher's eyes followed his every motion, a curious wonderment mirrored in them conflicting with the half-smile that wreathed her face.

Aaron put his books down, then smiling broadly, advanced toward the teacher's desk. His alert eyes were so bright with joy that they were almost frightening. The children were leaning forward in their seats, staring greedily at him; a restless anticipation was rampant within every breast.

Already the teacher sensed that Aaron had a present for her. Still smiling, he placed it on her desk and began to help her unwrap it. As the last piece of paper fell from the large frame, the teacher jerked her hand away from it suddenly, her eyes flickering unbelievingly. Amidst the rigid tension, her heavy breathing was distinct and frightening. Temporarily, there was no other sound in the room.

With a quick, involuntary movement I rose up from my desk. A series of submerged murmurs spread through the room, rising to a distinct monotone. The teacher turned toward the children, staring reproachfully. They did not move their eyes from the present that Aaron had brought her . . . . It was a large picture of Christ—painted black!

Aaron Crawford went back to his seat, a feeling of triumph reflecting in his every movement.

The teacher faced us. Her curious half-smile had blurred into a mild bewilderment. She searched the bright faces before her and started to smile again, occasionally stealing quick glances at the large picture propped on her desk, as though doing so were forbidden amusement.

"Aaron," she spoke at last, a slight tinge of uncertainty in her tone, "this is a most welcome present. Thanks. I will treasure it." She paused, then went on speaking, a trifle more coherent than before. "Looks like you are going to be quite an artist . . . . Suppose you come forward and tell the class how you came to paint this remarkable picture."

When he rose to speak, to explain about the picture, a hush fell tightly over the room, and the children gave him all of their attention . . . something they rarely did for the teacher. He did not speak at first; he just stood there in front of the room, toying absently with his hands, observing his audience carefully, like a great concert artist.

"It was like this," he said, placing full emphasis on every word. "You see, my uncle who lives in New York teaches classes in Negro History at the Y.M.C.A. When he visited us last year he was telling me about the many great black folks who have made history. He said black folks were once the most powerful people on earth. When I asked him about Christ, he said no one ever proved whether he was black or white. Somehow a feeling came over me that he was a black man, 'cause he was so kind and forgiving, kinder than I have ever seen white people be. So, when I painted his picture I couldn't help but paint it as I thought it was."

After this, the little artist sat down, smiling broadly, as if he had gained entrance to a great storehouse of knowledge that ordinary people could neither acquire nor comprehend.

The teacher, knowing nothing else to do under prevailing circumstances, invited the children to rise from their seats and come forward so they could get a complete view of Aaron's unique piece of art.

When I came close to the picture, I noticed it was painted with a kind of paint you get in the five and ten cent stores. Its shape was blurred slightly, as if someone had jarred the frame before the paint had time to dry. The eyes of Christ were deepset and sad, very much like those of Aaron's father, who was a deacon in the local Baptist Church. This picture of Christ looked much different from the one I saw hanging on the wall when I was in Sunday School. It looked more like a helpless Negro, pleading silently for mercy.

For the next few days, there was much talk about Aaron's picture.

The school term ended the following week and Aaron's picture, along with the best handwork done by the students that year, was on display in the assembly room. Naturally, Aaron's picture graced the place of honor.

There was no book work to be done on commencement day and joy was rampant among the children. The girls in their brightly colored dresses gave the school the delightful air of Spring awakening.

In the middle of the day all the children were gathered in the small assembly. On this day we were always favored with a visit from a man whom all the teachers spoke of with mixed esteem and fear. Professor Danual, they called him, and they always pronounced his name with reverence. He was supervisor of all the city schools, including those small and poorly equipped ones set aside for colored children.

The great man arrived almost at the end of our commencement exercises. On seeing him enter the hall, the children rose, bowed courteously, and sat down again, their eyes examining him as if he were a circus freak.

He was a tall white man with solid gray hair that made his lean face seem paler than it actually was. His eyes were the clearest blue I have ever seen. They were the only life-like things about him.

As he made his way to the front of the room the Negro principal, George Du Vaul, was walking ahead of him, cautiously preventing anything from getting in his way. As he passed me, I heard the teachers, frightened, sucking in their breath, felt the tension tightening.

A large chair was in the center of the rostrum. It had been daintily polished and the janitor had laboriously recushioned its bottom. The supervisor went straight to it without being guided, knowing that this pretty splendor was reserved for him.

Presently the Negro principal introduced the distinguished guest and he favored us with a short speech. It wasn't a very important speech. Almost at the end of it, I remember him saying something about he wouldn't be surprised if one of us boys grew up to be a great colored man, like Booker T. Washington.[2]

After he sat down, the school chorus sang two spirituals and the girls in the fourth grade did an Indian folk dance. This brought the commencement program to an end.

After this the supervisor came down from the rostrum, his eyes tinged with curiosity, and began to view the array of handwork on display in front of the chapel.

Suddenly his face underwent a strange rejuvenation. His clear blue eyes flickered in astonishment. He was looking at Aaron Crawford's picture of Christ. Mechanically he moved his stooped form closer to the picture and stood gazing fixedly at it, curious and undecided, as though it were a dangerous animal that would rise any moment and spread destruction.

We waited tensely for his next movement. The silence was

2. Booker T. Washington: (1856-1915) a black American educator, head of Tuskegee Institute in Alabama. He believed that Negroes should strive for economic equality before they tried for social equality.

almost suffocating. At last he twisted himself around and began to search the grim faces before him. The fiery glitter of his eyes abated slightly as they rested on the Negro principal, protestingly.

"Who painted this sacrilegious nonsense?" he demanded angrily.

"I painted it, sir." These were Aaron's words, spoken hesitantly. He wetted his lips timidly and looked up at the supervisor, his eyes voicing a sad plea for understanding.

He spoke again, this time more coherently. "Th' principal said a colored person have jes as much right paintin' Jesus black as a white person have paintin' him white. And he says . . . ." At this point he halted abruptly, as if to search for his next words. A strong tinge of bewilderment dimmed the glow of his solid black face. He stammered out a few more words, then stopped again.

The supervisor strode a few steps toward him. At last color had swelled some of the lifelessness out of his lean face.

"Well, go on!" he said, enragedly, ". . . .I'm still listening."

Aaron moved his lips pathetically but no words passed them. His eyes wandered around the room, resting finally, with an air of hope, on the face of the Negro principal. After a moment, he jerked his face in another direction, regretfully, as if something he had said had betrayed an understanding between him and the principal.

Presently the principal stepped forward to defend the school's prize student.

"I encouraged the boy in painting that picture," he said firmly. "And it was with my permission that he brought the picture into this school. I don't think the boy is so far wrong in painting Christ black. The artists of all other races have painted whatsoever God they worship to resemble themselves. I see no reason why we should be immune from that privilege. After all, Christ was born in that part of the world that had always been predominantly populated by colored people. There is a strong possibility that he could have been a Negro."

But for the monotonous lull of heavy breathing, I would have sworn that his words had frozen everyone in the hall. I had never heard the little principal speak so boldly to anyone, black or white.

The supervisor swallowed dumbfoundedly. His face was aglow in silent rage.

"Have you been teaching these children things like that?" he asked the Negro principal, sternly.

"I have been teaching them that their race has produced great kings and queens as well as slaves and serfs," the principal said. "The time is long overdue when we should let the world know that we erected and enjoyed the benefits of a splendid civilization long before the people of Europe had a written language."

The supervisor coughed. His eyes bulged menacingly as he spoke. "You are not being paid to teach such things in this school, and I am demanding your resignation for overstepping your limit as principal."

George Du Vaul did not speak. A strong quiver swept over his sullen face. He revolved himself slowly and walked out of the room towards his office.

The supervisor's eyes followed him until he was out of focus. Then he murmured under his breath: "There'll be a lot of fuss in this world if you start people thinking that Christ was a nigger."

Some of the teachers followed the principal out of the chapel, leaving the crestfallen children restless and in a quandry about what to do next. Finally we started back to our rooms. The supervisor was behind me. I heard him murmur to himself: "Damn, if niggers ain't getting smarter."

A few days later I heard that the principal had accepted a summer job as art instructor of a small high school somewhere in south Georgia and had gotten permission from Aaron's parents to take him along so he could continue to encourage him in his painting.

I was on my way home when I saw him leaving his office. He was carrying a large briefcase and some books tucked under his arm. He had already said good-by to all the teachers. And strangely, he did not look brokenhearted. As he headed for the large front door, he readjusted his horn-rimmed glasses, but did not look back. An air of triumph gave more dignity to his soldierly stride. He had the appearance of a man who had done a great thing, something greater than any ordinary man would do.

Aaron Crawford was waiting outside for him. They walked down the street together. He put his arm around Aaron's shoulder affectionately. He was talking sincerely to Aaron about something, and Aaron was listening, deeply earnest.

I watched them until they were so far down the street that their forms had begun to blur. Even from this distance I could see they were still walking in brisk, dignified strides, like two people who had won some sort of victory.

QUESTIONS FOR DISCUSSION AND WRITING

1. Why did Aaron Crawford's teacher once say, "If he were white he might, some day, become President"? What do you learn about Aaron during the story that helps explain what the teacher meant?
2. How did the teacher react when she had unwrapped Aaron's birthday present to her? Reread Aaron's explanation of why he painted Christ black. What is your reaction to his explanation?
3. When Professor Danual, the superintendent of schools, entered the commencement hall, how did the teachers react? Why? What does it show about him when he says that he thinks one of the boys "might grow up to be a great colored man, like Booker T. Washington?" How could he say this and also react to Aaron's picture as he did?
4. How does this principal come to Aaron's rescue when the boy is too afraid to explain why he painted Christ Black? How do the pupils react? How does the superintendent react? Why did it take courage for the principal to speak out as he did?
5. Reread the last paragraph of the story. What is the "victory" that is referred to? Victory over what?
6. The title of this group of two stories is "Lost Power Is Recovered." Why is this story included under that title? What power has been lost? Has power been recovered? How?

SUGGESTIONS FOR FURTHER WRITING OR DISCUSSION

1. Write a story or an account of some courageous deed done or words said against the force of hostile opinion or power.
2. Tell about a person you know who has some of the qualities of greatness. Make us see clearly how he or she is great.
3. Tell about a startlingly original creation like Aaron's painting (perhaps a work of art, a story, a speech, or something hand-made) and the effects it had on those who saw or heard it.

THE FEELING OF POWER

by Isaac Asimov

It is far in the future. Computers have taken over much of the activity of the human brain. The old arithmetic has been forgotten. Computer programmers are the most important citizens. A lowly Technician reveals a source of great power available to the men who govern. What does this story say about human intelligence and war?

Jehan Shuman was used to dealing with the men in authority on long-embattled Earth. He was only a civilian but he originated programming patterns that resulted in self-directing war computers of the highest sort. Generals consequently listened to him. Heads of congressional committees, too.

There was one of each in the special lounge of New Pentagon. General Weider was space-burnt and had a small mouth puckered almost into a cipher. Congressman Brant was smooth-cheeked and clear-eyed. He smoked Denebian tobacco with the air of one whose patriotism was so notorious, he could be allowed such liberties.

Shuman, tall, distinguished, and Programmer-first-class, faced them fearlessly.

He said, "This, gentlemen, is Myron Aub."

"The one with the unusual gift that you discovered quite by accident," said Congressman Brant placidly. "Ah." He inspected the little man with the egg-bald head with amiable curiosity.

The little man, in return, twisted the fingers of his hands anxiously. He had never been near such great men before. He was only an aging low-grade Technician who had long ago failed all tests designed to smoke out the gifted ones among mankind and had settled into the rut of unskilled labor. There was just this hobby of his that the great Programmer had found out about and was now making such a frightening fuss over.

General Weider said, "I find this atmosphere of mystery childish."

"You won't in a moment," said Shuman. "This is not something we can leak to the firstcomer.—Aub!" There was something imperative about his manner of biting off that one-syllable name, but then he was a great Programmer speaking to a mere Technician. "Aub! How much is nine times seven?"

Aub hesitated a moment. His pale eyes glimmered with a feeble anxiety. "Sixty-three," he said.

Congressman Brant lifted his eyebrows. "Is that right?"

"Check it for yourself, Congressman."

The congressman took out his pocket computer, nudged the milled edges twice, looked at its face as it lay there in the palm of his hand, and put it back. He said. "Is this the gift you brought us here to demonstrate. An illusionist?"

"More than that, sir. Aub has memorized a few operations and with them he computes on paper."

"A paper computer?" said the general. He looked pained.

"No, sir," said Shuman patiently. "Not a paper computer. Simply a sheet of paper. General, would you be so kind as to suggest a number?"

"Seventeen," said the general.

"And you, Congressman?"

"Twenty-three."

"Good! Aub, multiply those numbers and please show the gentlemen your manner of doing it."

"Yes, Programmer," said Aub, ducking his head. He fished a small pad out of one shirt pocket and an artist's hairline stylus out of the other. His forehead corrugated as he made painstaking marks on the paper.

General Weider interrupted him sharply. "Let's see that."

Aub passed him the paper, and Weider said, "Well, it looks like the figure seventeen."

Congressman Brant nodded and said, "So it does, but I suppose anyone can copy figures off a computer. I think I could make a passable seventeen myself, even without practice."

"If you will let Aub continue, gentlemen," said Shuman without heat.

Aub continued, his hand trembling a little. Finally he said in a low voice, "The answer is three hundred and ninety-one."

Congressman Brant took out his computer a second time and flicked it, "By Godfrey, so it is. How did he guess?"

"No guess, Congressman," said Shuman. "He computed that· result. He did it on this sheet of paper."

"Humbug," said the general impatiently. "A computer is one thing and marks on paper are another."

"Explain, Aub," said Shuman.

"Yes, Programmer.—Well, gentlemen, I write down seventeen and just underneath it, I write twenty-three. Next, I say to myself: seven times three—"

The congressman interrupted smoothly, "Now, Aub, the problem is seventeen times twenty-three."

"Yes, I know," said the little Technician earnestly, "but I *start* by saying seven times three because that's the way it works. Now seven times three is twenty-one."

"And how do you know that?" asked the congressman.

"I just remember it. It's always twenty-one on the computer. I've checked it any number of times."

"That doesn't mean it always will be, though, does it?" said the congressman.

"Maybe not," stammered Aub. "I'm not a mathematician. But I always get the right answers, you see."

"Go on."

"Seven times three is twenty-one, so I write down twenty-one. Then one times three is three, so I write down a three under the two of twenty-one."

"Why under the two?" asked Congressman Brant at once.

"Because—" Aud looked helplessly at his superior for support. "It's difficult to explain."

Shuman said, "If you will accept his work for the moment, we can leave the details for the mathematicians."

Brant subsided.

Aub said, "Three plus two makes five, you see, so the twenty-one becomes a fifty-one. Now you let that go for a while and start fresh. You multiply seven and two, that's fourteen, and one and two, that's two. Put them down like this and it adds up to thirty-four. Now if you put the thirty-four under the fifty-one this way and add them, you get three hundred and ninety-one and that's the answer."

There was an instant's silence and then General Weider said, "I don't believe it. He goes through this rigmarole and makes up numbers and multiplies and adds them this way and that, but I don't believe it. It's too complicated to be anything but hornswoggling."[1]

"Oh no, sir," said Aub in a sweat. "It only *seems* complicated because you're not used to it. Actually, the rules are quite simple and will work for any numbers."

"Any numbers, eh?" said the general. "Come then." He took

---

1. hornswoggling: deceiving or fooling.

out his own computer (a severely styled GI model) and struck it at random. "Make a five seven three eight on the paper. That's five thousand seven hundred and thirty-eight."

"Yes, sir," said Aub, taking a new sheet of paper.

"Now," (more punching of his computer), "seven two three nine. Seven thousand two hundred and thirty-nine."

"Yes, sir."

"And now multiply those two."

"It will take some time," quavered Aub.

"Take the time," said the general.

"Go ahead, Aub," said Shuman crisply.

Aub set to work, bending low. He took another sheet of paper and another. The general took out his watch finally and stared at it. "Are you through with your magic making, Technician?"

"I'm almost done, sir.—Here it is, sir. Forty-one million, five hundred and thirty-seven thousand, three hundred and eighty-two." He showed the scrawled figures of the result.

General Weider smiled bitterly. He pushed the multiplication contact on his computer and let the numbers whirl to a halt. And then he stared and said in a surprised squeak, "Great Galaxy, the fella's right."

The President of the Terrestrial Federation[2] had grown haggard in office and, in private, he allowed a look of settled melancholy to appear on his sensitive features. The Denebian war, after its early start of vast movement and great popularity, had trickled down into a sordid matter of maneuver and countermaneuver, with discontent rising steadily on Earth. Possibly, it was rising on Deneb, too.

And now Congressman Brant, head of the important Committee on Military Appropriations was cheerfully and smoothly spending his half-hour appointment spouting nonsense.

"Computing without a computer," said the president impatiently, "is a contradiction in terms."

"Computing," said the congressman, "is only a system for handling data. A machine might do it, or the human brain might. Let me give you an example." And, using the new skills he had learned, he worked out sums and products until the president, despite himself, grew interested.

"Does this always work?"

"Every time, Mr. President. It is foolproof."

2. Terrestrial Federation: a government of all the nations on Earth.

"Is it hard to learn?"

"It took me a week to get the real hang of it. I think you would do better."

"Well," said the president, considering, "it's an interesting parlor game, but what is the use of it?"

"What is the use of a newborn baby, Mr. President? At the moment there is no use, but don't you see that this points the way toward liberation from the machine. Consider, Mr. President," the congressman rose and his deep voice automatically took on some of the cadences he used in public debate, "that the Denebian war is a war of computer against computer. Their computers forge an impenetrable shield of counter-missiles against our missiles, and ours forge one against theirs. If we advance the efficiency of our computers, so do they theirs, and for five years a precarious and profitless balance has existed.

"Now we have in our hands a method for going beyond the computer, leapfrogging it, passing through it. We will combine the mechanics of computation with human thought; we will have the equivalent of intelligent computers; billions of them. I can't predict what the consequences will be in detail but they will be incalculable. And if Deneb beats us to the punch, they may be unimaginably catastrophic."

The president said, troubled, "What would you have me do?"

"Put the power of the administration behind the establishment of a secret project on human computation. Call it Project Number, if you like. I can vouch for my committee, but I will need the administration behind me."

"But how far can human computation go?"

"There is no limit. According to Programmer Shuman, who first introduced me to this discovery—"

"I've heard of Shuman, of course."

"Yes. Well, Dr. Shuman tells me that in theory there is nothing the computer can do that the human mind can not do. The computer merely takes a finite amount of data and performs a finite number of operations upon them. The human mind can duplicate the process."

The president considered that. He said, "If Shuman says this, I am inclined to believe him—in theory. But, in practice, how can anyone know how a computer works?"

Brant laughed genially. "Well, Mr. President, I asked the same question. It seems that at one time computers were designed directly by human beings. Those were simple computers, of course, this being before the time of the rational use of computers to design more advanced computers.

"Yes, yes. Go on."

"Technician Aub apparently had, as his hobby, the recon-
struction of some of these ancient devices and in so doing he
studied the details of their workings and found he could imitate
them. The multiplication I just performed for you is an imitation
of the workings of a computer."

"Amazing!"

The congressman coughed gently, "If I may make another
point, Mr. President—The further we can develop this thing, the
more we can divert our Federal effort from computer production
and computer maintenance. As the human brain takes over,
more of our energy can be directed into peacetime pursuits and
the impingement of war on the ordinary man will be less. This
will be most advantageous for the party in power, of course."

"Ah," said the president, "I see your point. Well, sit down,
Congressman, sit down. I want some time to think about this.
—But meanwhile, show me that multiplication trick again. Let's
see if I can't catch the point of it."

Programmer Shuman did not try to hurry matters. Loesser
was conservative, very conservative, and liked to deal wtih computers as his father and grandfather had. Still, he controlled the
West European computer combine, and if he could be persuaded
to join Project Number in full enthusiasm, a great deal would
be accomplished.

But Loesser was holding back. He said, "I'm not sure I like
the idea of relaxing our hold on computers. The human mind
is a capricious thing. The computer will give the same answer
to the same problem each time. What guarantee have we that
the human mind will do the same?"

"The human mind, Computer Loesser, only manipulates
facts. It doesn't matter whether the human mind or a machine
does it. They are just tools."

"Yes, yes. I've gone over your ingenious demonstration that
the mind can duplicate the computer but it seems to me a little
in the air. I'll grant the theory but what reason have we for
thinking that theory can be converted to practice?"

"I think we have reason, sir. After all, computers have not
always existed. The cave men with their triremes,[3] stone axes,
and railroads had no computers."

3. triremes: an ancient galley, usually a warship, having rowers arranged in
   groups of three.

"And possibly they did not compute."

"You know better than that. Even the building of a railroad or a ziggurat[4] called for some computing, and that must have been without computers as we know them."

"Do you suggest they computed in the fashion you demonstrate?"

"Probably not. After all, this method—we call it 'graphitics,' by the way, from the old European word 'grapho' meaning 'to write'—is developed from the computers themselves so it cannot have antedated them. Still, the cave men must have had *some* method, eh?"

"Lost arts! If you're going to talk about lost arts—"

"No, no. I'm not a lost art enthusiast, though I don't say there may not be some. After all, man was eating grain before hydroponics, and if the primitives ate grain, they must have grown it in soil. What else could they have done?"

"I don't know, but I'll believe in soil-growing when I see someone grow grain in soil. And I'll believe in making fire by rubbing two pieces of flint together when I see that, too."

Shuman grew placative. "Well, let's stick to graphitics. It's just part of the process of etherealization. Transportation by means of bulky contrivances is giving way to direct mass-transference. Communications devices become less massive and more efficient constantly. For that matter, compare your pocket computer with the massive jobs of a thousand years ago. Why not, then, the last step of doing away with computers altogether? Come, sir, Project Number is a going concern; progress is already headlong. But we want your help. If patriotism doesn't move you, consider the intellectual adventure involved."

Loesser said skeptically, "What progress? What can you do beyond multiplication? Can you integrate a transcendental function?"[5]

"In time, sir. In time. In the last month I have learned to handle division. I can determine, and correctly, integral quotients and decimal quotients."

"Decimal quotients? To how many places?"

Programmer Shuman tried to keep his tone casual. "Any number!"

Loesser's lower jaw dropped. "Without a computer?"

"Set me a problem."

"Divide twenty-seven by thirteen. Take it to six places."

4. ziggurat; ancient Babylonian terraced pyramid.
5. transcendantal function: a complicated mathematical operation.

Five minutes later, Shuman said, "Two point oh seven six nine two three."

Loesser checked it. "Well, now, that's amazing. Multiplication didn't impress me too much because it involved integers after all, and I thought trick manipulation might do it. But decimals—"

"And that is not all. There is a new development that is, so far, top secret and which, strictly speaking, I ought not to mention. Still—We may have made a break-through on the square root front."

"Square roots?"

"It involves some tricky points and we haven't licked the bugs yet, but Technician Aub, the man who invented the science and who has an amazing intuition in connection with it, maintains he has the problem almost solved. And he is only a Technician. A man like yourself, a trained and talented mathematician ought to have no difficulty."

"Square roots," muttered Loesser, attracted.

"Cube roots, too. Are you with us?"

Loesser's hand thrust out suddenly, "Count me in."

General Weider stumped his way back and forth at the head of the room and addressed his listeners after the fashion of a savage teacher facing a group of recalcitrant students. It made no difference to the general that they were the civilian scientists heading Project Number. The general was the over-all head, and he so considered himself at every waking moment.

He said, "Now square roots are all fine. I can't do them myself and I don't understand the methods, but they're fine. Still, the Project will not be sidetracked in what some of you call the fundamentals. You can play with graphitics any way you want to after the war is over, but right now we have specific and very practical problems to solve."

In a far corner, Technician Aub listened with painful attention. He was no longer a Technician, of course, having been relieved of his duties and assigned to the Project, with a fine-sounding title and good pay. But, of course, the social distinction remained and the highly placed scientific leaders could never bring themselves to admit him to their ranks on a footing of equality. Nor, to do Aub justice, did he, himself, wish it. He was as uncomfortable with them as they with him.

The general was saying, "Our goal is a simple one, gentlemen; the replacement of the computer. A ship that can navigate space without a computer on board can be constructed in one fifth the time and at one tenth the expense of a computer-laden ship. We could build fleets five times, ten times, as great as Deneb could if we could but eliminate the computer.

"And I see something even beyond this. It may be fantastic now; a mere dream; but in the future I see the manned missile!"

There was an instant murmur from the audience.

The general drove on. "At the present time, our chief bottleneck is the fact that missiles are limited in intelligence. The computer controlling them can only be so large, and for that reason they can meet the changing nature of anti-missile defenses in an unsatisfactory way. Few missiles, if any, accomplish their goal and missile warfare is coming to a dead end; for the enemy fortunately, as well as for ourselves.

"On the other hand, a missile with a man or two within, controlling flight by graphitics, would be lighter, more mobile, more intelligent. It would give us a lead that might well mean the margin of victory. Besides which, gentlemen, the exigencies of war compel us to remember one thing. A man is much more dispensable than a computer. Manned missiles could be launched in numbers and under circumstances that no good general would care to undertake as far as computer-directed missiles are concerned—"

He said much more but Technician Aub did not wait.

Technician Aub, in the privacy of his quarters, labored long over the note he was leaving behind. It read finally as follows:

"When I began the study of what is now called graphitics, it was no more than a hobby. I saw no more in it than an interesting amusement, an exercise of mind.

"When Project Number began, I thought that others were wiser than I; that graphitics might be put to practical use as a benefit to mankind, to aid in the production of really practical mass-transference devices perhaps. But now I see it is to be used only for death and destruction.

"I cannot face the responsibility involved in having invented graphitics."

He then deliberately turned the focus of a protein-depolarizer on himself and fell instantly and painlessly dead.

They stood over the grave of the little Technician while tribute was paid to the greatness of his discovery.

Programmer Shuman bowed his head along with the rest of them, but remained unmoved. The Technician had done his share and was no longer needed, after all. He might have started graphitics, but now that it had started, it would carry on by itself overwhelmingly, triumphantly, until manned missiles were possible with who knew what else.

Nine times seven, thought Shuman with deep satisfaction, is sixty-three, and I don't need a computer to tell me so. The computer is in my own head.

And it was amazing the feeling of power that gave him.

QUESTIONS FOR DISCUSSION AND WRITING

1. What does Isaac Asimov say about the far-future world when, in the first paragraph, he calls Jehan Shuman "only a civilian"? Why did generals and congressmen listen to him so carefully, however?
2. What lost powers has Myron Aub rediscovered? Why are the generals and congressmen so amazed?
3. When Congressman Brant explains human computation to the Terrestrial Federation President, he quotes Programmer Shuman as saying, "There is nothing the computer can do that the human mind cannot do." What is the importance of this discovery for the Federation? The idea doesn't seem amazing to us today; why did it amaze the President?
4. Notice the number of times Asimov used the ideas of "mind" and "computer" in exactly the opposite way from which we use them today. What is the purpose of the switch? Today we are "amazed" by what they tell us computers can do. Should we be?
5. What other arts besides arithmetic had been lost at the time the events of this story take place? Read the sentences that tell of these.
6. Why did Technician Aub commit suicide? How do you know that his suicide is in vain? What is it that gives Programmer Shuman the feeling of power?
7. What does the story say about brains and war? What is Asimov telling us about the way the world is going today?

SUGGESTION FOR FURTHER WRITING OR DISCUSSION

Write a future-fantasy based on the rapid development of some recent invention used today. (Snowmobiles? TV? Moving sidewalks? Computer-driven automobiles? Artificial manufacture of human growth cells?)

Animals Affect People

The fate of a turtle sparks an argument between a father and his son.

A young girl frantically searches for her dog.

A newborn colt creates a problem for its owner, a soldier in the midst of war.

THE TURTLE

by George Vukelich

It's just before dawn in the Wisconsin countryside when old Tony and his son Jimmy see a turtle ahead on the sandroad. They argue about what to do. Who wins the argument?

They were driving up to fish the White Creek for German Browns[1] and the false dawn was purpling the Wisconsin countryside when they spotted the huge hump-backed object in the middle of the sandroad and Jimmy coasted the station wagon to a stop.

"Pa," he said. "Turtle. Lousy snapper."

Old Tony sat up.

"Is he dead?"

"Not yet," Jimmy said. "Not yet he isn't." He shifted into neutral and pulled the handbrake. The snapper lay large and darkgreen in the headlight beams, and they got out and went around to look at it closely. The turtle moved a little and left razorlike clawmarks in the wet sand, and it waited.

"Probably heading for the creek," Jimmy said. "They kill trout like crazy."

They stood staring down.

"I'd run the wagon over him," Jimmy said. "Only he's too big."

He looked around and walked to the ditchway, and came back with a long finger-thick pine branch. He jabbed it into the turtle's face and the snakehead lashed out and struck like springsteel and the branch snapped like a stick of macaroni, and it all happened fast as a matchflare.

"Looka that!" Tony whistled.

"You bet, Pa. I bet he goes sixty pounds. Seventy maybe."

The turtle was darting its head around now in long stretching movements.

"I think he got some branch stuck in his craw," Jimmy said.

1. German Browns: a kind of trout.

First appeared in *The University of Kansas City Review*. Reprinted by permission of *The University of Kansas City Review*.

He got out a cigaret and lighted it, and flipped the match at the rockgreen shell.

"I wish now I'd brought the twenty-two,"[2] he said. "The pistol."

"You going to kill him?"

"Why not?" Jimmy asked. "They kill trout, don't they?"

They stood there smoking and not talking, and looking down at the unmoving shell.

"I could use the lug wrench on him," Jimmy said. "Only I don't think it's long enough. I don't want my hands near him."

Tony didn't say anything.

"You watch him," Jimmy said. "I'll go find something in the wagon."

Slowly Tony squatted down onto his haunches and smoked and stared at the turtle. Poor Old One, he thought. You had the misfortune to be caught in the middle of a sandroad, and you are very vulnerable on the sandroads, and now you are going to get the holy life beaten out of you.

The turtle stopped its stretching movements and was still. Tony looked at the full webbed feet and the nail claws and he knew the truth.

"It would be different in the water, turtle," he said. "In the water you could cut down anybody."

He thought about this snapper in the water and how it would move like a torpedo and bring down trout, and nobody would monkey with it in the water—and here it was in the middle of a sandroad, vulnerable as a baby and waiting to get its brains beaten out.

He finished his cigaret and field-stripped it,[3] and got to his feet and walked to the wagon and reached into the glove compartment for the thermos of coffee. What was he getting all worked up about a turtle for? He was an old man and he was acting like a kid, and they were going up to the White for German Browns, and he was getting worked up about a God-forsaken turtle in the middle of a God-forsaken sandroad. *God-forsaken*. He walked back to the turtle and hunched down and sipped at the strong black coffee and watched the old snapper watching him.

Jimmy came up to him holding the bumper jack.

"I want to play it safe," he said. "I don't think the lug wrench

---

2. twenty-two: a 22 caliber pistol.
3. field-stripped it: broke it apart.

is long enough." He squatted beside Tony. "What do you think?"

"He waits," Tony said. "What difference what I think?"

Jimmy squinted at him.

"I can tell something's eating you. What are you thinking, Pa?"

"I am thinking this is not a brave thing."

"What?"

"This turtle—he does not have a chance."

Jimmy lit a cigaret and hefted the bumper jack. The turtle moved ever so slightly.

"You talk like an old woman. An old tired woman."

"I can understand this turtle's position."

"He doesn't have a chance?"

"That's right."

"And that bothers you?"

Tony looked into Jimmy's face.

"That is right," he said. "That bothers me."

"Well of all the dumb stupid things," Jimmy said. "What do you want me to do? Get down on all fours and fight with him?"

"No," Tony said. "Not on all fours. Not on all fours." He looked at Jimmy. "In the water. Fight this turtle in the water. That would be a brave thing, my son."

Jimmy put down the bumper jack and reached for the thermos jug and didn't say anything. He drank his coffee and smoked his cigaret, and he stared at the turtle and didn't say anything.

"You're crazy," he said finally.

"It is a thought, my son. A thought. This helpless plodding old one like a little baby in this sandroad, eh? But in the water, his home. . ." Tony snapped his fingers with the suddenness of a switch blade. "In the water he could cut down anyone, anything . . . any man. Fight him in the water, Jimmy. Use your bumper jack in the water. . ."

"I think you're nuts," Jimmy said. "I think you're honest to goodness nuts."

Tony shrugged. "This does not seem fair for you, eh? To be in the water with this one." He motioned at the turtle. "This seems nuts to you. Crazy to you. Because in the water he could cripple you. Drown you. Because in the water you are not a match."

"What are you trying to prove, Pa?"

"Jimmy. This turtle is putting up his life. In the road here you are putting up nothing. You have nothing to lose at all. Not a finger or a hand or your life. Nothing. You smash him with a long steel bumper jack and he cannot get to you. He has as much chance as a ripe watermelon."

"So?"

"So I want you to put up something also. You should have something to lose or it is no match."

Jimmy looked at the old man and then at the turtle.

"Any fool can smash a watermelon," Tony said. "It does not take a brave man."

"Pa. It's only a turtle. You're making a federal case."

Old Tony looked at his son. "All right," he said. "Finish your coffee now and do what you are going to do. I say nothing more. Only for the next five minutes put yourself into this turtle's place. Put yourself into his shell and watch through his eyes. And try to think what he is thinking when he sees a coward coming to kill him with a long steel bumper jack."

Jimmy got to his feet and ground out his cigaret.

"All right, Pa," he said. "All right. You win."

Tony rose slowly from his crouch.

"No," he said, "Not me. You. You win."

"But Pa, they do kill trout."

"So," Tony said. "They kill trout. Nature put them here, and they kill trout. To survive. The trout are not extinct, eh? We kill trout also, we men. To survive? No, for sport. This old one, he takes what he needs. I do not kill him for being in nature's plan. I do not play God."

Jimmy walked to the rear of the wagon then and flung down the bumper jack and closed up the door and came back.

"Pa," he said. "Honest to goodness you got the nuttiest ideas I ever heard."

Old Tony walked around behind the snapper and gently prodded it with his boot toe, and the turtle went waddling forward across the road and toppled over the sand shoulder and disappeared in the brushy growth of the creek bank. Tony and his son climbed into the wagon and sat looking at each other. The sun was coming up strong now and the sky was cracking open like a shell and spilling reds and golds and blues, and Jimmy started the engine.

Tony put the thermos away and got out his cigarets and stuck one in his son's mouth.

"So?" he said.

They sat smoking for a full minute watching each other, and then Jimmy released the emergency and they rolled slowly along the drying sandroad and down past the huge cleansing dawn coming, and the pine forests growing tall in the rising mists, and the quickly quiet waters of the eternal creek.

QUESTIONS FOR DISCUSSION AND WRITING

1. As Old Tony squatted on the road and stared at the turtle, "he knew the truth." What truth did he know about the turtle and about himself?
2. What does Jimmy mean when he compares his father to "a tired old woman"? What crazy thing does Tony want his son to do? Why? In what sense is Tony "honest to goodness nuts"? In what sense is Jimmy the one who is nuts?
3. What names does Tony indirectly call Jimmy as they talk? How does the father finally persuade the son not to kill the turtle? Why doesn't he simply forbid him to do it? What does he mean when he replies to his son, "Not me. You. You win." What does he mean when he says, "I do not play God"? What is God's plan, according to Tony?
4. In the last sentence of the story the author shows without doubt who he thinks is right in the argument. Why does he use the phrases "cleansing dawn," "rising mists," and "eternal creek"?

SUGGESTIONS FOR FURTHER WRITING OR DISCUSSION

1. Read again the several places where George Vukelich describes the turtle and its actions. Think of an animal you know, or find an animal and observe it carefully, and then describe it. If you want, make it a part of a story.
2. In "The Turtle," Tony, the father, is a good ecologist; he does not want to destroy the plan of nature. Write a paper giving your opinion on whether or not men are justified in killing animals for sport. Or write a dialogue—a conversation— between a person who favors hunting or fishing for sport and one who opposes them.

THE APPRENTICE

by Dorothy Canfield Fisher

*Thirteen-year-old Peg feels constantly annoyed by her
parents. Then late one afternoon, Rollie, her collie, disap-
pears. It is sheep country, and collies kill sheep. What understanding does Peg come to after she finds Rollie?*

The day had been one of the unbearable ones, when every
sound had set her teeth on edge like chalk creaking on a blackboard, when every word her father or mother said to her or did
not say to her seemed an intentional injustice. And of course
it would happen, as the fitting end to such a day, that just as
the sun went down back of the mountain and the long twilight
began, she noticed that Rollie was not around.

Tense with exasperation at what her mother would say, she
began to call him in a carefully casual tone—she would simply
explode if Mother got going: "Here, Rollie! He-ere, boy! Want
to go for a walk, Rollie?" Whistling to him cheerfully, her heart
full of wrath at the way the world treated her, she made the
rounds of his haunts: the corner of the woodshed, where he liked
to curl up on the wool of Father's discarded old sweater; the
hay barn, the cow barn, the sunny spot on the side porch. No
Rollie.

Perhaps he had sneaked upstairs to lie on her bed, where
he was not supposed to go—not that *she* would have minded!
That rule was a part of Mother's fussiness, part, too, of Mother's
bossiness. It was *her* bed, wasn't it? But was she allowed the
say-so about it? Not on your life. They *said* she could have things
the way she wanted in her own room, now she was in her teens,
but— Her heart burned at unfairness as she took the stairs
stormily, two steps at a time, her pigtails flopping up and down
on her back. If Rollie was there, she was just going to let him
stay there, and Mother could say what she wanted to.

But he was not there. The bedspread and pillow were
crumpled, but that was where she had flung herself down to
cry that afternoon. Every nerve in her had been twanging dis-

---

cordantly, but she couldn't cry. She could only lie there, her hands doubled up hard, furious that she had nothing to cry about. Not really. She was too big to cry just over Father's having said to her, severely, "I told you if I let you take the chess set, you were to put it away when you got through with it. One of the pawns was on the floor of our bedroom this morning. I stepped on it. If I'd had my shoes on, I'd have broken it."

Well, he *had* told her that. And he hadn't said she mustn't ever take the set again. No, the instant she thought about that, she knew she couldn't cry about it. She could be, and was, in a rage about the way Father kept on talking long after she'd got his point: "It's not that I care so much about the chess set. It's because if you don't learn how to take care of things, you yourself will suffer for it. You'll forget or neglect something that will be really important for *you*. We *have* to try to teach you to be responsible for what you've said you'll take care of. If we—" on and on.

She stood there, dry-eyed, by the bed that Rollie had not crumpled and thought, *I hope Mother sees the spread and says something about Rollie—I just hope she does.*

She heard her mother coming down the hall, and hastily shut her door. She had a right to shut the door to her own room, hadn't she? She had *some* rights, she supposed, even if she was only thirteen and the youngest child. If her mother opened it to say, "What are you doing in here that you don't want me to see?" she'd say—she'd just say—

But her mother did not open the door. Her feet went steadily on along the hall, and then, carefully, slowly, down the stairs. She probably had an armful of winter things she was bringing down from the attic. She was probably thinking that a tall, thirteen-year-old daughter was big enough to help with a chore like that. But she wouldn't *say* anything. She would just get out that insulting look of a grownup silently putting up with a crazy, unreasonable kid. She had worn that expression all day; it was too much to be endured.

Up in her bedroom behind her closed door the thirteen-year-old stamped her foot in a gust of uncontrollable rage, none the less savage and heartshaking because it was mysterious to her.

But she had not located Rollie. She would be cut into little pieces before she would let her father and mother know she had lost sight of him, forgotten about him. They would not scold her, she knew. They would do worse; they would look at her. And in their silence she would hear, droning on reproachfully, what they had said when she had been begging to keep for her own the sweet, woolly collie puppy in her arms.

How warm he had felt! Astonishing how warm and alive a puppy was compared with a doll! She had never liked her dolls much after she had held Rollie, feeling him warm against her breast, warm and wriggling, bursting with life, reaching up to lick her face. He had loved her from that first instant. As he felt her arms around him, his liquid, beautiful eyes had melted in trusting sweetness. And they did now, whenever he looked at her. Her dog was the only creature in the world who *really* loved her, she thought passionately.

And back then, at the very minute when, as a darling baby dog, he was beginning to love her, her father and mother were saying, so cold, so reasonable—gosh, how she *hated* reasonableness!—"Now, Peg, remember that, living where we do, with sheep on the farms around us, it is a serious responsibility to have a collie dog. If you keep him, you've got to be the one to take care of him. You'll have to be the one to train him to stay at home. We're too busy with you children to start bringing up a puppy, too."

Rollie, nestling in her arms, let one hind leg drop awkwardly. It must be uncomfortable. She looked down at him tenderly, tucked his leg up under him, and gave him a hug. He laughed up in her face—he really did laugh, his mouth stretched wide in a cheerful grin. Now he was snug in a warm little ball.

Her parents were saying, "If you want him, you can have him. But you must be responsible for him. If he gets to running sheep, he'll just have to be shot, you know that."

They had not said, aloud, "Like the Wilsons' collie." They never mentioned that awfulness—her racing unsuspectingly down across the fields just at the horrible moment when Mr. Wilson shot his collie, caught in the very act of killing sheep. They probably thought that if they never spoke about it, she would forget it—*forget* the crack of that rifle, and the collapse of the great beautiful dog! Forget the red, red blood spurting from the hole in his head. She hadn't forgotten. She never would. She knew as well as they did how important it was to train a collie puppy about sheep. They didn't have to rub it in like that. They always rubbed everything in. She had told them, fervently, indignantly, that of *course* she would take care of him, be responsible for him, teach him to stay at home. Of course. Of course. *She* understood!

And now, when he was six months old, tall, rangy, power-

ful, standing up far above her knee, nearly to her waist, she
didn't know where he was. But of course he must be somewhere
around. He always was. She composed her face to look natural
and went downstairs to search the house. He was probably asleep
somewhere. She looked every room over carefully. Her mother
was nowhere visible. It was safe to call him again, to give the
special piercing whistle which always brought him racing to her,
the white-feathered plume of his tail waving in elation that she
wanted him.

But he did not answer. She stood still on the front porch
to think.

Could he have gone up to their special place in the edge
of the field where the three young pines, their branches growing
close to the ground, made a triangular, walled-in space, completely hidden from the world? Sometimes he went up there with
her, and when she lay down on the dried grass to dream he,
too, lay down quietly, his head on his paws, his beautiful eyes
fixed adoringly on her. He entered into her every mood. If she
wanted to be quiet, all right, he did too. It didn't seem as though
he would have gone alone there. Still— She loped up the steep
slope of the field rather fast, beginning to be anxious.

No, he was not there. She stood irresolutely in the roofless,
green-walled triangular hide-out, wondering what to do next.

Then, before she knew what thought had come into her
mind, its emotional impact knocked her down. At least her knees
crumpled under her. The Wilsons had, last Wednesday, brought
their sheep down from the far upper pasture to the home farm.
They were—she herself had seen them on her way to school,
and like an idiot had not thought of Rollie—on the river meadow.

She was off like a racer at the crack of the starting pistol,
her long, strong legs stretched in great leaps, her pigtails flying.
She took the short cut, regardless of the brambles. Their thorn-
spiked, wiry stems tore at her flesh, but she did not care. She
welcomed the pain. It was something she was doing for Rollie,
for her Rollie.

She was in the pine woods now, rushing down the steep,
stony path, tripping over roots, half falling, catching herself just
in time, not slackening her speed. She burst out on the open
knoll above the river meadow, calling wildly, "Rollie, here, Rollie,
here, boy! Here! Here!" She tried to whistle, but she was crying
too hard to pucker her lips.

There was nobody to see or hear her. Twilight was falling
over the bare, grassy knoll. The sunless evening wind slid down

the mountain like an invisible river, engulfing her in cold. Her teeth began to chatter. "Here, Rollie, here, boy, here!" She strained her eyes to look down into the meadow to see if the sheep were there. She could not be sure. She stopped calling him as she would a dog, and called out his name despairingly as if he were her child, "Rollie! Oh, *Rollie*, where are you?"

The tears ran down her cheeks in streams. She sobbed loudly, terribly; she did not try to control herself, since there was no one to hear. "Hou! Hou! Hou!" she sobbed, her face contorted grotesquely. "Oh, Rollie! Rollie! Rollie!" She had wanted something to cry about. Oh, how terribly now she had something to cry about.

She saw him as clearly as if he were there beside her, his muzzle and gaping mouth all smeared with the betraying blood (like the Wilsons' collie). "But he didn't *know* it was wrong!" she screamed like a wild creature. "Nobody *told* him it was wrong. It was my fault. I should have taken better care of him. I will now, I will!"

But no matter how she screamed, she could not make herself heard. In the cold gathering darkness, she saw him stand, poor, guiltless victim of his ignorance, who should have been protected from his own nature, his beautiful soft eyes looking at her with love, his splendid plumed tail waving gently. "It was my fault. I promised I would bring him up. I should have *made* him stay at home. I was responsible for him. It was my fault."

But she could not make his executioners hear her. The shot rang out. Rollie sank down, his beautiful liquid eyes glazed, the blood spurting from the hole in his head—like the Wilsons' collie. She gave a wild shriek, long, soul-satisfying, frantic. It was the scream at sudden, unendurable tragedy of a mature, full-blooded woman. It drained dry the girl of thirteen. She came to herself. She was standing on the knoll, trembling and quaking with cold, the darkness closing in on her.

Her breath had given out. For once in her life she had wept all the tears there were in her body. Her hands were so stiff with cold she could scarcely close them. How her nose was running! Simply streaming down her upper lip. And she had no handkerchief. She lifted her skirt, fumbled for her slip, stooped, blew her nose on it, wiped her eyes, drew a long quavering breath—and heard something! Far off in the distance, a faint sound, like a dog's muffled bark.

She whirled on her heels and bent her head to listen. The sound did not come from the meadow below the knoll. It came

from back of her, from the Wilsons' maple grove higher up. She
held her breath. Yes, it came from there. She began to run again,
but now she was not sobbing. She was silent, absorbed in her
effort to cover ground. If she could only live to get there, to see
if it really were Rollie. She ran steadily till she came to the fence,
and went over this in a great plunge. Her skirt caught on a
nail. She impatiently pulled at it, not hearing or not heeding
the long sibilant[1] tear as it came loose. She was in the dusky
maple woods, stumbling over the rocks as she ran. As she tore
on up the slope, she knew it was Rollie's bark.

She stopped short and leaned weakly against a tree, sick
with the breathlessness of her straining lungs, sick in the reaction of relief, sick with anger at Rollie, who had been here having
a wonderful time while she had been dying, just dying in terror
about him.

For she could now not only hear that it was Rollie's bark;
she could hear, in the dog language she knew as well as he,
what he was saying in those excited yips; that he had run a
woodchuck into a hole in the tumbled stone wall, that he almost
had him, that the intoxicating wild-animal smell was as close
to him—almost—as if he had his jaws on his quarry. Yip! Woof!
Yip! Yip!

The wild, joyful quality of the dog talk enraged the girl.
She was trembling in exhaustion, in indignation. So that was
where he had been, when she was killing herself trying to take
care of him. Plenty near enough to hear her calling and whistling
to him, if he had paid attention. Just so set on having his foolish
good time, he never thought to listen for her call.

She stooped to pick up a stout stick. She would teach him!
It was time he had something to make him remember to listen.
She started forward.

But she stopped, stood thinking. One of the things to remember about collies—everybody knew that—was their sensitive-
ness. A collie who had been beaten was never "right" again.
His spirit was broken. "Anything but a broken-spirited collie,"
the farmers often said. They were no good after that.

She threw down her stick. Anyhow, she thought, he was
too young to know, really, that he had done wrong. He was still
only a puppy. Like all puppies, he got perfectly crazy over wild-
animal smells. Probably he really and truly hadn't heard her calling and whistling.

---

1. sibiliant: hissing.

All the same, all the same—she stared intently into the twilight—he couldn't be let to grow up just as he wanted to. She would have to make him understand that he mustn't go off this way by himself. He must be trained to know how to do what a good dog does—not because *she* wanted him to, but for his own sake.

She walked on now, steady, purposeful, gathering her inner strength together, Olympian[2] in her understanding of the full meaning of the event.

When he heard his own special young god approaching, he turned delightedly and ran to meet her, panting, his tongue hanging out. His eyes shone. He jumped up on her in an ecstasy of welcome and licked her face.

But she pushed him away. Her face and voice were grave. "No, Rollie, *no!*" she said severely. "You're *bad.* You know you're not to go off in the woods without me! You are—a—*bad—dog.*"

He was horrified. Stricken into misery. He stood facing her, frozen, the gladness going out of his eyes, the erect waving plume of his tail slowly lowered to slinking, guilty dejection.

"I know you were all wrapped up in that woodchuck. But that's no excuse. You *could* have heard me calling you, whistling for you, if you'd paid attention," she went on. "You've got to learn, and I've got to teach you."

With a shudder of misery he lay down, his tail stretched out limp on the ground, his head flat on his paws, his ears drooping—ears ringing with doomsday awfulness of the voice he so loved and revered. He must have been utterly wicked. He trembled and turned his head away from her august look of blame, groveling in remorse for whatever mysterious sin he had committed.

She sat down by him, as miserable as he. "I don't *want* to scold you. But I have to! I have to bring you up right, or you'll get shot, Rollie. You *mustn't* go away from the house without me, do you hear, *never!*"

Catching, with his sharp ears yearning for her approval, a faint overtone of relenting affection in her voice, he lifted his eyes to her, humbly, soft in imploring fondness.

"Oh, Rollie!" she said, stooping low over him. "I *do* love you. I do. But I *have* to bring you up. I'm responsible for you, don't you see?"

He did not see. Hearing sternness or something else he did

2. Olympian: like a god, very great.

not recognize in the beloved voice, he shut his eyes tight in sorrow, and made a little whimpering lament in his throat.

She had never heard him cry before. It was too much. She sat down by him and drew his head to her, rocking him in her arms, smoothing him with inarticulate³ small murmurs.

He leaped in her arms and wriggled happily as he had when he was a baby; he reached up to lick her face as he had then. But he was no baby now. He was half as big as she, a great, warm, pulsing, living armful of love. She clasped him closely. Her heart was brimming full, but calmed, quiet. The blood flowed in equable⁴ gentleness all over her body. She was deliciously warm. Her nose was still running a little. She sniffed and wiped it on her sleeve.

It was almost dark now. "We'll be late to supper, Rollie," she said responsibly. Pushing him gently off, she stood up. "Home, Rollie, home!"

Here was a command he could understand. At once he trotted along the path toward home. His plumed tail, held high, waved cheerfully. His short dog memory had dropped into oblivion the suffering just back of him.

Her human memory was longer. His prancing gait was as carefree as a young child's. Plodding heavily like a serious adult, she trod behind him. Her very shoulders seemed bowed by what she had lived through. She felt, she thought, like an old, old woman of thirty. But it was all right now. She knew she had made an impression on him.

When they came out into the open pasture, Rollie ran back to get her to play with him. He leaped around her in circles, barking in cheerful yawps, jumping up on her, inviting her to run a race with him, to throw him a stick, to come alive.

His high spirits were ridiculous. But infectious. She gave one little leap to match his. Rollie pretended that this was a threat to him, planted his forepaws low, and barked loudly at her, laughing between yips. He was so funny, she thought, when he grinned that way. She laughed back and gave another mock-threatening leap at him. Radiant that his sky was once more clear, he sprang high on his spring-steel muscles in an explosion of happiness, and bounded in circles around her.

Following him, not noting in the dusk where she was going, she felt the grassy slope drop steeply. Oh, yes, she knew where

---

3. inarticulate: not in understandable words.
4. equable: steady, even.

she was. They had come to the rolling-down hill just back of the house. All the kids rolled down there, even the little ones, because it was soft grass without a stone. She had rolled down that slope a million times—years and years ago, when she was a kid herself. It was fun. She remembered well the whirling dizziness of the descent, all the world turning over and over crazily. And the delicious giddy staggering when you first stood up, the earth still spinning under your feet.

"All right, Rollie, let's go," she cried, and flung herself down in the rolling position, her arms straight up over her head.

Rollie had never seen this skylarking before. It threw him into almost hysterical amusement. He capered around the rapidly rolling figure, half-scared, mystified, enchanted.

His wild frolicsome barking might have come from her own throat, so accurately did it sound the way she felt—crazy, foolish, like a little kid no more than five years old, the age she had been when she had last rolled down that hill.

At the bottom she sprang up, on muscles as steel-strong as Rollie's. She staggered a little, and laughed aloud.

The living-room windows were just before them. How yellow lighted windows looked when you were in the darkness going home. How nice and yellow. Maybe Mother had waffles for supper. She was a swell cook, Mother was, and she certainly gave her family all the breaks, when it came to meals.

"Home, Rollie, home!" She burst open the door to the living room. "Hi, Mom, what you got for supper?"

From the kitchen her mother announced coolly, "I hate to break the news to you, but it's waffles."

"Oh, *Mom!*" she shouted in ecstasy.

Her mother could not see her. She did not need to. "For goodness' sakes, go and wash," she called.

In the long mirror across the room she saw herself, her hair hanging wild, her long bare legs scratched, her broadly smiling face dirt-streaked, her torn skirt dangling, her dog laughing up at her. Gosh, was it a relief to feel your own age, just exactly thirteen years old!

QUESTIONS FOR DISCUSSION AND WRITING

1. At one point early in the story (page 86), Peg "stamped her foot in a gust of uncontrollable rage, none the less savage . . . because it was mysterious to her." Why does she feel

as she does toward her parents? Does she have any legiti-
mate reasons for complaint against them? What, if any, reasons do they have for complaining about her?

2. In the middle part of the story, Peg feels a frantic concern
   for Rollie. Why? What event does she remember? Then she
   screams, "It was my fault. I should have taken better care
   of him." How, at this point (page 89) has she begun to understand her parents better?

3. What is Peg's first reaction when she finds Rollie excitedly
   yapping at a woodchuck? Then what is her second reaction?
   Read again what she says to him (page 91). She is trying
   to teach him something. What is she really teaching herself?

4. At the beginning of the story, Peg is thirteen and miserable.
   Find places in the story where she feels different ages, older
   and younger. Why does she feel this way? At the end of the
   story she is still thirteen. Is she a different thirteen because
   of her experience? Why or why not?

5. Why is the story called "The Apprentice"? Who is the apprentice? An apprentice in what?

SUGGESTIONS FOR FURTHER WRITING OR DISCUSSION

1. Write an account of a relationship between a person and
   an animal, or a story about such a relationship.

2. Tell about an experience from which you learned better the
   meaning of responsibility on your part or on someone else's
   part.

3. Peg learns that it is important to train Rollie. Write a
   description or a story about training an animal.

THE COLT

by Mikhail Sholokhov

For two years after the Russian Revolution of 1917, there was a civil war in Russia during which the new Communist government's Red Army struggled to put down a resistance. In the midst of a bloody battle in this war, much of it fought on horseback, a colt was born to the mare of a Red Army soldier, Trofim. How does the colt present a problem for Trofim and his squadron?

He struggled out of his mother's body in broad daylight, head first. His spindly front legs stretched out near a pile of manure buzzing with emerald flies, and the first thing he saw was the dove-gray puff of a shrapnel explosion melting overhead. The roar of a cannon split the air and threw his little wet body under his mother's legs. Terror was the first feeling he knew on this earth.

An ill-smelling hail of grapeshot rattled on the tiled roof of the stable and sprinkled the ground below. The frightened mother jumped to her feet and with a shrill neigh dropped down again, her sweating flank resting against the sheltering dung heap.

She was soldier Trofim's mare.

In the sultry silence that followed, the buzzing of the flies could be heard more clearly. A rooster, scared by the gunfire and not daring to jump to the top of the fence, flapped his wings several times somewhere in the safety of the bushes, and crowed there with abandon. From the hut came the tearful groans of a wounded machine-gunner. He cried out repeatedly in a voice sharp yet hoarse, and his cries were mingled with fierce oaths. Bees were humming among the silky heads of the poppies in the small garden. Beyond the village a machine gun was finishing off its belt, and to the rhythm of its wierdly cheerful chatter, in the interval between the cannon shots, the mare lovingly licked her firstborn. And the colt, lowering himself to his moth-

From *Fierce and Gentle Warriors* by Mikhail Sholokhov, translated by Miriam Morton. Reprinted by permission of Doubleday & Company Inc.

er's swollen udder, sensed for the first time the fullness of life and the unforgettable sweetness of a mother's caresses.

After the second shell had crashed somewhere behind the barn, Trofim emerged from the hut, slammed the door, and walked toward the stable. As he was passing the manure pile, he shielded his eyes from the sun with the palm of his hand and, seeing the colt quiver with the strain of sucking at his mare, he was spellbound and dumbfounded. With trembling hands he fumbled for his tobacco pouch. After rolling himself a cigarette, he regained his power of speech:

"So-o-o! I see you've gone and foaled! You've picked a fine time, I must say!" There was a bitter note of injury in his last remark.

Scrub grass and dry dung clung to the mare's shaggy flanks. She looked indecently thin and loose, but her eyes beamed with a proud joy touched with weariness, and her satiny upper lip curled back in a grin. Or so at least it seemed to Trofim. He led his mare into the stable. She snorted as she shook the bag of grain he hung from her head. Trofim leaned against the door-post and, looking crossly at the colt, asked his mother dryly:

"What the devil am I going to do with him?"

The sound of grain being crunched could be heard in the dimness and stillness of the stable. A crooked sunbeam, like a column of golden dust, shed its light through a chink in the closed door and shone on Trofim's cheek. His whiskers and the brush of his beard were tinged with a reddish hue. The lines around his mouth curved in dark furrows. The colt stood on its thin, downy legs like a wooden toy horse.

"Will I have to kill him?" Trofim said, pointing his tobacco-stained forefinger in the direction of the newborn.

The mare rolled her bloodshot eyeballs, blinked, and gave her master a sidelong, mocking glance.

That evening, inside the best room of the hut, Trofim had a conversation with the Squadron Commander:

". . . I could tell my mare was in foal, she couldn't trot, I couldn't get her to canter, and she kept getting short of breath. I had taken a good look at her one day and it turned out she was in foal. And what care she took of it! Such care! You know, the colt is a sort of bay color . . . That's how . . ." Trofim told his story, hesitating between the details.

The Squadron Commander clutched the copper mug of tea in his fist as he would clutch a sabre hilt before going into battle, and kept staring at the lamp with tired eyes. Above the yellow flame moths flew about in a frenzy. They had flown in through the open window and were burning themselves against the lamp's glass chimney, one after another.

"It makes no difference—bay or black—it's all the same. Shoot it! With a colt around we'll be like a gypsy camp, not a cavalry squadron," the Commander said.

Trofim muttered something.

"What? . . . That's what I said, just like gypsies. And if the Chief were to show up, what then? There he'll be, reviewing the regiment, and the colt will come prancing out with its tail up . . . . The whole Red Army will be ashamed and disgraced. I don't understand how you could have allowed such a thing, Trofim. Here we are, at the very height of the Civil War, and suddenly, there is this kind of thing going on. Why, it's downright disgraceful! Give the hostlers[1] the strictest orders to keep the stallions away from the mares."

Next morning Trofim came out of the hut carrying his rifle. The sun hadn't yet fully risen. The grass was sparkling with roseate dew. The meadow, marked with traces of the infantry's boots and dug up for trenches, reminded one of a girl's tear-stained, sorrowful face. The cooks were bustling around the field kitchen. On the porch of the hut the Commander was sitting in a threadbare undershirt. As he sat there, shaping a ladle out of wood, his fingers, now more accustomed to the chilly touch of a revolver, were awkward at this task. The feel and fragrance of the damp wood brought back to him the forgotten past of village life.

As Trofim went by he asked, with a show of interest:

"Making a dumpling ladle?"

The Commander finished off the handle and said through his teeth:

"That woman, that pest of a housekeeper, kept after me: 'Do, please make me one . . . .' At one time I was good at this sort of thing, but now somehow it doesn't come out right."

"No, on the contrary . . . I think it's quite good," Trofim praised his Commander's handiwork.

He brushed the chips off his knees and asked Trofim:

"Going to shoot the colt?"

Trofim waved his hand and said nothing. After a moment's pause he walked on toward the stable.

With head bent, the Commander waited for the sound of

---

1. hostlers: stablemen.

the shot. A minute passed, then another, but he heard nothing. Trofim reappeared from around the corner of the stable. He looked distressed.

"Well?"

"Something must be wrong with the hammer of the rifle. It won't strike the percussion cap."

"Let me have a look at it."

Trofim reluctantly handed over his rifle. The Commander pulled the bolt back and forth, and screwed up his eyes.

"You have no bullets in it."

"Can't be!" Trofim exclaimed.

"I tell you it's empty."

"Guess I must have dropped them somewhere . . . maybe behind the stable."

The Commander laid the rifle aside and spent some time turning over the new ladle in his hands. The scent of the moist wood was so strong that his nostrils quickened to the fragrance of flowering alders and of newly plowed earth. He thought longingly of past toil amost forgotten in the endless conflagration of war.

"All right! The devil with him! Let him stay near his mother. For the time being let him live . . . then we'll see. When the war is over he may yet be of some use—maybe for plowing . . . . And if anything goes wrong, the Chief will understand that the colt is a suckling and must be allowed to nurse . . . the Chief was once a suckling himself . . . and we have nursed too . . . and since it is the way of nature, that's all there is to it! But there's nothing whatever wrong with your rifle."

It so happened that a month later, not far from the village of Ust-Khopersk, Trofim's squadron was engaged in battle with a company of enemy Cossacks. The two sides opened fire at twilight. It was getting dark as they rode into attack, sabres bared. Halfway in the charge Trofim had fallen behind his platoon. Neither the whip nor the bit, which Trofim pulled so hard that his mare's mouth bled, could get her to break into a gallop. Tossing her head high, she neighed hoarsely and stamped the ground until the colt, waving his tail, caught up with her. Trofim leaped from his saddle, thrust his sabre into its scabbard, and, his face contorted with rage, tore the rifle from his shoulder. The men on the right flank were already in hand-to-hand combat with the enemy. Near a cliff a group of fighters was moving back and forth as if swayed by a strong wind. They brandished their sabres in silence. Only the dull thud of the horses' hoofs could be heard. Trofim glanced in their direction for a second, then aimed at the colt's narrow head. His hand may have trembled in his exasperation, or perhaps there was some other reason for it, but he missed his aim. After the shot the colt merely kicked up his heels stupidly, neighed in a thin voice and, throwing up clumps of gray dirt, circled around and came to a standstill a little way off. Trofim fired several more bullets at the little devil. Then, convinced that the shots had caused neither injury nor the death of his mare's offspring, he leaped on to her back, and swearing monstrously, rode off at a jogtrot to where bearded, red-faced Cossacks were pressing his Squadron Commander and three other Red Army men toward a gully.

The squadron spent that night in the steppe,[2] near a shallow gully. The men smoked little. They didn't unsaddle the horses. A reconnaissance returning from the Don reported that considerable enemy forces had gathered to prevent the Reds from crossing the river.

As Trofim lay dozing, his feet wrapped in the folds of a rubber cloak, he could not stop thinking of the events of the past day.

Before dawn, the Commander came over and squatted down beside him in the darkness.

"Trofim, are you asleep?"

"Just dozing."

Looking up at the fading stars, the Commander said:

"Get rid of that colt. He's causing trouble in battle. When I look at him my hand shakes . . . I can't use my sabre. It's all because he reminds us of home . . . and we can't have that sort of thing in war . . . it turns the soldier's heart from stone to a limp rag. And, besides, when the horses went into attack the scamp got between their legs and they wouldn't tread on him." The Commander was silent a moment, then smiled sadly. But Trofim did not see the smile. "Do you understand, Trofim?" he continued. "That colt's tail . . . seeing that tail . . . the way he puts it over his back, kicks up his heels . . . and his tail is just like a fox's . . . . It's a marvelous tail! . . ."

Trofim remained silent. He drew his coat over his head and, shivering in the dewy dampness, fell asleep with astonishing speed.

2. steppe: plain.

Opposite a certain ancient monastery, the Don strikes against projecting cliffs and dashes past them with reckless swiftness. At the bend the water spins in little whirlpools, and the green, white-maned waves rush to fling themselves against the chalk rocks scattered into the river by the spring floods.

The enemy had occupied the shore where the current was weaker and the river broader and calmer. They were on the right bank. They were now aiming their fire at the foothills across from their vantage point. To avoid the line of fire, the Squadron Commander could not do otherwise than have his men cross the rushing river opposite the monastery. He rode down from the sandbank beneath the cliffs and led the way into the water with his bay horse. The rest of the squadron followed him with a thunderous splash—one hundred and eight half-naked swimmers and the same number of horses of varied colors. The saddles were piled into three canoes. Trofim was steering one of them. He had entrusted his mare to the platoon[3] leader, Nechepurenko. From the middle of the river Trofim could see the leading horses wading deeply, forced to gulp water. Their riders urged them on. In less than a minute, some one hundred and fifty feet from the shore, the water was thickly dotted with horses' heads, snorting in a variety of sounds. The men swam at their sides, clinging to their manes, clothes and knapsacks tied to rifles which they held above their heads.

Throwing his oar into the boat, Trofim rose to his full height and screwing up his eyes against the sun, looked anxiously for his mare's head among the swimming horses. The squadron resembled a gaggle of geese scattered over the sky by hunters' shots. Right in front was the Squadron Commander's bay, his glossy back rising high out of the water. Behind it was a dark cloud of animals and, last of all, falling more and more behind the others, as Trofim could see, came platoon leader Nechepurenko's bristling head, with the pointed ears of Trofim's mare on his left. Straining his eyes, Trofim also caught sight of the colt. He was swimming in spurts, rising high out of the water, then sinking till his nostrils were barely visible.

And then the wind passing over the Don carried to Trofim's ears a plaintive neigh, as thin as a spider's thread.

The cry sounded over the water as sharp and keen as the point of a sabre. It struck right at Trofim's heart, and something extraordinary happened to the man: he had gone through five

---

3. platoon: a small group of men, part of a squadron.

years of war, death had gazed like a temptress into his eyes
again and again, and who knows what else. But now he went
pale under his red bushy beard, turning the color of ashes.
Snatching up the oar, he sent the boat back against the current,
toward the spot where the exhausted colt was spinning in a
whirlpool. And some sixty feet away, Nechepurenko was struggling with the mare but could not hold her back. She was swimming toward that whirlpool, whinnying in distress. Trofim's
friend, Steshka Yefremov, sitting on a pile of saddles in another
canoe, shouted to him:

"Don't take a fool's chances. Make for the shore. Look!
There they are—the Cossacks!"

"I'll shoot him!" Trofim cried, his breath coming hard as
he tugged at his rifle strap.

The current had carried the colt to where the squadron was
crossing. The small whirlpool swung him around and around
smoothly, lapping against him with its green, foam-capped waves.
Trofim worked his oar desperately as the boat lurched violently.
He could see the Cossacks rushing out of a ravine on the right
shore. A Maxim gun began its rapid drumming. The bullets
hissed as they smacked into the water. An enemy officer in a
torn canvas shirt shouted something, waving his rifle.

The colt whinnied more and more rarely, the short, piercing
cry grew fainter and fainter. And that cry sounded so much like
the cry of an infant that it sent a chill of horror through all
who heard it.

Nechepurenko, abandoning the mare, easily swam back to
the left shore. Trembling, Trofim seized his rifle and fired, aiming just below the small head being sucked down by the whirlpool. Then he kicked off his boots and, stretching out his arms
dived into the river with a dull moan.

On the right bank the officer in the canvas shirt bellowed:
"Cease fire!"

Within five minutes Trofim reached the colt. With his left
hand he supported his chilled body, and panting and coughing
in spasms, made for the left shore. Not a shot was fired from
the opposite side.

Sky, forest, sand—all glowingly green, transparent . . . .
With one last tremendous effort Trofim's feet felt the ground.
He dragged the colt's slippery body onto the shore, and, sobbing,
spat up the green water as he groped over the sand with his
hands. From the forest across the Don came the muffled voices
of his squadron that had made the crossing. Somewhere beyond

the sandbank on the opposite side rifle shots rang out. The mare stood at Trofim's side, shaking herself and licking her colt. From her tail a rainbow stream was dripping, making small holes in the sand.

Swaying, Trofim rose to his feet, took a few steps, then sprang into the air and dropped on his side. He felt as though a hot arrow had pierced his chest. He heard the shot as he fell. A single shot in the back, from the opposite shore. There the officer in the torn canvas shirt casually rattled his carbine lock ejecting the smoking cartridge case, while on the sand, two paces from the colt, Trofim twitched and his rough blue lips, which for five years had not kissed a child, smiled for the last time.

QUESTIONS FOR DISCUSSION AND WRITING

1. The story begins with the stark contrast between the pain, cruelty, terror and death of war and the delicacy of the newborn colt being lovingly licked by its mother. Reread the first paragraphs of the story. What details does Sholokhov give to show this contrast?

2. Why does the colt present a problem to Trofim, to the commander, and to the whole cavalry squadron? How is the problem more than just a physical one?

3. Trofim cannot make himself obey the order to shoot the colt. Is this strange for a man in a war who has been shooting other men? How does the Commander find out that his order was not obeyed? What makes the Commander decide: "For the time being, let him live"? Before you answer, read carefully the short paragraph that precedes his words.

4. A month later, how do the colt and mare endanger the squadron during a life-and-death battle? Why does Trofim fail to kill the colt?

5. That night the Commander again orders Trofim to kill the colt. Why? What effects is the colt having on the fighting power of the soldiers?

6. Trofim's company of men and horses are swimming across the Don River to avoid deadly enemy gunfire when Trofim hears the plaintive neigh of the drowning colt. What happens to the colt? Why did Trofim allow himself to get into a position where he could so easily be shot? Does Sholokhov give us any clue as to how Trofim felt as he died? Explain.

7. Earlier in the story (page 101), Sholokhov says about Trofim, "Death had gazed like a temptress into his eyes again and again." Why is death described as a temptress?
8. What is Sholokhov saying in this story about men and war. (The collection of which this story is a part is called *Fierce and Gentle Warriors*.)

SUGGESTIONS FOR FURTHER WRITING OR DISCUSSION

1. Tell about a person, real or made up, who combines fierceness and gentleness.
2. This is a story of self-sacrifice. Write an account of some sort of sacrifice of self (not necessarily by death) that you know of or can imagine.
3. Write a story of an experience in which a baby animal makes life more difficult for the people around him.

Six Fables: Stories with a Moral

THREE FABLES BY AESOP

retold by Anne Terry White

One of the greatest story-tellers of Ancient Greece was Aesop. Here are three of his famous fables, each with its moral or lesson.

THE COUNTRY MOUSE AND THE CITY MOUSE

"My dear, how are you?" said the Country Mouse. She kissed her cousin the City Mouse and made her welcome in her snug little hole.

"How good of you to travel all this way to visit me," she went on. "Well, you shall see how we country folk live. Not badly at all."

With that she began to carry food out of the house. The best of everything should be put on the table for her guest. They would eat outdoors in the fresh air under a tree and the birds would sing to them while they feasted.

It took a long time to carry out the moldy crust, the cheese parings, the bacon rind, and the dry peas and beans she had stored up. But all was ready at last. The dessert would be two stalks of fresh wheat which she had brought home from the field that very day. She laid them proudly on a mushroom, and very pretty they looked, too.

The Country Mouse ate heartily, but the City Mouse only nibbled at the food. She was used to better things. After the dessert she said:

"My dear, how can you bear to live in this poky way? I call this starving. You don't know what happiness is. Come with me and let me show you my way of life. You will be done with loneliness. You will live in plenty and enjoy all the pleasures your heart desires."

The Country Mouse saw nothing wrong with her way of life, but she agreed to go with her cousin and they set off at once. It was night when they reached the city.

"This is my house," the City Mouse said and led the way

up the stairs and into the dining room. It was brightly lighted. On the table were the remains of a fine feast, for there had been a party that night.

"Help yourself," the City Mouse invited her cousin.

The Country Mouse scampered over the snowy cloth and stared at the dishes. She could hardly believe it wasn't all a dream. She didn't know which to taste first—the pudding, the cheese, the cakes, the jellies, or the nuts. She sniffed at the grapes and pears. They didn't look real, but yes, they were. She was very thirsty, so first of all she took a sip out of a tall, sparkling glass.

"How silly I have been to waste my life in the country," she thought. "This is heaven!"

Then she started nibbling on a piece of cake. But she had taken no more than two bites when the doors flew open. In came the servants with their friends and a couple of roaring dogs. They were going to enjoy the leavings of the feast too.

The mice ran for their lives and hid in a corner. They lay trembling, hardly daring to breathe. Not till everybody had gone away did they dare to creep out.

"Well, my dear," said the Country Mouse, "if this is city life, good-by. I'll go back to the country. I would rather have my moldy crusts and dry peas in my own quiet hole than feast like this in fear of my life."

Crusts eaten in peace are better than cakes eaten in fear.

THE GRASSHOPPER AND THE ANT

All summer long the Grasshopper could be heard in the fields. He hopped and leaped and he sang away at the top of his voice. "The sun is warm!" he sang. "The leaves taste good! It is so nice to be alive!"

The summer days passed quickly. It seemed to the Hopper he had barely turned around when already it was fall. The cold wind was blowing. All the flowers and grasses in the field were dead. The bushes and the trees had stripped themselves for their winter sleep. And there was nothing to eat—simply nothing.

The Grasshopper no longer sang about how nice it was to be alive. Indeed, how could he live at all if somebody didn't help him?

"Please," he said, stumbling over to an Ant, "will you give me something to eat?"

The Ant was busy. She was dragging a dead fly into the nest. It was one of a hundred insects she had lugged home. For she had worked, worked, worked all summer, storing up food for the winter.

She stopped a moment to stare at the beggar.

"Something to eat?" she asked sternly. "And what, if you please, were you doing all summer? That is the time when sensible folk provide for the winter."

"I had no time to work," the Grasshopper said. "Please don't be cross with me. All summer long I hopped and leaped and sang."

"What? All you did was sing and prance?" cried the Ant, turning her back on him. "Well, my good fellow, now you can dance!"

Prepare today for the needs of tomorrow.

THE MILKMAID AND HER PAIL

Milkmaid Sally was on her way to market. On her pretty head she carried the pail of milk she was going to sell. And inside the pretty head she was thinking busy thoughts.

"With the money I get for my milk," she said to herself as she walked along, "I shall buy a good hen. She will lay me a whole nestful of eggs—twenty at least. But I shall not sell them. I shall let her hatch out the whole lot.

"How cute twenty little yellow chicks will be, running around the yard! I shall feed them well, and when they are of good size, I shall sell them. With the money I shall buy a fine new dress and a ribbon to go with it. I'll wear them to the fair. All the lads will be crazy about me. But I shall act proud and not look at one of them."

Here she tossed her pretty head to show how she would scorn the boys. And down fell the pail of milk, spilling every drop.

Don't count your chickens before they are hatched.

QUESTIONS FOR DISCUSSION AND WRITING

Before you read the Thurber fables, reread the moral of each Aesop fable. Do you agree with it? Can you think of or make up a counter-moral, one that will say just the opposite and yet have some truth in it? (For example, a famous true saying is: "Never put off until tomorrow what you can do today;" but a saying, perhaps equally famous and equally true, is: "Eat, drink and be merry, for tomorrow we die.")

THREE FABLES FOR OUR TIME

by James Thurber

Another well-known story-teller, this one of modern America, was James Thurber. And here are three of his Fables for Our Time, *which make a bit of fun of Aesop's fables and also draw their own slightly cock-eyed morals.*

THE SCOTTY WHO KNEW TOO MUCH

Several summers ago there was a Scotty who went to the country for a visit. He decided that all the farm dogs were cowards because they were afraid of a certain animal that had a white stripe down its back. "You are a pussy-cat and I can lick you," the Scotty said to the farm dog who lived in the house where the Scotty was visiting. "I can lick the little animal with the white stripe, too. Show him to me." "Don't you want to ask any questions about him?" said the farm dog. "Naw," said the Scotty. "*You* ask the questions."

So the farm dog took the Scotty into the woods and showed him the white-striped animal and the Scotty closed in on him, growling and slashing. It was all over in a moment and the Scotty lay on his back. When he came to, the farm dog said, "What happened?" "He threw vitriol,"[1] said the Scotty, "but he never laid a glove on me."

A few days later the farm dog told the Scotty there was another animal all the farm dogs were afraid of. "Lead me to him," said the Scotty. "I can lick anything that doesn't wear horseshoes." "Don't you want to ask any questions about him?" said the farm dog. "Naw," said the Scotty. "Just show me where he hangs out." So the farm dog led him to a place in the woods and pointed out the little animal when he came along. "A clown," said the Scotty, "a pushover," and he closed in, leading with his left and exhibiting some mighty fancy footwork. In less than a

1. vitriol: sulfuric acid, which burns the skin.

second the Scotty was flat on his back, and when he woke up the farm dog was pulling quills out of him. "What happened?" said the farm dog. "He pulled a knife on me," said the Scotty, "but at least I have learned how you fight out here in the country, and now I am going to beat *you* up." So he closed in on the farm dog, holding his nose with one front paw to ward off the vitriol and covering his eyes with the other front paw to keep out the knives. The Scotty couldn't see his opponent and he couldn't smell his opponent and he was so badly beaten that he had to be taken back to the city and put in a nursing home.

Moral: It is better to ask some of the questions than to know all the answers.

THE SHRIKE AND THE CHIPMUNKS

Once upon a time there were two chipmunks, a male and a female. The male chipmunk thought that arranging nuts in artistic patterns was more fun than just piling them up to see how many you could pile up. The female was all for piling up as many as you could. She told her husband that if he gave up making designs with the nuts there would be room in their large cave for a great many more and he would soon become the wealthiest chipmunk in the woods. But he would not let her interfere with his designs, so she flew into a rage and left him.

"The shrike will get you," she said, "because you are helpless and cannot look after yourself." To be sure, the female chipmunk had not been gone three nights before the male had to dress for a banquet and could not find his studs or shirt or suspenders. So he couldn't go to the banquet, but that was just as well, because all the chipmunks who did go were attacked and killed by a weasel.

The next day the shrike began hanging around outside the chipmunk's cave, waiting to catch him. The shrike couldn't get in because the doorway was clogged up with soiled laundry and dirty dishes. "He will come out for a walk after breakfast and I will get him then," thought the shrike. But the chipmunk slept all day and did not get up and have breakfast until after dark. Then he came out for a breath of air before beginning work on a new design. The shrike swooped down to snatch up the chipmunk, but could not see very well on account of the dark, so he batted his head against an alder branch and was killed.

A few days later the female chipmunk returned and saw the awful mess the house was in. She went to the bed and shook her husband. "What would you do without me?" she demanded. "Just go on living, I guess," he said. "You wouldn't last five days," she told him. She swept the house and did the dishes and sent out the laundry, and then she made the chipmunk get up and wash and dress. "You can't be healthy if you lie in bed all day and never get any exercise," she told him. So she took him for a walk in the bright sunlight and they were both caught and killed by the shrike's brother, a shrike named Stoop.

Moral: Early to rise and early to bed makes a male healthy and wealthy and dead.

THE UNICORN IN THE GARDEN

Once upon a sunny morning a man who sat in a breakfast nook looked up from his scrambled eggs to see a white unicorn with a gold horn quietly cropping the roses in the garden. The man went up to the bedroom where his wife was still asleep and woke her. "There's a unicorn in the garden," he said. "Eating roses." She opened one unfriendly eye and looked at him. "The unicorn is a mythical beast," she said, and turned her back on him. The man walked slowly downstairs and out into the garden. The unicorn was still there; he was now browsing among the tulips. "Here, unicorn," said the man, and he pulled up a lily and gave it to him. The unicorn ate it gravely. With a high heart, because there was a unicorn in his garden, the man went upstairs and roused his wife again. "The unicorn," he said, "ate a lily." His wife sat up in bed and looked at him coldly. "You are a booby," she said, "and I am going to have you put in the booby hatch."[2] The man, who had never liked the words "booby" and "booby hatch," and who liked them even less on a shining morning when there was a unicorn in the garden, thought for a moment. "We'll see about that," he said. He walked over to the door. "He has a golden horn in the middle of his forehead,"

2. booby hatch: insane asylum (slang)

he told her. Then he went back to the garden to watch the unicorn, but the unicorn had gone away. The man sat down among the roses and went to sleep.

As soon as the husband had gone out of the house, the wife got up and dressed as fast as she could. She was very excited and there was a gloat in her eye. She telephoned the police and she telephoned a psychiatrist; she told them to hurry to her house and bring a strait jacket. When the police and the psychiatrist arrived, they sat down in chairs and looked at her with great interest. "My husband," she said, "saw a unicorn this morning." The police looked at the psychiatrist and the psychiatrist looked at the police. "He told me it ate a lily," she said. The psychiatrist looked at the police and the police looked at the psychiatrist. "He told me it had a golden horn in the middle of its forehead," she said. At a solemn signal from the psychiatrist, the police leaped from their chairs and seized the wife. They had a hard time subduing her, for she put up a terrific struggle, but they finally subdued her. Just as they got her into the strait ʼacket, the husband came back into the house.

"Did you tell your wife you saw a unicorn?" asked the police. "Of course not," said the husband. "The unicorn is a mythical beast." "That's all I wanted to know," said the psychiatrist. "Take her away. I'm sorry, sir, but your wife is as crazy as a jay bird." So they took her away, cursing and screaming, and shut her up in an institution. The husband lived happily ever after.

Moral: Don't count your boobies until they are hatched.

QUESTIONS FOR DISCUSSION AND WRITING

The three Aesop fables and the three Thurber fables were chosen to go in pairs. Which Aesop would you pair with each Thurber? Explain why. Although Aesop is basically serious and Thurber is mostly having fun, there is some truth in Thurber's fables too. Which moral in each pair, seriously, do you agree with more, Aesop's or Thurber's? Be ready to defend your choice. (Of course, one of Thurber's morals is based on a pun. Is there any more to it than the mere pun?)

SUGGESTION FOR FURTHER WRITING OR DISCUSSION

Write a fable of your own. Probably the best way to do it is to choose a moral or a lesson first and then plan the fable to illustrate the truth of the moral. Use animals as your characters, if you wish. Probably you will want to use dialogue too. Give your fable a title; end it with the moral, underlined for emphasis.

Escaping Reality

An intelligent young woman with a bright future finds that she cannot face her past.
Her injured pride leads a young governess to make a decision.
A boy in a reformatory attempts to conceal his loneliness.

MOLLY MORGAN

by John Steinbeck

Molly Morgan, an intelligent young woman just out of Teachers' College, is interviewed for a job in an isolated community in California, the Pastures of Heaven. What do you learn about her past life that explains her actions at the end of the story?

Molly Morgan got off the train in Salinas and waited three quarters of an hour for the bus. The big automobile was empty except for the driver and Molly.

"I've never been to the Pastures of Heaven, you know," she said. "Is it far from the main road?"

"About three miles," said the driver.

"Will there be a car to take me into the valley?"

"No, not unless you're met."

"But how do people get in there?"

The driver ran over the flattened body of a jack rabbit with apparent satisfaction. "I only hit 'em when they're dead," he apologized. "In the dark, when they get caught in the lights, I try to miss 'em."

"Yes, but how am I going to get into the Pastures of Heaven?"

"I dunno. Walk, I guess. Most people walk if they ain't met."

When he set her down at the entrance to the dirt sideroad, Molly Morgan grimly picked up her suitcase and marched toward the draw in the hills. An old Ford truck squeaked up beside her.

"Goin' into the valley, ma'am?"

"Oh—yes, yes, I am."

"Well, get in, then. Needn't be scared. I'm Pat Humbert. I got a place in the Pastures."

Molly surveyed the grimy man and acknowledged his introduction. "I'm the new schoolteacher, I mean, I think I am. Do you know where Mr. Whiteside lives?"

"Sure, I go right by there. He's clerk of the board. I'm on the school board myself, you know. We wondered what you'd look like." Then he grew embarrassed at what he had said, and flushed under his coating of dirt. "'Course I mean what you'd *be* like. Last teacher we had gave a good deal of trouble. She was all right, but she was sick—I mean, sick and nervous. Finally quit because she was sick."

Molly picked at the fingertips of her gloves. "My letter says I'm to call on Mr. Whiteside. Is he all right? I don't mean that. I mean—is he—what kind of a man is he?"

"Oh, you'll get along with him all right. He's a fine old man. Born in that house he lives in. Been to college, too. He's a good man. Been clerk of the board for over twenty years."

When he put her down in front of the big old house of John Whiteside, she was really frightened. "Now it's coming," she said to herself. "But there's nothing to be afraid of. He can't do anything to me." Molly was only nineteen. She felt that this moment of interview for her first job was a tremendous inch in her whole existence.

The walk up to the door did not reassure her, for the path lay between tight little flower beds hedged in with clipped box, seemingly planted with the admonition, "Now grow and multiply, but don't grow too high, nor multiply too greatly, and above all things, keep out of this path!" There was a hand on those flowers, a guiding and a correcting hand. The large white house was very dignified. Venetian blinds of yellow wood were tilted down to keep out the noon sun. Halfway up the path she came in sight of the entrance. There was a veranda as broad and warm and welcoming as an embrace. Through her mind flew the thought, "Surely you can tell the hospitality of a house by its entrance. Suppose it had a little door and no porch." But in spite of the welcoming of the wide steps and the big doorway, her timidities clung to her when she rang the bell. The big door opened, and a large, comfortable woman stood smiling at Molly.

"I hope you're not selling something," said Mrs. Whiteside. "I never want to buy anything and I always do, and then I'm mad."

Molly laughed. She felt suddenly very happy. Until that moment she hadn't known how frightened she really was. "Oh, no," she cried. "I'm the new schoolteacher. My letter says I'm to interview Mr. Whiteside. Can I see him?"

"Well, it's noon, and he's just finishing his dinner. Did you have dinner?"

"Oh, of course. I mean, no."

Mrs. Whiteside chuckled and stood aside for her to enter. "Well, I'm glad you're sure." She led Molly into a large dining room, lined with mahogany, glass-fronted dish closets. The square table was littered with the dishes of a meal. "Why, John must have finished and gone. Sit down, young woman. I'll bring back the roast."

"Oh, no. Really, thank you, no, I'll just talk to Mr. Whiteside and then go along."

"Sit down. You'll need nourishment to face John."

"Is—is he very stern, with new teachers, I mean?"

"Well," said Mrs. Whiteside. "That depends. If they haven't had their dinner, he's a regular bear. He shouts at them. But when they've just got up from the table, he's only just fierce."

Molly laughed happily. "You have children," she said. "Oh, you've raised lots of children—and you like them."

Mrs. Whiteside scowled. "One child raised me. Raised me right through the roof. It was too hard on me. He's out raising cows now, poor devils. I don't think I raised him very high."

When Molly had finished eating, Mrs. Whiteside threw open a side door and called, "John, here's someone to see you." She pushed Molly through the doorway into a room that was a kind of a library, for big bookcases were loaded with thick, old, comfortable books, all filigreed in gold. And it was a kind of a sitting room. There was a fireplace of brick with a mantel of little red tile bricks and the most extraordinary vases on the mantel. Hung on a nail over the mantel, slung really, like a rifle on a shoulder strap, was a huge meerschaum pipe in the Jaeger fashion. Big leather chairs with leather tassels hanging to them, stood about the fireplace, all of them patent rocking chairs with the kind of springs that chant when you rock them. And lastly, the room was a kind of an office, for there was an old-fashioned roll-top desk, and behind it sat John Whiteside. When he looked up, Molly saw that he had at once the kindest and the sternest eyes she had ever seen, and the whitest hair, too. Real blue-white, silky hair, a great cluster of it.

"I am Mary Morgan," she began formally.

"Oh, yes, Miss Morgan, I've been expecting you. Won't you sit down?"

She sat in one of the big rockers, and the springs cried with sweet pain. "I love these chairs," she said. "We used to have one when I was a little girl." Then she felt silly. "I've come to interview you about this position. My letter said to do that."

"Don't be so tense, Miss Morgan. I've interviewed every teacher we've had for years. And," he said, smiling, "I still don't know how to go about it."

"Oh—I'm glad, Mr. Whiteside. I never asked for a job before. I was really afraid of it."

"Well, Miss Mary Morgan, as near as I can figure, the purpose of this interview is to give me a little knowledge of your past and of the kind of person you are. I'm supposed to know something about you when you've finished. And now that you know my purpose, I suppose you'll be self-conscious and anxious to give a good impression. Maybe if you just tell me a little about yourself, everything'll be all right. Just a few words about the kind of girl you are, and where you came from."

Molly nodded quickly. "Yes, I'll try to do that, Mr. Whiteside," and she dropped her mind back into the past.

There was the old, squalid, unpainted house with its wide back porch and the round washtubs leaning against the rail. High in the great willow tree her two brothers, Joe and Tom, crashed about crying, "Now I'm an eagle." "I'm a parrot." "Now I'm an old chicken." "Watch me!"

The screen door on the back porch opened, and their mother leaned tiredly out. Her hair would not lie smoothly no matter how much she combed it. Thick strings of it hung down beside her face. Her eyes were always a little red, and her hands and wrists painfully cracked. "Tom, Joe," she called. "You'll get hurt up there. Don't worry me so, boys! Don't you love your mother at all?" The voices in the tree were hushed. The shrieking spirits of the eagle and the old chicken were drenched in self-reproach. Molly sat in the dust, wrapping a rag around a stick and doing her best to imagine it a tall lady in a dress. "Molly, come in and stay with your mother. I'm so tired today."

Molly stood up the stick in the deep dust. "You, miss," she whispered fiercely. "You'll get whipped on your bare bottom when I come back." Then she obediently went into the house.

Her mother sat in a straight chair in the kitchen. "Draw up, Molly. Just sit with me for a little while. Love me, Molly! Love your mother a little bit. You are mother's good little girl, aren't you?" Molly squirmed on her chair. "Don't you love your mother, Molly?"

The little girl was very miserable. She knew her mother would cry in a moment, and then she would be compelled to stroke the stringy hair. Both she and her brothers knew they should love their mother. She did everything for them. They were ashamed that they hated to be near her, but they couldn't help it. When she called to them and they were not in sight, they pretended not to hear, and crept away, talking in whispers.

"Well, to begin with, we were very poor," Molly said to John Whiteside. "I guess we were really poverty-stricken. I had two brothers a little older than I. My father was a traveling salesman, but even so, my mother had to work. She worked terribly hard for us."

About once in every six months a great event occurred. In the morning the mother crept silently out of the bedroom. Her hair was brushed as smoothly as it could be; her eyes sparkled, and she looked happy and almost pretty. She whispered, "Quiet, children! Your father's home."

Molly and her brothers sneaked out of the house, but even in the yard they talked in excited whispers. The news traveled quickly about the neighborhood. Soon the yard was filled with whispering children. "They say their father's home." "Is your father really home?" "Where's he been this time?" By noon there were a dozen children in the yard, standing in expectant little groups, cautioning one another to be quiet.

About noon the screen door on the porch sprang open and whacked against the wall. Their father leaped out. "Hi," he yelled. "Hi, kids!" Molly and her brothers flung themselves upon him and hugged his legs, while he plucked them off and hurled them into the air like kittens.

Mrs. Morgan fluttered about, clucking with excitement, "Children, children. Don't muss your father's clothes."

The neighbor children threw handsprings and wrestled and shrieked with joy. It was better than any holiday.

"Wait till you see," their father cried. "Wait till you see what I brought you. It's a secret now." And when the hysteria had quieted a little he carried his suitcase out on the porch and opened it. There were presents such as no one had ever seen, mechanical toys unknown before—tin bugs that crawled, and astounding steam shovels that worked in sand. There were superb glass marbles with bears and dogs right in their centers. He had something for everyone, several things for everyone. It was all the great holidays packed into one.

Usually it was midafternoon before the children became calm enough not to shriek occasionally. But eventually George Morgan sat on the steps, and they all gathered about while he told his adventures. This time he had been to Mexico while there was a revolution. Again he had gone to Honolulu, had seen the volcano and had himself ridden on a surfboard. Always there were cities and people, strange people; always adventures and a hundred funny incidents, funnier than anything they had ever heard. It couldn't all be told at one time. After school they had to gather to hear more and more. Throughout the world George Morgan tramped, collecting glorious adventures.

"As far as my home life went," Miss Morgan said, "I guess I almost didn't have any father. He was able to get home very seldom from his business trips."

John Whiteside nodded gravely.

Molly's hands rustled in her lap and her eyes were dim.

One time he brought a dumpy, woolly puppy in a box, and it wet on the floor immediately.

"What kind of a dog is it?" Tom asked in his most sophisticated manner.

Their father laughed loudly. He was so young! He looked twenty years younger than their mother. "It's a dollar and a half dog," he explained. "You get an awful lot of kinds of dog for a dollar and a half. It's like this. . . . Suppose you go into a candy store and say, 'I want a nickel's worth of peppermints and gumdrops and licorice and raspberry chews.' Well, I went in and said, 'Give me a dollar and a half's worth of mixed dog.' That's the kind it is. It's Molly's dog, and she has to name it."

"I'm going to name it George," said Molly.

Her father bowed strangely to her, and said, "Thank you, Molly." They all noticed that he wasn't laughing at her, either.

Molly got up very early the next morning and took George about the yard to show him the secrets. She opened the hoard where two pennies and a gold policeman's button were buried. She hooked his little front paws over the back fence so he could look down the street at the schoolhouse. Lastly she climbed into the willow tree, carrying George under one arm. Tom came out of the house and sauntered under the tree. "Look out you don't drop him," Tom called, and just at that moment the puppy squirmed out of her arms and fell. He landed on the hard ground with a disgusting little thump. One leg bent out at a crazy angle, and the puppy screamed long, horrible screams, with sobs between breaths. Molly scrambled out of the tree, dull and stunned by the accident. Tom was standing over the puppy, his face white and twisted with pain, and George, the puppy, screamed on and on.

"We can't let him," Tom cried. "We can't let him." He ran to the woodpile and brought back a hatchet. Molly was too stupe-

*fied to look away, but Tom closed his eyes and struck. The
screams stopped suddenly. Tom threw the hatchet from him and
leaped over the back fence. Molly saw him running away as
though he were being chased.*

*At that moment Joe and her father came out of the back
door. Molly remembered how haggard and thin and gray her
father's face was when he looked at the puppy. It was something
in her father's face that started Molly to crying. "I dropped him
out of the tree, and he hurt himself, and Tom hit him, and then
Tom ran away." Her voice sounded sulky. Her father hugged
Molly's head against his hip.*

*"Poor Tom!" he said. "Molly, you must remember never to
say anything to Tom about it, and never to look at him as though
you remembered." He threw a gunny sack over the puppy. "We
must have a funeral," he said. "Did I ever tell you about the
Chinese funeral I went to, about the colored paper they throw
in the air, and the little fat roast pigs on the grave?" Joe edged
in closer, and even Molly's eyes took on a gleam of interest.
"Well, it was this way...."*

Molly looked up at John Whiteside and saw that he seemed
to be studying a piece of paper on his desk. "When I was twelve
years old, my father was killed in an accident," she said.

*The great visits usually lasted about two weeks. Always
there came an afternoon when George Morgan walked out into
the town and did not come back until late at night. The mother
made the children go to bed early, but they could hear him come
home, stumbling a little against the furniture, and they could
hear his voice through the wall. These were the only times when
his voice was sad and discouraged. Lying with held breaths, in
their beds, the children knew what that meant. In the morning
he would be gone, and their hearts would be gone with him.*

*They had endless discussions about what he was doing.
Their father was a glad argonaut, a silver knight. Virtue and
Courage and Beauty—he wore a coat of them. "Sometime," the
boys said, "sometime when we're big, we'll go with him and see
all those things."*

"I'll go, too," Molly insisted.

"Oh, you're a girl. You couldn't go, you know."

*"But he'd let me go, you know he would. Sometime he'll
take me with him. You see if he doesn't."*

When he was gone their mother grew plaintive again, and

her eyes reddened. Querulously she demanded their love, as though it were a package they could put in her hand.

One time their father went away, and he never came back. He had never sent any money, nor had he ever written to them, but this time he just disappeared for good. For two years they waited, and then their mother said he must be dead. The children shuddered at the thought, but they refused to believe it, because no one so beautiful and fine as their father could be dead. Some place in the world he was having adventures. There was some good reason why he couldn't come back to them. Some day when the reason was gone, he would come. Some morning he would be there with finer presents and better stories than ever before. But their mother said he must have had an accident. He must be dead. Their mother was distracted. She read those advertisements which offered to help her make money at home. The children made paper flowers and shamefacedly tried to sell them. The boys tried to develop magazine routes, and the whole family nearly starved. Finally, when they couldn't stand it any longer, the boys ran away and joined the navy. After that Molly saw them as seldom as she had seen her father, and they were so changed, so hard and boisterous, that she didn't even care, for her brothers were strangers to her.

"I went through high school, and then I went to San Jose and entered Teachers' College. I worked for my board and room at the home of Mrs. Allen Morit. Before I finished school my mother died, so I guess I'm kind of an orphan, you see."

"I'm sorry," John Whiteside murmured gently.

Molly flushed. "That wasn't a bid for sympathy, Mr. Whiteside. You said you wanted to know about me. Everyone has to be an orphan some time."

Molly worked for her board and room. She did the work of a full time servant, only she received no pay. Money for clothes had to be accumulated by working in a store during summer vacation. Mrs. Morit trained her girls. "I can take a green girl, not worth a cent," she often said, "and when that girl's worked for me six months, she can get fifty dollars a month. Lots of women know it, and they just snap up my girls. This is the first schoolgirl I've tried, but even she shows a lot of improvement. She reads too much though. I always say a servant should be asleep by ten o'clock, or else she can't do her work right."

Mrs. Morit's method was one of constant criticism and nag-

ging, carried on in a just, firm tone. "Now, Molly, I don't want to find fault, but if you don't wipe the silver drier than that, it'll have streaks."—"The butter knife goes this way, Molly. Then you can put the tumbler here."

　　"I always give a reason for everything," she told her friends.

　　In the evening after the dishes were washed, Molly sat on her bed and studied, and when the light was off, she lay on her bed and thought of her father. It was ridiculous to do it, she knew. It was a waste of time. Her father came up to the door, wearing a cutaway coat, and striped trousers and a top hat. He carried a huge bouquet of red roses in his hand. "I couldn't come before, Molly. Get on your coat quickly. First we're going down to get that evening dress in the window of Prussia's, but we'll have to hurry. I have tickets for the train to New York tonight. Hurry up, Molly! Don't stand there gawping." It was silly. Her father was dead. No, she didn't really believe he was dead. Somewhere in the world he lived beautifully, and sometime he would come back.

　　Molly told one of her friends at school, "I don't really believe it, you see, but I don't disbelieve it. If I ever knew he was dead, why it would be awful. I don't know what I'd do then. I don't want to think about knowing *he's dead."*

　　When her mother died, she felt little besides shame. Her mother had wanted so much to be loved, and she hadn't known how to draw love. Her importunities had bothered the children and driven them away.

　　"Well, that's about all," Molly finished. "I got my diploma, and then I was sent down here."

　　"It was about the easiest interview I ever had," John Whiteside said.

　　"Do you think I'll get the position, then?"

　　The old man gave a quick, twinkly glance at the big meerschaum hanging over the mantel.

　　"That's his friend," Molly thought. "He has secrets with that pipe."

　　"Yes, I think you'll get the job. I think you have it already. Now, Miss Morgan, where are you going to live? You must find board and room some place."

　　Before she knew she was going to say it, she had blurted, "I want to live here."

　　John Whiteside opened his eyes in astonishment. "But we never take boarders, Miss Morgan."

"Oh, I'm sorry I said that. I just like it so much here, you see."

He called, "Willa," and when his wife stood in the half-open door, "This young lady wants to board with us. She's the new teacher."

Mrs. Whiteside frowned. "Couldn't think of it. We never take boarders. She's too pretty to be around that fool of a Bill. What would happen to those cows of his? It'd be a lot of trouble. You can sleep in the third bedroom upstairs," she said to Molly. "It doesn't catch much sun anyway."

Life changed its face. All of a sudden Molly found she was a queen. From the first day the children of the school adored her, for she understood them, and what was more, she let them understand her. It took her some time to realize that she had become an important person. If two men got to arguing at the store about a point of history or literature or mathematics, and the argument deadlocked, it ended up, "Take it to the teacher! If she doesn't know, she'll find it." Molly was very proud to be able to decide such questions. At parties she had to help with the decorations and to plan refreshments.

"I think we'll put pine boughs around everywhere. They're pretty, and they smell so good. They smell like a party." She was supposed to know everything and to help with everything, and she loved it.

At the Whiteside home she slaved in the kitchen under the mutterings of Willa. At the end of six months, Mrs. Whiteside grumbled to her husband, "Now if Bill only had any sense. But then," she continued, "if *she* has any sense—" and there she left it.

At night Molly wrote letters to the few friends she had made in Teachers' College, letters full of little stories about her neighbors, and full of joy. She must attend every party because of the social prestige of her position. On Saturdays she ran about the hills and brought back ferns and wild flowers to plant about the house.

Bill Whiteside took one look at Molly and scuttled back to his cows. It was a long time before he found the courage to talk to her very much. He was a big, simple young man who had neither his father's balance nor his mother's humor. Eventually, however, he trailed after Molly and looked after her from distances.

One evening, with a kind of feeling of thanksgiving for her happiness, Molly told Bill about her father. They were sitting in canvas chairs on the wide veranda, waiting for the moon. She told him about the visits, and then about the disappearance. "Do you see what I have, Bill?" she cried. "My lovely father is some place. He's mine. You think he's living, don't you, Bill?"

"Might be," said Bill. "From what you say, he was a kind of an irresponsible cuss, though. Excuse me, Molly. Still, if he's alive, it's funny he never wrote."

Molly felt cold. It was just the kind of reasoning she had successfully avoided for so long. "Of course," she said stiffly, "I know that. I have to do some work now, Bill."

High up on a hill that edged the valley of the Pastures of Heaven, there was an old cabin which commanded a view of the whole country and of all the roads in the vicinity. It was said that the bandit Vasquez had built the cabin and lived in it for a year while the posses went crashing through the country looking for him. It was a landmark. All the people of the valley had been to see it at one time or another. Nearly everyone asked Molly whether she had been there yet. "No," she said, "but I will go up some day. I'll go some Saturday. I know where the trail to it is." One morning she dressed in her new hiking boots and corduroy skirt. Bill sidled up and offered to accompany her. "No," she said. "You have work to do. I can't take you away from it."

"Work be hanged!" said Bill.

"Well, I'd rather go alone. I don't want to hurt your feelings, but I just want to go alone, Bill." She was sorry not to let him accompany her, but his remark about her father had frightened her. "I want to have an adventure," she said to herself. "If Bill comes along, it won't be an adventure at all. It'll just be a trip." It took her an hour and a half to climb up the steep trail under the oaks. The leaves on the ground were as slippery as glass, and the sun was hot. The good smell of ferns and dank moss and yerba buena filled the air. When Molly came at last to the ridge crest, she was damp and winded. The cabin stood in a small clearing in the brush, a little square wooden room with no windows. Its doorless entrance was a black shadow. The place was quiet, the kind of humming quiet that flies and bees and crickets make. The whole hillside sang softly in the sun. Molly approached on tiptoe. Her heart was beating violently.

"Now I'm having an adventure," she whispered. "Now I'm right in the middle of an adventure at Vasquez' cabin." She peered in at the doorway and saw a lizard scuttle out of sight. A cobweb fell across her forehead and seemed to try to restrain her. There was nothing at all in the cabin, nothing but the dirt floor and the rotting wooden walls, and the dry, deserted smell of the earth that has long been covered from the sun. Molly was filled with excitement. "At night he sat in there. Sometimes when he heard noises like men creeping up on him, he went out of the door like a ghost of a shadow, and just melted into the darkness." She looked down on the valley of the Pastures of Heaven. The orchards lay in dark green squares; the grain was yellow, and the hills behind, a light brown washed with lavender. Among the farms the roads twisted and curled, avoiding a field, looping around a huge tree, half circling a hill flank. Over the whole valley was stretched a veil of heat shimmer. "Unreal," Molly whispered, "fantastic. It's a story, a real story, and I'm having an adventure." A breeze rose out of the valley like the sigh of a sleeper, and then subsided.

"In the daytime that young Vasquez looked down on the valley just as I'm looking. He stood right here, and looked at the roads down there. He wore a purple vest braided with gold, and the trousers on his slim legs widened at the bottom like the mouths of trumpets. His spur rowels were wrapped with silk ribbons to keep them from clinking. Sometimes he saw the posses riding by on the road below. Lucky for him the men bent over their horses' necks, and didn't look up at the hilltops. Vasquez laughed, but he was afraid, too. Sometimes he sang. His songs were soft and sad because he knew he couldn't live very long."

Molly sat down on the slope and rested her chin in her cupped hands. Young Vasquez was standing beside her, and Vasquez had her father's gay face, his shining eyes as he came on the porch shouting, "Hi, Kids!" This was the kind of adventure her father had. Molly shook herself and stood up. "Now I want to go back to the first and think it all over again."

In the late afternoon Mrs. Whiteside sent Bill out to look for Molly. "She might have turned an ankle, you know." But Molly emerged from the trail just as Bill approached it from the road.

"We were beginning to wonder if you'd got lost," he said. "Did you go up to the cabin?"

"Yes."

"Funny old box, isn't it? Just an old woodshed. There are a dozen just like it down here. You'd be surprised, though, how many people go up there to look at it. The funny part is, nobody's sure Vasquez was ever there."

"Oh, I think he must have been there."

"What makes you think that?"

"I don't know."

Bill became serious. "Everybody thinks Vasquez was a kind of a hero, when really he was just a thief. He started in stealing sheep and horses and ended up robbing stages. He had to kill a few people to do it. It seems to me, Molly, we ought to teach people to hate robbers, not worship them."

"Of course, Bill," she said wearily. "You're perfectly right. Would you mind not talking for a little while, Bill? I guess I'm a little tired, and nervous, too."

The year wheeled around. Pussywillows had their kittens, and wild flowers covered the hills. Molly found herself wanted and needed in the valley. She even attended school board meetings. There had been a time when those secret and august conferences were held behind closed doors, a mystery and a terror to everyone. Now that Molly was asked to step into John Whiteside's sitting room, she found that the board discussed crops, told stories, and circulated mild gossip.

Bert Munroe had been elected early in the fall, and by the springtime he was the most energetic member. He it was who planned dances at the schoolhouse, who insisted upon having plays and picnics. He even offered prizes for the best report cards in the school. The board was coming to rely pretty much on Bert Munroe.

One evening Molly came down late from her room. As always, when the board was meeting, Mrs. Whiteside sat in the dining room. "I don't think I'll go in to the meeting," Molly said. "Let them have one time to themselves. Sometimes I feel that they would tell other kinds of stories if I weren't there."

"You go on in, Molly! They can't hold a board meeting without you. They're so used to you, they'd be lost. Besides. I'm not at all sure I want them to tell those other stories."

Obediently Molly knocked on the door and went into the sitting room. Bert Munroe paused politely in the story he was narrating. "I was just telling about my new farm hand, Miss Morgan. I'll start over again, 'cause it's kind of funny. You see, I needed a hay hand, and I picked this fellow up under the Salinas River bridge. He was pretty drunk, but he wanted a job. Now I've got him, I find he isn't worth a cent as a hand, but I can't get rid of him. That son of a gun has been every place. You ought to hear him tell about the places he's been. My kids wouldn't let me get rid of him if I wanted to. Why he can take the littlest thing he's seen and make a fine story out of it. My kids just sit around with their ears spread, listening to him. Well, about twice a month he walks into Salinas and goes on a bust. He's one of those dirty, periodic drunks. The Salinas cops always call me up when they find him in a gutter, and I have to drive in to get him. And you know, when he comes out of it, he's always got some kind of present in his pocket for my kid Manny. There's nothing you can do with a man like that. He disarms you. I don't get a dollar's worth of work a month out of him."

Molly felt a sick dread rising in her. The men were laughing at the story. "You're too soft, Bert. You can't afford to keep an entertainer on the place. I'd sure get rid of him quick."

Molly stood up. She was dreadfully afraid someone would ask the man's name. "I'm not feeling very well tonight," she said. "If you gentlemen will excuse me, I think I'll go to bed." The men stood up while she left the room. In her bed she buried her head in the pillow. "It's crazy," she said to herself. "There isn't a chance in the world. I'm forgetting all about it right now." But she found to her dismay that she was crying.

The next few weeks were agonizing to Molly. She was reluctant to leave the house. Walking to and from school she watched the road ahead of her. "If I see any kind of a stranger I'll run away. But that's foolish. I'm being a fool." Only in her own room did she feel safe. Her terror was making her lose color, was taking the glint out of her eyes.

"Molly, you ought to go to bed," Mrs. Whiteside insisted. "Don't be a little idiot. Do I have to smack you the way I do Bill to make you go to bed?" But Molly would not go to bed. She thought too many things when she was in bed.

The next time the board met, Bert Munroe did not appear. Molly felt reassured and almost happy at his absence.

"You're feeling better, aren't you, Miss Morgan?"

"Oh, yes. It was only a little thing, a kind of a cold. If I'd gone to bed I might have been really sick."

The meeting was an hour gone before Bert Munroe came in. "Sorry to be late," he apologized. "The same old thing happened. My so-called hay hand was asleep in the street in Salinas. What a mess! He's out in the car sleeping it off now. I'll have to hose the car out tomorrow."

Molly's throat closed with terror. For a second she thought she was going to faint. "Excuse me, I must go." she cried, and ran out of the room. She walked into the dark hallway and steadied herself against the wall. Then slowly and automatically she marched out of the front door and down the steps. The night was filled with whispers. Out in the road she could see the black

mass that was Bert Munroe's car. She was surprised at the way
her footsteps plodded down the path of their own volition. "Now
I'm killing myself," she said. "Now I'm throwing everything away.
I wonder why." The gate was under her hand, and her hand
flexed to open it. Then a tiny breeze sprang up and brought
to her nose the sharp foulness of vomit. She heard a blubbering,
drunken snore. Instantly something whirled in her head. Molly
spun around and ran frantically back to the house. In her room
she locked the door and sat stiffly down, panting with the effort
of her run. It seemed hours before she heard the men go out
of the house, calling their good-nights. Then Bert's motor started,
and the sound of it died away down the road. Now that she
was ready to go she felt paralyzed.

John Whiteside was writing at his desk when Molly entered
the sitting room. He looked up questioningly at her. "You aren't
well, Miss Morgan. You need a doctor."

She planted herself woodenly beside the desk. "Could you
get a substitute teacher for me?" she asked.

"Of course I could. You pile right into bed and I'll call a
doctor."

"It isn't that, Mr. Whiteside. I want to go away tonight."

"What are you talking about? You aren't well."

"I told you my father was dead. I don't know whether he's
dead or not. I'm afraid—I want to go away tonight."

He stared intently at her. "Tell me what you mean," he said
softly.

"If I should see that drunken man of Mr. Munroe's—"she
paused, suddenly terrified at what she was about to say.

John Whiteside nodded very slowly.

"No," she cried. "I don't think that. I'm sure I don't."

"I'd like to do something, Molly."

"I don't want to go, I love it here—But I'm afraid. It's so
important to me."

John Whiteside stood up and came close to her and put
his arm about her shoulders. "I don't think I understand, quite,"
he said. "I don't think I want to understand. That isn't necessary." He seemed to be talking to himself. "It wouldn't be quite
courteous—to understand."

"Once I'm away I'll be able not to believe it," Molly whim-
pered.

He gave her shoulders one quick squeeze with his encircling
arm. "You run upstairs and pack your things, Molly," he said.
"I'll get out the car and drive you right in to Salinas now."

QUESTIONS FOR DISCUSSION AND WRITING

1. "Molly Morgan" is several stories combined into one. There is the story of the job interview, the teaching job, and of Molly's life in the Pastures of Heaven. There is the story of Molly's early family life with her mother and the other children. There is the story of Molly's father. There is the brief story of the bandit Vasquez. Tell in the simplest way possible the facts of each of these stories. How are they all made into one story?

2. Who do you think are the two main characters in "Molly Morgan"? Explain.

3. For Mr. Whiteside, Molly's job interview turns out to be "about the easiest" he ever had. Why? Look over the story and read only the words that Molly tells Mr. Whiteside. Why do you think she tells only such a small part of what Steinbeck tells you, the reader, of her past life?

4. Molly's relationship with her mother and with her father were a contrast. Explain what you think the influence of each of them was on her.

5. Who said of Molly's father, "He was kind of an irresponsible cuss"? To what extent is this a correct description of him? What else is there to say about him? Why was he so important to Molly?

6. Bill and Molly see the bandit Vasquez quite differently. Bill says, "Really he was just a thief." How does Molly see him?

7. Why does Molly say, on page 130, as she walks toward the car where the hay hand was sleeping off his drunk, "Now I'm killing myself"? Why in the end, despite her love of the Pastures, does she have to escape? What is she escaping from?

SUGGESTIONS FOR FURTHER WRITING OR DISCUSSION

1. Perhaps you have known a supposed "no-good" character. If so describe him, or make him part of a story.

2. Write a story or an experience where a person had to get away, had to escape, even if only for a short while.

3. Molly had some illusions about her father and the wonderful man she wanted to think he was. She could not stand facing the disillusionment of knowing he was an incurable drunk. Tell an experience of disillusionment in which you, or someone else, had to face a bad truth when you wanted only to see good.

THE LOST BROOCH

by Anton Chekhov

*A valuable brooch is stolen. A sensitive girl's room is
searched. The master of the house reveals himself sur-
prisingly. For whom is the need to escape the greatest?
Don't be confused by the names in the story.*
Mashenka Pavletsky *is the governess.*
Nicolai Sergeitch Kushkin *is the master of the
house.*
Theodosia Vasilevny Kushkina—*the a makes the
name feminine—is the mistress of the house. Her
husband calls her by her nickname,* Fenya.
The other names are of minor characters, all servants.

Mashenka Pavletsky, a young girl who had just finished her
studies at boarding school, returning home from a walk, to the
house of the Kushkins, where she was living as a governess,
came upon an extraordinary commotion. The doorman, Michael, who let her in, was agitated and red as a lobster. A commotion could be heard from upstairs.

"The mistress is probably having one of her spells," Mashenka thought, "or she has been quarreling with her husband."

In the reception room and in the hall she ran into some
of the maids. One servant was crying. Then Mashenka saw the
master himself run out of her room. This Nicolai Sergeitch,
though not yet old, had a flabby face and a big bald spot. He
was red in the face. He shuddered. Taking no notice of the governess, he went past her and throwing up his hands, exclaimed,
"Oh, how ghastly this is! How tactless! How stupid, absurd! It's
abominable!"

Mashenka stepped into her room and there, for the first
time in her life, she experienced in all of its acuteness the feeling
which is so familiar to all timid people in a subordinate position,
living on the bread of the rich and powerful. They were making
a search of her room. The mistress, Theodosia Vasilevny, a
plump, broadshouldered woman with heavy black eyebrows
under her cap, uncouth, with a slight growth of mustache, with
red hands and face, and in her manners resembling a rude country cook, was standing at her table and putting back into her

workbag balls of wool, scraps, and slips of paper. Evidently the appearance of the governess took her by surprise, as, looking up and catching sight of her white, astonished face, she became somewhat embarrassed and stammered, "Pardon, I . . . accidentally spilled . . . I caught my sleeve . . ."

And still mumbling something, Madame Kushkina gave a swish to her train and went out. Mashenka looked around her room with amazement, and understanding nothing, not knowing what to think, shrugged her shoulders and turned cold with fear. What was Theodosia Vasilevny looking for in her bag? If, as she said, she had really caught her sleeve in it and spilled it, then why had Nicolai Sergeitch dashed out of her room looking so red and excited? Why was one of the table drawers partly open? The money box, in which the governess kept coins and old stamps locked up, was unfastened. They had opened it, but they had not been able to lock it, although they had covered the whole lock with scratches. The bookstand, the top of the table, the bed—all bore fresh traces of the search. And the basket with the linen, too. The linen was neatly folded, but not in that order in which Mashenka had left it on going out of the house. This meant that it was really a search, but what was the object of it? What had happened? Mashenka recalled the agitation of the doorman, the commotion, which was still going on, the crying servant; didn't all this have some connection with the search that had just taken place in her room? Wasn't she involved in some terrible affair? Mashenka turned pale, and, cold all over, she sank down on the linen basket.

A servant came into the room.

"Liza, don't you know that they . . . have been searching in my room?" asked the governess.

"A brooch of the mistress worth two thousand rubles has been lost."

"Yes, but why search me?"

"They searched everybody, Miss. They went through everything of mine, too. They stripped us all stark naked and searched us. And there I was, Miss, as before God. I never even went near her toilet table, let alone touching the brooch. And I shall tell that to the police, too."

"But . . . why search me?" continued the governess, unable to understand.

"Someone stole the brooch, I tell you. . .The mistress herself searched everybody with her own hands. They even searched Michael, the doorman, himself. A downright scandal! Nicolai

Sergeitch just looks on, cackling like a hen. But there's no need for you to be upset about this, Miss. They didn't find anything in your room! As long as you didn't take the brooch there's nothing for you to be afraid of."

"But this is vile, Liza . . . insulting," said Mashenka, choking with indignation. "This is baseness, meanness! What right had she to suspect me and to ransack my things?"

"You are living amongst strangers, Miss," sighed Liza. "Although you are a young lady, yet . . . it's as if you were a servant . . . . This isn't like being at home with papa and mama."

Mashenka threw herself down on the bed and began to sob bitterly. Never before had such an outrage been perpetrated against her, never had she been so deeply insulted as now. . . .They had suspected her, a well-bred, sensitive girl, the daughter of a professor, of stealing; they had searched her like a woman of the streets! It would be impossible, seemingly, to conceive of any insult greater than that. And to this feeling of outrage was added another heavy fear: what might happen now? All sorts of absurd ideas came into her mind. If they were capable of suspecting her of stealing, then that meant that they might arrest her, strip her stark naked and search her, and then lead her through the street under guard, imprison her in a dark, cold cell with mice and vermin, in just the sort of place they put Princess Tarakanova. Who would intercede for her? Her people lived far away in the provinces; they hadn't the money to come to her. She was alone in the great city as in a great field, without relatives, without acquaintances. They could do with her what they wished.

"I shall run to all the judges and lawyers," thought Mashenka shuddering. "I shall explain to them, I shall take oath. . . .They will prove that I cannot be the thief."

Mashenka recalled that in her room in the basket, under the sheets, were lying some sweets, that, following an old habit established at boarding school, she had put into her pocket at dinner and had carried off to her room with her. The thought that this little secret of hers was already known to her master and mistress threw her into a fever, and the result of all this, the fear, the shame, the insult, was that her heart began to palpitate violently and made itself felt in her temples, her hands, and deep within her.

"Dinner is served!" They were calling Mashenka. Should she go down or not? Mashenka smoothed her hair, wiped her face with a wet towel, and went into the dining room. There dinner was already begun. At one end of the table sat Theodosia Vasilevny, pompous, with a grave, stupid face; at the other end was Nicolai Sergeitch. At the sides sat the guests and the children. Two footmen in frock coats and white gloves served the dinner. Everybody knew that there had been a commotion in the house, that the mistress was upset, and all kept silent. Nothing was heard but their chewing and the clatter of the spoons against the plates.

The mistress herself opened the conversation.

"What have we for the third course?" she asked the footman in a dull, martyred voice.

"Sturgeon *á la russe*," answered the footman.

"I ordered that, Fenya," Nicolai Sergeitch made haste to say. "I was hungry for fish. If you don't like it, my dear, then don't have them serve it. You see I . . . among the rest . . ."

Theodosia Vasilevny did not like dishes that she had not ordered herself, and now her eyes filled with tears.

"There, there, let's not get upset," said Mamikov, her family doctor, in a syrupy voice as he lightly patted her hand and smiled sweetly. "We are nervous enough without that. Let's forget about the brooch. One's health is more precious than two thousand rubles."

"I don't care about the miserable two thousand!" answered the mistress, and a big tear ran down her cheek. "The fact itself fills me with indignation! I have never put up with stealing in my house. I am not sorry, I am not sorry about anything. But to steal in my house—that is such ungratefulness! To repay me in such a way for my kindness!"

Everyone looked at his plate, but it seemed to Mashenka that after what the mistress said everyone was staring at her. Suddenly a lump came into her throat; she began to cry and pressed her handkerchief to her face.

"Pardon. . ." she stammered, "I cannot. My head aches. I am going."

And she rose from the table, awkwardly banging her chair and more disconcerted than ever went out.

"God knows," said Nicolai Sergeitch, "there was no need to make a search in her room. How ridiculous that was, really!"

"I do not say that she took the brooch," said Theodosia Vasilevny, "but you can vouch for her, I suppose? I confess, I put little trust in these learned paupers."

"Really, Fenya, it is beside the point. Excuse me, Fenya, but according to law you haven't the right to search anyone."

"I don't know anything about your laws. I only know that my brooch is gone, that is all. And I'm going to find that brooch," and she hit her fork against her plate, her eyes flashing with anger. "And you go ahead and eat and don't interfere with my affairs."

Nicolai Sergeitch meekly dropped his eyes and sighed. Meanwhile, Mashenka, having reached her room threw herself on the bed. She was no longer frightened or ashamed, but a violent desire obsessed her to slap the face of this hard, this arrogant, stupid, smug woman.

As she lay there, breathing hard into the pillow, she dreamed how sweet it would be to go right now and buy the most costly brooch and fling it into the face of this stupid and unreasonable woman. If God would only let Theodosia Vasilevny be brought to ruin, so that she would have to go begging and might understand all the horror of poverty and of not being one's own master, and if the outraged Mashenka might only offer her charity. Oh, if she might only fall heir to a large fortune, buy a carriage, and ride dashingly past her windows that she might envy her.

But all this was daydreaming; in reality there was only one thing to do, to go away as quickly as possible, not to remain here even a single hour. True, it was terrible to give up her place, to go back to her people who had nothing, but what could she do? Mashenka couldn't look at her mistress again, nor at her little room; she was stifled here, full of horror. Theodosia Vasilevny, daft on the subject of diseases and of her would-be aristocracy, was so repulsive to her that it seemed as if everything in the world became gross and ugly because of the fact that this woman was in existence. Mashenka jumped up from the bed and began to pack.

"May I come in?" asked Nicolai Sergeitch at the door; he had come to the door noiselessly and spoke in a soft, gentle voice. "May I?"

"Come in." He came in and remained standing at the door. His eyes looked dim and his little red nose shone. He had been drinking beer after dinner, and this was evidenced in his gait and in his weak flabby hands.

"What does this mean?" he asked pointing to the basket.

"I am packing. I am sorry, Nicolai Sergeitch, but I can't stay in your house any longer. This search has offended me deeply!"

"I understand. Only there's no need of doing this. Why?

Your room was searched, but you . . . what difference does that make to you? You will lose nothing because of that."

Mashenka was silent and went on packing. Nicolai Sergeitch kept worrying his mustache as if trying to think what else to say and continued in a wheedling voice:

"I understand, of course, but you must be forbearing. You know my wife is excitable, flighty; you mustn't judge her harshly."

Mashenka said nothing.

"If you are so offended," continued Nicolai Sergeitch, "well, then . . . I am ready to apologize before you. I am sorry."

Mashenka made no answer but only bent lower over her trunk. This hollow-cheeked, spineless creature was of no significance whatever in the house. He played the miserable part of a weakling and somebody always in the way even for the servants; and his apology, likewise, meant nothing.

"M-m- . . . you say nothing? This isn't enough for you? In that case I apologize for my wife. In the name of my wife. . . . She didn't behave with much tact, I admit like a gentleman."

Nicolai Sergeitch walked about, sighed, and went on: "That means you want to keep on gnawing me here, beneath my heart. . . . You want my conscience to torment me."

"I know, Nicolai Sergeitch, you are not to blame," said Mashenka, looking straight into his face with her big, tear-stained eyes. "Why then do you fret yourself?"

"Of course, but for all that . . . don't go away . . . I beg you."

Mashenka shook her head in sign of negation. Nicolai Sergeitch remained standing at the window and began drumming on the window with his finger tips.

"For me such misunderstandings are simply torture," he said. "How about my getting down on my knees before you, eh, how would that be? Your pride has been offended, and here you are crying and getting ready to go away; but here I am with some pride, too, and you have no mercy on it. Or do you want me to tell you what I shall not tell even in confession? Listen, you want me to confess to what I shall not confess to a soul even in the face of death?"

Mashenka did not answer.

"I took my wife's brooch!" said Nicolai Sergeitch quickly. "Are you satisfied now? Does that make it all right? Yes, I . . . took it. . . Only, of course, I count on your discretion. For God's sake, not a word to anyone, not half a hint!"

Mashenka, amazed and startled, went on packing; she caught up her things, crumpled them, and without any kind of order stuffed them into the trunk and the basket. Now, after the outspoken confession made by Nicolai Sergeitch, she could not remain a minute longer, and she no longer understood how she had been able to live in this house before.

"And it's no wonder . . . " continued Nicolai Sergeitch after a long silence. "The usual story. I need money, and she doesn't give me any. This house and all these things belonged to my father. All this is mine, and the brooch belonged to my mother, and . . . everything is mine. But she has siezed everything, taken possession of everything . . . I can't go to court with her . . . you agree. I beg you earnestly, forgive me . . . and stay. *Tout comprendre, tout pardonner.*[1] Will you stay?"

"No," said Mashenka with decision, beginning to tremble. "Let me alone, I beg you."

"Well, God be with you," sighed Nicolai Sergeitch, sitting down on a stool near the trunk.

"I confess, I like those people who can still be offended, who can feel scorn, and so on. I could sit here a hundred years and look at your indignant face. . . .So then, you won't stay? I understand. . . .It has to be so . . . yes, of course. It is easy for you, but for me—tsk, tsk . . . . And not a step out of this cellar. I might go to one of our estates but there are those scoundrels of my wife everywhere . . . agronomists,[2] stewards, devil take them. They mortgage and remortgage . . . . You mustn't catch the fish, keep off the grass—don't break the trees."

"Nicolai Sergeitch!" Theodosia Vasilevny's voice was heard from the drawing room. "Agnia, call the master."

"So you won't stay?" asked Nicolai Sergeitch, rising hastily and moving toward the door. "You might just as well stay. In the evenings I could drop in to see you . . . we could talk, eh? Will you stay? If you go, in the whole house there won't be one human face. Oh, this is awful!"

The pallid, hollow-cheeked face of Nicolai Sergeitch implored her, but Mashenka shook her head, and with a wave of the hand he went out.

In half an hour she was already on her way.

---

1. *Tout comprendre, tout pardonner:* To understand all is to forgive all.
2. agronomists: crop experts.

QUESTIONS FOR DISCUSSION AND WRITING

1. When we first see Nicolai Sergeitch he is helplessly criticizing his wife: "Oh, how ghastly this is! How tactless!" Little by little, we come to see his true relationship to his wife. What is it? What events and actions of his show us?
2. Mashenka is outraged by having her room searched. She is not comforted when told by the servant Liza, "They searched everybody, Miss." Why not? And what little secret of hers has been discovered? Why did this upset her so?
3. Reread page 135. Why is Madame Kushkina so repulsive and hateful to Mashenka?
4. Why does Nicolai Sergeitch confess that he stole the brooch? Why did he steal it? Why is he so eager to have Mashenka stay? What does he mean when he says, "I like people who can still be offended"?
5. It might be said that this is the story of the weakness of strong people and the strength of weak people. Explain. Who is the strongest character in the story? Explain your choice.

SUGGESTIONS FOR FURTHER DISCUSSION AND WRITING

1. Write about an incident of theft and its consequences. Perhaps you can show how the theft grows out of a need a person thinks he can't meet any other way.
2. In "The Lost Brooch" a husband is dominated by his wife. Write about another dominating relationship that you know of or make up.
3. Mashenka had her little secret, the stolen sweets. Tell about another person's little—or perhaps not so little—secret and how it affected the person.
4. Have you ever felt a desire to hurt a person who was hateful to you? Tell about the situation and the person's and your actions and feelings.

HA'PENNY

by Alan Paton

This is the story of a poor boy in a reformatory in South Africa. He has a secret. How does the school's discovery of his secret affect him?

Of the six hundred boys at the reformatory, about one hundred were from ten to fourteen years of age. My Department had from time to time expressed the intention of taking them away, and of establishing a special institution for them, more like an industrial school than a reformatory. This would have been a good thing, for their offences were very trivial, and they would have been better by themselves. Had such a school been established, I should have liked to have been Principal of it myself, for it would have been an easier job; small boys turn instinctively towards affection, and one controls them by it, naturally and easily.

Some of them, if I came near them, either on parade or in school or at football, would observe me watchfully, not directly or fully, but obliquely and secretly; sometimes I would surprise them at it, and make some small sign of recognition, which would satisfy them so that they would cease to observe me, and would give their full attention to the event of the moment. But I knew that my authority was thus confirmed and strengthened.

These secret relations with them were a source of continuous pleasure to me. Had they been my own children I would no doubt have given a greater expression to it. But often I would move through the silent and orderly parade, and stand by one of them. He would look straight in front of him with a little frown of concentration that expressed both childish awareness of and manly indifference to my nearness. Sometimes I would tweak his ear, and he would give me a brief smile of acknowledgment, or frown with still greater concentration. It was natural I suppose to confine these outward expressions to the very smallest, but they were taken as symbolic, and some older boys would observe them and take themselves to be included. It was a relief, when the reformatory was passing through times of turbulence

and trouble, and when there was danger of estrangement between authority and boys, to make these simple and natural ges-
tures, which were reassurances both to me and them that nothing important had changed.

On Sunday afternoon when I was on duty, I would take
my car to the reformatory and watch the free boys being signed
out at the gate. This simple operation was also watched by many
boys not free, who would tell each other "in so many weeks I'll
be signed out myself." Amongst the watchers were always some
of the small boys, and these I would take by turns in the car.
We would go out to the Potchefstroom Road with its ceaseless
stream of traffic, and to the Baragwanath crossroads, and come
back by the Van Wyksrus road to the reformatory. I would talk
to them about their families, their parents, their sisters and brothers, and I would pretend to know nothing of Durban, Port
Elizabeth, Potchefstroom, and Clocolan,[1] and ask them if these
places were bigger than Johannesburg.

One of the small boys was Ha'penny,[2] and he was about
twelve years old. He came from Bloemfontein and was the biggest talker of them all. His mother worked in a white person's
house, and he had two brothers and two sisters. His brothers
were Richard and Dickie and his sisters Anna and Mina.

"Richard and Dickie?" I asked.

"Yes, *meneer.*"[3]

"In English," I said, "Richard and Dickie are the same
name."

When we returned to the reformatory, I sent for Ha'penny's
papers; there it was plainly set down, Ha'penny was a waif, with
no relatives at all. He had been taken in from one home to another, but he was naughty and uncontrollable, and eventually had
taken to pilfering at the market.

I then sent for the Letter Book, and found that Ha'penny
wrote regularly, or rather that others wrote for him till he would
write himself, to Mrs. Betty Maarman, of 48 Vlak Street, Bloemfontein. But Mrs. Maarman had never once replied to him. When
questioned, he had said, perhaps she is sick. I sat down and
wrote at once to the Social Welfare Officer at Bloemfontein, asking him to investigate.

The next time I had Ha'penny out in the car, I questioned
him again about his family. And he told me the same as before,

1. Durban . . . Clocolan: South African cities or towns.
2. Ha'penny: the coin of smallest value in the money system (a half penny).
3. meneer: sir (in South African Dutch).

his mother, Richard and Dickie, Anna and Mina. But he softened the "D" of "Dickie," so that it sounded now like Tickie.

"I thought you said Dickie," I said.

"I said Tickie," he said.

He watched me with concealed apprehension, and I came to the conclusion that this waif of Bloemfontein was a clever boy, who had told me a story that was all imagination, and had changed one single letter of it to make it safe from any question. And I thought I understood it all too, that he was ashamed of being without a family, and had invented them all, so that no one might discover that he was fatherless and motherless, and that no one in the world cared whether he was alive or dead. This gave me a strong feeling for him, and I went out of my way to manifest towards him that fatherly care that the State, though not in those words, had enjoined upon me by giving me this job.

Then the letter came from the Social Welfare Officer in Bloemfontein, saying that Mrs. Betty Maarman of 48 Vlak Street was a real person, and that she had four children, Richard and Dickie, Anna and Mina, but that Ha'penny was no child of hers, and she knew him only as a derelict[4] of the streets. She had never answered his letters, because he wrote to her as *mother*, and she was no mother of his, nor did she wish to play any such role. She was a decent woman, a faithful member of the church, and she had no thought of corrupting her family by letting them have anything to do with such a child.

But Ha'penny seemed to me anything but the usual delinquent, his desire to have a family was so strong, and his reformatory record was so blameless, and his anxiety to please and obey so great, that I began to feel a great duty towards him. Therefore I asked him about his "mother."

He could not speak enough of her, nor with too high praise. She was loving, honest, and strict. Her home was clean. She had affection for all her children. It was clear that the homeless child, even as he had attached himself to me, would have attached himself to her; he had observed her even as he had observed me, but did not know the secret of how to open her heart, so that she would take him in, and save him from the lonely life that he led.

"Why did you steal when you had such a mother?" I asked.

He could not answer that; not all his brains nor his courage

4. derelict: tramp.

could find an answer to such a question, for he knew that with such a mother he would not have stolen at all.

"The boy's name is Dickie," I said, "not Tickie."

And then he knew the deception was revealed. Another boy might have said, "I told you it was Dickie," but he was too intelligent for that; he knew that if I had established that the boy's name was *Dickie*, I must have established other things too. I was shocked by the immediate and visible effect of my action. His whole brave assurance died within him, and he stood there exposed, not as a liar, but as a homeless child who had surrounded himself with mother, brothers, and sisters, who did not exist. I had shattered the very foundations of his pride, and his sense of human significance.

He fell sick at once, and the doctor said it was tuberculosis. I wrote at once to Mrs. Maarman, telling her the whole story, of how this small boy had observed her, and had decided that she was the person he desired for his mother. But she wrote back saying that she could take no responsibility for him. For one thing, Ha'penny was a Mosuto,[5] and she was a coloured[6] woman; for another, she had never had a child in trouble, and how could she take such a boy?

Tuberculosis is a strange thing; sometimes it manifests itself suddenly in the most unlikely host, and swiftly sweeps to the end. Ha'penny withdrew himself from the world, from all Principals and mothers, and the doctor said there was little hope. In desperation I sent money for Mrs. Maarman to come.

She was a decent homely woman, and seeing that the situation was serious, she, without fuss or embarrassment, adopted Ha'penny for her own. The whole reformatory accepted her as his mother. She sat the whole day with him, and talked to him of Richard and Dickie, Anna and Mina, and how they were all waiting for him to come home. She poured out her affection on him, and had no fear of his sickness, nor did she allow it to prevent her from satisfying his hunger to be owned. She talked to him of what they would do when he came back, and how he would go to the school, and what they would buy for Guy Fawkes night.[7]

He in turn gave his whole attention to her, and when I visited him he was grateful, but I had passed out of his world.

5. Mosuto: a Black African tribe.
6. coloured: of mixed race. In South Africa, where whites have maintained strict anti-black laws, people of mixed races have more rights and status.
7. Guy Fawkes night: night of an annual celebration of the failure of a British revolutionary's attempt to blow up Parliament and the King in 1605.

I felt judged in that I had sensed only the existence and not the measure of his desire. I wished I had done something sooner, more wise, more prodigal.[8]

We buried him on the reformatory farm, and Mrs. Maarman said to me, "When you put up the cross, put he was my son."

"I'm ashamed," she said, "that I wouldn't take him."

"The sickness," I said, "the sickness would have come."

"No," she said, shaking her head with certainty. "It wouldn't have come. And if it had come at home, it would have been different."

So she left for Bloemfontein, after her strange visit to a reformatory. And I was left too, with the resolve to be more prodigal in the task that the State, though not in so many words, had enjoined on me.[9]

8. prodigal: very generous, extravagant.
9. enjoined on me: required of me.

QUESTIONS FOR DISCUSSION AND WRITING

1. Describe the relationship between the teller of the story and the little boys in his charge. What does it mean to him? What does he think it means to them? What makes him think so?

2. Why did Ha'penny make up the story about his relationship with a family? By what small thing was he able to tell that the teller of the story had discovered that he really had no family? Find the paragraph on page 143 that tells the effect on him of this discovery and reread it. Why was the effect so serious?

3. It seems cruel of the teller to have forced the truth out of Ha'penny, doesn't it? What other actions of his, however, show that he was truly concerned about the boy? What does he mean when he says, "I wished I had done something sooner, more wise, more prodigal"?

4. Why didn't Mrs. Maarman respond sooner to the boy's needs? Would you call her an insensitive woman, or was she more sensitive than most of us would be in a similar situation? Discuss.

5. The narrator describes the boy's need as "a hunger to be owned." What does that mean? What does the phrase show

us about the boy? What does it reveal about the man who uses it?

6. In what way is this a story of escape?
7. How were the teller and Mrs. Maarman changed by their experience with Ha'penny?

SUGGESTION FOR FURTHER WRITING OR DISCUSSION

Write about the relationship between a teacher and a pupil that you know. Try to show, if you can, what the relationship meant to each person as each understood it. It will probably be best to use made-up names.

Who Is Blind?

A prosperous businessman listens to a blind beggar's story.
A girl's efforts to help a blind classmate are rebuffed.

A MAN WHO HAD NO EYES

by MacKinlay Kantor

What did Mr. Parsons have that the blind beggar did not?

A beggar was coming down the avenue just as Mr. Parsons emerged from his hotel.

He was a blind beggar, carrying the traditional battered cane and thumping his way before him with the cautious, half-furtive effort of the sightless. He was a shaggy, thick-necked fellow; his coat was greasy about the lapels and pockets, and his hand splayed over the cane's crook with a futile sort of clinging. He wore a black pouch slung over his shoulder. Apparently he had something to sell.

The air was rich with spring; sun was warm and yellowed on the asphalt. Mr. Parsons, standing there in front of his hotel and noting the clack-clack approach of the sightless man, felt a sudden and foolish sort of pity for all blind creatures.

And, thought Mr. Parsons, he was very glad to be alive. A few years ago he had been little more than a skilled laborer; now he was a successful, respected, admired . . . . Insurance . . . . And he had done it alone, unaided, struggling beneath handicaps . . . . And he was still young. The blue air of spring, fresh from its memories of windy pools and lush shrubbery, could thrill him with eagerness.

He took a step forward just as the tap-tapping blind man passed him by. Quickly the shabby fellow turned.

"Listen, guv'nor. Just a minute of your time."

Mr. Parsons said, "It's late. I have an appointment. Do you want me to give you something?"

"I ain't no beggar, guv'nor. You bet I ain't. I got a handy little article here"—he fumbled until he could press a small object into Mr. Parsons' hand—"that I sell. One buck. Best cigarette lighter made."

Mr. Parsons stood there, somewhat annoyed and embarrassed. He was a handsome figure, with his immaculate gray

suit and gray hat and malacca stick.[1] Of course the man with
the cigarette lighters could not see him . . . . "But I don't
smoke," he said.

"Listen. I bet you know plenty people who smoke. Nice little
present," wheedled the man. "And, mister, you wouldn't mind
helping a poor guy out?" He clung to Mr. Parsons' sleeve.

Mr. Parsons sighed and felt in his vest pocket. He brought
out two half dollars and pressed them into the man's hand. "Certainly. I'll help you out. As you say, I can give it to someone.
Maybe the elevator boy would—" He hesitated, not wishing to
be boorish and inquisitive, even with a blind peddler. "Have you
lost your sight entirely?"

The shabby man pocketed the two half dollars. "Fourteen
years, guv'nor." Then he added with an insane sort of pride:
"Westbury, sir. I was one of 'em."

"Westbury," repeated Mr. Parsons. "Ah, yes. The chemical
explosion . . . . The papers haven't mentioned it for years. But
at the time it was supposed to be one of the greatest disasters
in—"

"They've all forgot about it." The fellow shifted his feet wearily. "I tell you, guv'nor, a man who was in it don't forget about
it. Last thing I ever saw was C shop going up in one grand
smudge, and that awful gas pouring in at all the busted windows."

Mr. Parsons coughed. But the blind peddler was caught up
with the train of his one dramatic reminiscence. And, also, he
was thinking that there might be more half dollars in Mr. Parsons' pocket.

"Just think about it, guv'nor. There was a hundred and eight
people killed, about two hundred injured, and over fifty of them
lost their eyes. Blind as bats—" He groped forward until his dirty
hand rested against Mr. Parsons' coat. "I tell you, sir, there
wasn't nothing worse than that in the war. If I had lost my eyes
in the war, okay. I would have been well took care of. But I
was just a workman, working for what was in it. And I got it.
You're so right I got it, while the capitalists were making their
dough! They was insured, don't worry about that. They—"

"Insured," repeated his listener. "Yes. That's what I sell—"

"You want to know how I lost my eyes?" cried the man.
"Well, here it is!" His words fell with the bitter and studied drama
of a story often told, and told for money. "I was there in C shop,

---

1. malacca stick: a cane made from Malayan palm wood.

last of all the folks rushing out. Out in the air there was a chance, even with buildings exploding right and left. A lot of guys made it safe out the door and got away. And just when I was about there, crawling along between those big vats, a guy behind me grabs my leg. He says, 'Let me past, you——!' Maybe he was nuts. I dunno. I try to forgive him in my heart, guv'nor. But he was bigger than me. He hauls me back and climbs right over me! Tramples me into the dirt. And he gets out, and I lie there with all that poison gas pouring down on all sides of me, and flame and stuff . . . ." He swallowed—a studied sob—and stood dumbly expectant. He could imagine the next words: Tough luck, my man. Awfully tough. Now, I want to— "That's the story, guv'nor."

The spring wind shrilled past them, damp and quivering.

"Not quite," said Parsons.

The blind peddler shivered crazily. "Not quite? What you mean, you—?"

"The story is true," Mr. Parsons said, "except that it was the other way around."

"Other way around?" He croaked unamiably. "Say, guv'-nor—"

"I was in C shop," said Mr. Parsons. "It was the other way around. You were the fellow who hauled back on me and climbed over me. You were bigger than I was, Markwardt."

The blind man stood for a long time, swallowing hoarsely. He gulped: "Parsons. By heaven! By heaven! I thought you—" And then he screamed fiendishly: "Yes. Maybe so. Maybe so. But I'm blind! I'm blind, and you've been standing here letting me spout to you, and laughing at me every minute! I'm blind!"

People in the street turned to stare at him.

"You got away, but I'm blind! Do you hear! I'm—"

"Well," said Mr. Parsons, "don't make such a row about it, Markwardt . . . . So am I."

QUESTIONS FOR DISCUSSION AND WRITING

1. How in the first four paragraphs of the story does MacKinlay Kantor contrast the beggar and Mr. Parsons? As you reread these paragraphs, knowing now that Parsons, too, was blind, do you find any details that a blind man might not have been aware of? Is the author being unfair to the reader by leading him astray in any way?

2. There are two surprises, one near the end, one right at the end. What are they? How does the first one set the reader up perfectly for the second one—like a one, two punch?

SUGGESTION FOR FURTHER WRITING OR DISCUSSION

Tell a story of an accident or disaster that you know about. Perhaps you can make it part of a story.

YOUR HALO IS SHOWING

by M. de Koning Hoag

*Andrew cannot see, but lack of eyesight is not the
only kind of blindness. In this story, who else is blind?*

The laugh was spontaneous: a guffaw from two boys, a titter
from a ring of girls as the trash can, which the custodian had
set just outside the common room door, vomited papers across
the walk. Andrew (they didn't know his full name yet) had
stumbled into the can and tipped it. Sara and Linda and Tim
and their friends stood watching as the new boy in school hesitated, bewildered, on the walk. How much of an idiot could a
guy be, how could he have been so stupid as to walk right into
a trash can and thereby make himself vulnerable to them?

Andrew stepped back, turned and moved uncertainly in the
direction from which he had come as the custodian called:
"Okay, which kid?" knowing he wouldn't get an answer.

"None of us, honest, Mr. Houseman. It was a new kid, a
real shaker!" Smiling, they drifted apart. The bell rang and they
headed for classes, leaving Mr. Houseman with his spilled trash.

During third period Sara, delivering attendance slips to the
office, saw the boy again. He was sitting straight against the
wall outside the counselor's room. When Mr. Trevor came out
and put a hand on Andrew's arm, Andrew rose hastily and
jumbled words of apology.

"I knocked something down out there. It wasn't there last
weekend when I walked around the buildings."

With that interesting bit of information Sara raced back
to class.

"He walked around campus last weekend. Get that! New
kid in school and he sneaks over by himself and walks around
the buildings!"

"It's something about the way he walks," Tim said, catching
his breath. "Like he pretends he knows but isn't too sure where

he's going. And that pile of notebooks and those shades he wears, like a turn-on." Sara and Linda nudged each other.

By the end of class they were ready to forget him, but Sara was not so lucky. European lit class had just started when he walked in. Mrs. Keely went to the door.

"So you're Andrew," she said. (*Well*, thought Sara, *a special greeting*.) "We have a new student, class: Andrew Estes." She walked him to a front-row seat right next to Sara. There went that class—a clumsy teacher's pet next to her! Sara had hoped for someone new and exciting, but never an Andrew.

Mrs. Kelly stood before the class again. "Andrew comes from a high school which has a special program for unsighted students. He prefers to be here. It won't be easy for him but he's very capable and you don't have to give him any special consideration—just common courtesy. Unless he asks, of course."

The class was tensely quiet. Sara sat at her desk, too embarrassed to look at Andrew. The word "unsighted" stood large in her vision. It meant *blind*. That explained the trash can and Mr. Trevor's concern and walking around the buildings. Remembering her eager, unkind words, she felt a momentary remorse and then a flash of anger. How was she to know? It really wasn't her fault: no one had warned her.

The class kept its collective eyes away from Andrew, their faces turned to their texts, unforgiving of his putting them in such a position.

In the cafeteria Sara told Linda, "He's in my European lit class. He's blind. How can he read books when he can't see?"

"Beats me," said Linda, who lost interest as soon as she realized Andrew wasn't going to be an asset to her dating list. "How does he get a lunch tray from the counter to the table?" They all looked around curiously.

"Someone picked him up for lunch," Tim volunteered

Walking around the quad after lunch, Sara began seriously thinking about Andrew. She told herself she really was interested, not just curious. She could hardly wait for European lit class the next day. Even if someone read the books to him, it would take monstrous time, and what about tests?

That second morning Andrew dropped his ball-point pen and it rolled under Sara's desk. He leaned over, groping on the floor. The room was hushed, expectant. Andrew's face flushed, and his words came out tonelessly.

"You don't have to wait for me." He was fingering in his pocket for another pen. Sara picked up his pen and held it out to him, feeling stupid when she realized he couldn't see the gesture.

"It's right here," she said, and when his hand opened, she put the pen in it and smiled at his thanks, another wasted gesture. From the corner of her eye she could see the heavy plastic-bound book on his desk, the pages dotted in pinpricks, his long fingers touching them with gentleness.

"Andrew uses braille texts," Mrs. Kelly explained. "He also has tapes of some of the longer works. I guarantee he'll give you some competition. He's a great reader." It sounded funny but not to be laughed at.

After class Sara followed him into the hall.

"I'm Sara," she said. "I can help you find your next class." He was already striding confidently down the corridor, next to the wall, his lips moving as if counting doorways.

"I can find it, Sara. But thanks. Here it is, algebra." She watched his enter the classroom, walk unerringly to a front seat. She felt somehow rebuffed. No special consideration, Mrs. Keely had said, just common courtesy. Even her common courtesy seemed unwelcome. Turning away she closed her eyes to create darkness and started down the hall. She bumped into two people who were openly offended at her clumsiness.

"I guess he's pretty shy, not having any friends. How can you have friends when you can't go to games and dances and do sports?" she asked later, on the way home from school. Tim spoke up to say that Andrew did go in for phys ed, not the games but the exercises.

"He's pretty well set up for a handicapped kid," Tim said.

"I tried playing blind in the hall," Sara reported. "It was ghastly; I bumped into people. I don't see how he can do it so well."

"He's been conditioned." This brought a small laugh from Linda.

"At least," Linda said, "if I were like that I'd have wanted it to happen after I'd been around awhile. So I'd know what things look like. If not, how could you ever relate?"

"Got to learn to, I guess," said Sara, suddenly feeling very much on top of it. She had been testing a beautiful idea and it was testing out well. She too had wondered how Andrew could manage. But he must have wanted to if he'd chosen their school. Without help he could never become a real member of the human race. And if someone like Sara didn't trouble to help him, who *was* there?

"I'm going to see he makes it here," she announced bravely.

"Who's got the time? It could be kind of a drag, you know."

"I don't care. From now on I am really, truly his friend."

She turned off at her house, full of high purpose and good thoughts. People would think of Sara with admiration as the girl who "did so much for that blind boy."

To befriend Andrew seemed to Sara very simple. It wasn't.

Andrew was willing to talk European lit, to show Sara his braille texts and how he read them (with fingers moving softly across the page, line by line, tracking the small dots that were words to him). When Sara touched them they meant nothing.

Listening to the tapes was better. They spent a long afternoon in the library hearing a Tolstoi tape, which was more fun than reading because they could talk about it at the same time. Being close to him in the recording room, sharing this intimacy, made Sara feel purposeful. Each gesture, each word that made her feel part of his life fascinated Sara. She reported her progress to anyone who would listen.

Yet in spite of her hopes, her efforts and her sympathy, Sara did not go far in her relationship with Andrew. By his own reluctance, he limited their relationship. She never saw him outside of school hours.

She tried to get him to go to the school play, but he declined politely. She went with Tim and, as they were leaving, she saw Andrew with someone else, an adult. Sara was angered by the rejection.

"He's so hung up," she complained to Tim later. "He could have fun if he'd let me help him."

"Ever hear of pride, Sara?"

"Tim, he can't afford pride if it cuts him off from people."

"Sara, quit trying so hard. You're great to be with him so much and keep so interested, but it looks as if what you want to be is 'do-good-Sara,' not really a friend."

"You must be crazy!"

She invited Andrew to dinner at her house, but he refused.

"Andy, my family is fine, really. They understand about that kind of thing."

"What kind of thing, Sara?"

Oh, honestly!

"I mean that you can't do everything." Andrew turned away.

He must be psycho, she thought. After all those years of missing things, he ought to be eager to experience them. But their relationship was like a closed-off room with high walls. Outside of school hours he walked alone.

"How about the tryouts for the choral concert?" she asked one day. "Or isn't music your thing either?"

"Music is very much my thing. But you don't have to push it."

Hurt, Sara went to the tryouts alone. Andrew was with a boy from one of his classes. She complained again to Tim.

"That guy is getting to you, Sara. Why don't you stop the charity case treatment?"

"Tim! You are absolutely stupid! Andy and I are friends. One helps one's friends."

"Your halo is showing, girl."

That really hurt. She didn't need Tim all that much, she decided.

Walking with Andrew to his algebra class on Monday, she said, "How come I'm not good enough to go to an old music tryout with, Andy? I am trying to be your friend. What more do you expect?"

"I don't expect anything, Sara. So don't try so hard. It's as though you want to get inside my head. You can't make it, you know. I don't need you there."

"But I want to!"

"You're telling yourself you want to, Sara. But I'm outside your life. Let's leave it that way, huh?"

"I don't want you outside, Andy."

"Maybe *I* do though. It's different for me, Sara. I have to go at things from another angle. I don't want to be your blind-friend-Andy that you're helping."

"Then what do you want to be?"

"Myself, just myself."

How ungrateful could he be anyway? She would have to try harder. Something had to get to him because by now, of course, Sara was psychologically incapable of dropping her role.

There came a soft fall day, a day of autumn leaves in the air that held its last warmth before winter. Foliage was a profusion of color, and she ached to share it.

"Can I have the car a little while, Dad?"

"Of course, sweetie. Need some extra money for shopping?"

"No, just the keys. And a little luck."

She pulled into the driveway at Andrew's house.

To his mother at the door she said, "I'm Sara. I've got the car for a while and I want to take Andy somewhere." His mother looked doubtful.

"That's good of you, Sara. I hope he'll go."

"How can I get him to go?"

"He doesn't like to have things done for him, you know."

"Don't I know?" She laughed sharply.

She followed Andrew's mother down a long hall and could hear music, a stereo playing the familiar *Hey, Jude*. Then she heard something else, a new sound blending with the music, something she hadn't heard before.

"Sara is here," Andrew's mother said at the door.

Sara stepped into the room distressed to feel her heart hammering. Andrew stood up from the bed, looking large and ungainly in the almost-naked room. Besides the bare walls and simple bed there was only a circle of amp boxes and the stereo. *Jude* wound to a stop. She saw that Andy cupped a harmonica in one hand.

"Andy, that was just great!" She touched his arm gently.

"Sara, what are you doing here?" He looked annoyed.

"I was going for a ride. I've got the car and I thought you'd like to go."

"Thanks, but no thanks."

"Why not, Andy?"

"I'm doing fine here. You don't have to take pocr old Andy for a ride."

"I know, Andy. I heard you doing fine. I didn't know you played. You really are good."

"Good because it's played good or good because Andy's playing? You shouldn't have come."

Anger hit at Sara. What he said was close to truth, but he shouldn't have said it. She had made a fool of herself, and Andy, too, had made a fool of her. He needed her and he just didn't know it. But however proud and untouchable he might be, he didn't have the right to cut her down. Defeat was hard to take. Everyone would know, and what was worse, would remind Sara that they had known all along.

"Okay, Andy. I give up. I do like you and I like your playing and I really wanted you to come for a drive with me."

"What's the matter with your other friends?"

"I didn't want them. I know a place where there are fall leaves and a little pond. I thought of you. I guess what I mean,

Andy, is that I didn't want to go alone. But what I want doesn't count. Just what you want. Okay, Andy, sit down in your room and play in it and think in it, and don't let any of yourself out. Don't share yourself. Because I've just decided that I don't need you after all."

She said it cruelly, hopelessly, and turning, walked out of his room and down the long hall.

Sitting in the car, she thought that probably nobody had ever talked to Andy that way. It was a weird thought. How really crippling to be treated all your life as if you were special, some-one to be carefully handled. Was it really living at all if no one ever yelled at you, blamed or criticized or ever hurt you? You could live without a lot of hurt, but without *all* of it? Sara felt sorry for Andrew but realized at the same time that feeling sorry wasn't the way to help a person live.

Just as she turned the ignition key, she saw Andy's front door open. He walked out and felt his way to the car door. He opened it and slid into the passenger seat.

"I didn't mean to hurt you, Sara. I know I'm supposed to need you; I'm just trying not to."

"You don't need me, Andy," she said, backing out and driving down the street, onto the highway. The air blew into the wide-open windows, and she said, "Smell it, Andy. It's almost winter."

"I smell it, Sara."

"Shall we walk awhile? I'd like to show you this place I mentioned. It'll be frozen over soon."

"Let's walk, then," said Andrew.

They walked, holding hands, into the woods. She knew that touching was for guidance but she tried not to guide. They bent under branches, stepped over tree trunks, felt the brush of golden leaves against their faces. When he seemed unsure, the pressure of his hand bit into hers, but she did not respond. Once when he stumbled, she managed not to pull at him.

"I'm going to sit down," she said when they came near the edge of a small pond. He sat with her, his face relaxed behind the dark glasses.

"Isn't it beautiful and quiet, Andy?"

"Yes. Beautiful and quiet. Is the water just ahead here? Is it good for swimming?"

"About twenty feet in front of you. It's muddy at the bottom."

"Let's wade in it." He was pulling off his shoes and socks eagerly, rolling up his jeans. Sara yanked at her laces. It would be cold; it would be muddy. She didn't much like the feel of mud.

He walked ahead of her but stopped as water washed over his white feet.

"It's squishy." He was laughing. She caught up with him and then he moved again into the water. Mud churned around his knees.

"It's freezing," he said and laughter remained in his voice. She knew that the pond, shallow as it was, could still be treacherous. But why tell him, warn him? Why spoil his joy? One false step and he might fall and lose his balance in the mud. But maybe he wouldn't make that step.

He stood with water lapping at his legs. As he stepped forward, the water went over his knees.

"Wow!" he said. She almost reached for him.

"I'm all right," Andy said.

"I know you are." And she did know. By not touching him, not urging him, not frightening him, she had let him keep his pride and let him into a corner of her world without pushing him there.

They stood so a long time. Then he turned and pulled wet muddy feet sucking from the pond.

They put on socks and shoes, which stuck over their heels. Then he put out his hand, found hers, held it crushingly. With her other hand she reached up and gently lifted his glasses from his face, exposing the sightless eyes in which no light shone.

"Hey, Andy," she said, her face close to his. "Did you know your eyes are blue?"

His free hand touched her face, her eyes, her hair.

"Yes, Sara, I know. Tell me something, Sara, are you beautiful?"

She felt a slow blush rise and laughed a little as a mental vision of herself formed in her mind: the long, dark hair, the straight mouth above the wide, unfeminine jaw, the too-pointed nose and the uneven brows (one higher than the other) shading the brown, almost black eyes. Who in the world had ever thought Sara beautiful? Nice, interesting, intelligent, friendly, yes. Beautiful? But she was sure she would be forgiven a small lie for the boy who sat next to her, hoping she was beautiful.

"Not really, Andy. I mean really really. But you make me feel beautiful and that's what counts."

"Sara," he was deadly earnest, "I do need you, you know. I need people all the time, only I don't want to. If they give

me something, I always hope it's because of me, not because
I'm blind. Today you made me feel kind of like maybe you need
me too. That was something very different."

She *had* needed him—for ego builder. But she wasn't going
to admit that now.

"Sara," he said, his head bending close to hers. "Tell me,
Sara, what color are your eyes?" She tried to imagine in her
mind what it would be like not even to know what colors were,
never to have lived in a world that was golden or green, only
gray or black, or maybe opague.

She stood up, brushing at her slacks.

"I have to take the car back, Andy. Sorry, but maybe we
can come again sometime." He stood up beside her and a smile
creased his face, and she knew that whatever she asked of him
from now on, he would probably say yes. So now she would have
to be careful.

"Sara, you didn't answer. What color are your eyes?"

"My eyes, Andy? Why, they're blue. Not quite as blue as
yours, but blue."

After all, she had known him for quite some time. And it
was only her second lie.

QUESTIONS FOR DISCUSSION AND WRITING

1. What is the attitude toward "new kids" in general at Sara's
   school? What actions of the students demonstrate this attitude? What is their attitude toward the special new kid, Andrew?
2. The students discuss Andrew, and Sara becomes very much
   interested in helping him. Why does she want to help him?
   How does he react to her attempts? Why? Do you think Tim
   is fair to her when he says, "Your halo is showing, girl"?
   Had she made some mistakes in her efforts to be helpful?
3. Andrew is unsighted. Is he blind in any other way? Reread
   Sara's remarks to Andy after he says to her (page 157), "What's
   the matter with your other friends?" How did the remarks
   affect Andy? Why? What does he do then?
4. When Andy wades into the pond, what does Sara make herself do, or not do? How does this affect Andy?
5. Toward the end of the story Andy says to Sara, "Today you
   made me feel like maybe you kind of need me too. That was

something very different." What does he mean by this? Why was it so important to him?

6. At the end Sara says her eyes are not as blue as Andy's and that this was only her second lie to him. What was her first lie?

7. Mr. Hoag does not explain everything to us, the readers, but sometimes lets us figure it out for ourselves. Toward the end he writes: "She knew that whatever she asked of him from now on, he would probably say yes. So now she would have to be careful." Why would he say yes? Why would she have to be careful?

SUGGESTIONS FOR FURTHER WRITING OR DISCUSSION

1. Write a story or tell an experience about helping, either giving or receiving help. See if you can show us something about the motives of the helper and the effects on the helper and the helped.

2. A blind lady who objected strenuously to being called blind once said, "I happen not to be able to see through my eyes, but everyone has some kind of blindness." Describe a case of blindness other than lack of eyesight.

Cruel Surprises

Fate intervenes in an old family feud.
A sniper finds out who is his victim.
A confident young man loses control of his car—and his life.

THE INTERLOPERS[1]

by Saki (H. H. Munro)

Two families of eastern Europe carry on an old feud over the ownership of a poor piece of border-forest. After their leaders, Ulrich and Georg, meet, what great change comes over them and what are its results?

In a forest of mixed growth somewhere on the eastern spurs of the Carpathians,[2] a man stood one winter night watching and listening, as though he waited for some beast of the woods to come within range of his vision, and later, of his rifle. But the game for whose presence he kept so keen an outlook was none that figured in the sportsman's calendar as lawful and proper for the chase; Ulrich von Gradwitz patrolled the dark forest in quest of a human enemy.

The forest lands of Gradwitz were of wide extent and well stocked with game; the narrow strip of precipitous woodland that lay on its outskirt was not remarkable for the game it harbored or the shooting it afforded, but it was the most jealously guarded of all its owner's territorial possessions. A famous lawsuit, in the days of his grandfather, had wrested it from the illegal possession of a neighboring family of petty landowners; the dispossessed party had never acquiesced in the judgment of the courts and a long series of poaching forays[3] and similar scandals had embittered the relationships between the families for three generations. The neighbor feud had grown into a personal one since Ulrich had come to be head of his family; if there was a man in the world whom he detested and wished ill to it was Georg Znaeym, the inheritor of the quarrel and the tireless game-snatcher and raider of the disputed border-forest. The feud might, perhaps, have died down or been compromised if the personal ill will of the two men had not stood in the way; as boys

1. interlopers: intruders, meddlers.
2. Carpathians: mountains in eastern Europe running through Czechoslavakia, Hungary, and the Soviet Union.
3. poaching forays: raids to steal game.

From *The Short Stories of Saki* by H. H. Munro. Reprinted by permission of The Viking Press, Inc.

they had thirsted for one another's blood, as men each prayed that misfortune might fall on the other, and this wind-scourged winter night Ulrich had banded together his foresters to watch the dark forest, not in quest of four-footed quarry, but to keep a lookout for the prowling thieves whom he suspected of being afoot from across the land boundary. The roebuck,[4] which usually kept in the sheltered hollows during a storm wind, were running like driven things tonight, and there was movement and unrest among the creatures that were wont to sleep through the dark hours. Assuredly there was a disturbing element in the forest, and Ulrich could guess the quarter from whence it came.

He strayed away by himself from the watchers whom he had placed in ambush on the crest of the hills, and wandered far down the steep slopes amid the wild tangle of undergrowth, peering through the tree trunks and listening through the whistling and skirling of the wind and the restless beating of the branches for sight or sound of the marauders. If only on this wild night, in this dark, lone spot, he might come across Georg Znaeym, man to man, with none to witness—that was the wish that was uppermost in his thoughts. And as he stepped around the trunk of a huge beech he came face to face with the man he sought.

The two enemies stood glaring at one another for a long silent moment. Each had a rifle in his hand, each had hate in his heart and murder uppermost in his mind. The chance had come to give full play to the passions of a lifetime. But a man who has been brought up under the code of a restraining civilization cannot easily nerve himself to shoot down his neighbor in cold blood and without word spoken, except for an offense against his hearth and honor. And before the moment of hesitation had given way to action a deed of Nature's own violence overwhelmed them both. A fierce shriek of the storm had been answered by a splitting crash over their heads, and ere they could leap aside a mass of falling beech tree had thundered down on them. Ulrich von Gradwitz found himself stretched on the ground, one arm numb beneath him and the other held almost as helplessly in a tight tangle of forked branches, while both legs were pinned beneath the fallen mass. His heavy shooting boots had saved his feet from being crushed to pieces, but if his fractures were not as serious as they might have been, at least it was evident that he could not move from his present

4. roebuck: small deer.

position till someone came to release him. The descending twigs had slashed the skin of his face, and he had to wink away some drops of blood from his eyelashes before he could take in a general view of the disaster. At his side, so near that under ordinary circumstances he could almost have touched him, lay Georg Znaeym, alive and struggling, but obviously as helplessly pinioned down as himself. All round them lay a thick-strewn wreckage of splintered branches and broken twigs.

Relief at being alive and exasperation at his captive plight brought a strange medley of pious thank offerings and sharp curses to Ulrich's lips. Georg, who was nearly blinded with the blood which trickled across his eyes, stopped his struggling for a moment to listen, and then gave a short, snarling laugh.

"So you're not killed, as you ought to be, but you're caught anyway," he cried, "caught fast. Ho, what a jest— Ulrich von Gradwitz snared in his stolen forest. There's a real justice for you!"

And he laughed again, mockingly and savagely.

"I'm caught in my own forest land," retorted Ulrich. "When my men come to release us you will wish, perhaps, that you were in a better plight than caught poaching on a neighbor's land, shame on you."

Georg was silent for a moment; then he answered quietly: "Are you sure that your men will find much to release? I have men, too, in the forest tonight, close behind me, and *they* will be here first and do the releasing. When they drag me out from under these branches it won't need much clumsiness on their part to roll this mass of trunk right over on the top of you. Your men will find you dead under a fallen beech tree. For form's sake I shall send my condolences[5] to your family."

"It is a useful hint," said Ulrich fiercely. "My men have orders to follow in ten minutes' time, seven of which must have gone by already, and when they get me out — I will remember the hint. Only as you will have met your death poaching on my lands I don't think I can decently send any message of condolence to your family."

"Good," snarled Georg, "good. We fight this quarrel out to the death, you and I and our foresters, with no cursed interlopers to come between us. Death and damnation to you, Ulrich von Gradwitz."

---

5. condolences: messages of sympathy.

"The same to you, Georg Znaeym, forest-thief, game-snatcher."

Both men spoke with the bitterness of possible defeat before them, for each knew that it might be long before his men would seek him out or find him; it was a bare matter of chance which party would arrive first on the scene.

Both had now given up the useless struggle to free themselves from the mass of wood that held them down; Ulrich limited his endeavors to an effort to bring his one partially free arm near enough to his outer coat pocket to draw out his wine flask. Even when he had accomplished that operation it was long before he could manage the unscrewing of the stopper or get any of the liquid down his throat. But what a Heaven-sent draught it seemed! It was an open winter, and little snow had fallen as yet, hence the captives suffered less from the cold than might have been the case at that season of the year; nevertheless, the wine was warming and reviving to the wounded man, and he looked across with something like a throb of pity to where his enemy lay, just keeping the groans of pain and weariness from crossing his lips.

"Could you reach this flask if I threw it over to you?" asked Ulrich suddenly. "There is good wine in it, and one may as well be as comfortable as one can. Let us drink, even if tonight one of us dies."

"No, I can scarcely see anything; there is so much blood caked round my eyes," said Georg, "and in any case I don't drink wine with an enemy."

Ulrich was silent for a few minutes, and lay listening to the weary screeching of the wind. An idea was slowly forming and growing in his brain, an idea that gained strength every time that he looked across at the man who was fighting so grimly against pain and exhaustion. In the pain and languor[6] that Ulrich himself was feeling the old fierce hatred seemed to be dying down.

"Neighbor," he said presently, "do as you please if your men come first. It was a fair compact. But as for me, I've changed my mind. If my men are the first to come you shall be the first to be helped, as though you were my guest. We have quarreled like devils all our lives over this stupid strip of forest, where the trees can't even stand upright in a breath of wind. Lying

6. languor: feeling of weakness and tiredness.

here tonight, thinking, I've come to think we've been rather fools; there are better things in life than getting the better of a boundary dispute. Neighbor, if you will help me to bury the old quarrel I—I will ask you to be my friend."

Georg Znaeym was silent for so long that Ulrich thought, perhaps, he had fainted with the pain of his injuries. Then he spoke slowly and in jerks.

"How the whole region would stare and gabble if we rode into the market square together. No one living can remember seeing a Znaeym and a von Gradwitz talking to one another in friendship. And what peace there would be among the forester folk if we ended our feud tonight. And if we choose to make peace among our people there is none other to interfere, no interlopers from outside . . . . You would come and keep the Sylvester night[7] beneath my roof, and I would come and feast on some high day at your castle . . . . I would never fire a shot on your land, save when you invited me as a guest; and you should come and shoot with me down in the marshes where the wildfowl are. In all the countryside there are none that could hinder if we willed to make peace. I never thought to have wanted to do other than hate you all my life, but I think I have changed my mind about things too, this last half-hour. And you offered me your wine flask . . . . Ulrich von Gradwitz, I will be your friend."

For a space both men were silent, turning over in their minds the wonderful changes that this dramatic reconciliation would bring out. In the cold, gloomy forest, with the wind tearing in fitful gusts through the naked branches and whistling round the tree trunks, they lay and waited for the help that would now bring release and succor to both parties. And each prayed a private prayer that his men might be the first to arrive, so that he might be the first to show honorable attention to the enemy that had become a friend.

Presently, as the wind dropped for a moment, Ulrich broke silence.

"Let's shout for help," he said. "In this lull our voices may carry a little way."

"They won't carry far through the trees and undergrowth," said Georg, "but we can try. Together, then."

The two raised their voices in a prolonged hunting call.

"Together again," said Ulrich a few minutes later, after listening in vain for an answering halloo.

---

7. Sylvester night: the night of December 31, in honor of St. Sylvester.

"I heard something that time, I think," said Ulrich.

"I heard nothing but the pestilential wind," said Georg hoarsely.

There was silence again for some minutes, and then Ulrich gave a joyful cry.

"I can see figures coming through the wood. They are following in the way I came down the hillside."

Both men raised their voices in as loud a shout as they could muster.

"They hear us! They've stopped. Now they see us. They're running down the hill toward us," cried Ulrich.

"How many of them are there?" asked Georg.

"I can't see distinctly," said Ulrich. "Nine or ten."

"Then they are yours," said Georg. "I had only seven out with me."

"They are making all the speed they can, brave lads," said Ulrich gladly.

"Are they your men?" asked Georg. "Are they your men?" he repeated impatiently as Ulrich did not answer.

"No," said Ulrich with a laugh, the idiotic chattering laugh of a man unstrung with hideous fear.

"Who are they?" asked Georg quickly, straining his eyes to see what the other would gladly not have seen.

"*Wolves.*"

QUESTIONS FOR DISCUSSION AND WRITING

1. In the first paragraph what do we learn is unusual about the hunting quest? Then, as the narrator gives us the historical background of the family feud, he creates an atmosphere of terror and wildness. How does he do this? Find the sentence which then starts the actual events of the story.

2. After the beech tree pins the two men down, what is their attitude towards each other? Read bits of conversation to show this. Then find words that show a beginning of change in their attitude. What causes this change? What is the plan they gradually work up togehter? What will be its effects?

3. Do you learn what becomes of the plan? How? Is there any doubt? Nature has intervened—interloped—twice in the story? How? What were the effects of each intervention?

4. What does the story seem to say about people and their territories, or perhaps about nations and their territories? Do you think "The Interlopers" is a serious story or merely a tricky one? Defend your point of view.

SUGGESTIONS FOR FURTHER WRITING OR DISCUSSION

1. Describe a situation—real or made-up—in which an event of nature drastically affected the lives of some people, or the life of a single person.
2. Write about a long-term enmity, perhaps between two people you really know, or perhaps as the main idea of a story. Try to make your readers understand and share the feelings of the people involved.

THE SNIPER

by Liam O'Flaherty

Here is another story of a struggle between two men, each representing a group. In this case, the events are part of the civil war that broke out in Ireland in the 1920's over the question of whether the country should become an independent republic or a "Free State" within the British Commonwealth. Feelings were so bitter and strong that even members of the same family were set against each other. What does this story say to you about violence and killing?

The long June twilight faded into night. Dublin lay enveloped in darkness, but for the dim light of the moon, that shone through fleecy clouds, casting a pale light as of approaching dawn over the streets and the dark waters of the Liffey. Around the beleaguered Four Courts the heavy guns roared. Here and there through the city machine guns and rifles broke the silence of the night, spasmodically, like dogs barking on lone farms. Republicans and Free Staters were waging civil war.

On a rooftop near O'Connell Bridge, a Republican sniper lay watching. Beside him lay his rifle and over his shoulders were slung a pair of field-glasses. His face was the face of a student—thin and ascetic, but his eyes had the cold gleam of the fanatic. They were deep and thoughtful, the eyes of a man who is used to looking at death.

He was eating a sandwich hungrily. He had eaten nothing since morning. He had been too excited to eat. He finished the sandwich, and taking a flask of whiskey from his pocket, he took a short draught. Then he returned the flask to his pocket. He paused for a moment, considering whether he should risk a smoke. It was dangerous. The flash might be seen in the darkness and there were enemies watching. He decided to take the risk. Placing a cigarette between his lips, he struck a match, inhaled the smoke hurriedly and put out the light. Almost immediately, a bullet flattened itself against the parapet of the roof.

From *Spring Sowing* by Liam Flaherty. Reprinted by permission of Harcourt Brace Jovanovich, Inc. Also from *The Short Stories of Liam Flaherty.* Reprinted by permission of Jonathan Cape Ltd.

The sniper took another whiff and put out the cigarette. Then he swore softly and crawled away to the left.

Cautiously he raised himself and peered over the parapet. There was a flash and a bullet whizzed over his head. He dropped immediately. He had seen the flash. It came from the opposite side of the street.

He rolled over the roof to a chimney stack in the rear, and slowly drew himself up behind it, until his eyes were level with the top of the parapet. There was nothing to be seen—just the dim outline of the opposite housetop against the blue sky. His enemy was under cover.

Just then an armoured car came across the bridge and advanced slowly up the street. It stopped on the opposite side of the street fifty yards ahead. The sniper could hear the dull panting of the motor. His heart beat faster. It was an enemy car. He wanted to fire, but he knew it was useless. His bullets would never pierce the steel that covered the grey monster.

Then round the corner of a side street came an old woman, her head covered by a tattered shawl. She began to talk to the man in the turret of the car. She was pointing to the roof where the sniper lay. An informer.

The turret opened. A man's head and shoulders appeared, looking towards the sniper. The sniper raised his rifle and fired. The head fell heavily on the turret wall. The woman darted toward the side street. The sniper fired again. The woman whirled round and fell with a shriek into the gutter.

Suddenly from the opposite roof a shot rang out and the sniper dropped his rifle with a curse. The rifle clattered to the roof. The sniper thought the noise would wake the dead. He stooped to pick the rifle up. He couldn't lift it. His forearm was dead. "I'm hit," he muttered.

Dropping flat on to the roof, he crawled back to the parapet. With his left hand he felt the injured right forearm. The blood was oozing through the sleeve of his coat. There was no pain— just a deadened sensation, as if the arm had been cut off.

Quickly he drew his knife from his pocket, opened it on the breastwork of the parapet and ripped open the sleeve. There was a small hole where the bullet had entered. On the other side there was no hole. The bullet had lodged in the bone. It must have fractured it. He bent the arm below the wound. The arm bent back easily. He ground his teeth to overcome the pain.

Then, taking out his field dressing, he ripped open the packet with his knife. He broke the neck of the iodine bottle and let the bitter fluid drip into the wound. A paroxysm of pain swept through him. He placed the cotton wadding over the wound and wrapped the dressing over it. He tied the end with his teeth.

Then he lay still against the parapet, and closing his eyes, he made an effort of will to overcome the pain.

In the street beneath all was still. The armoured car had retired speedily over the bridge, with the machine gunner's head hanging lifeless over the turret. The woman's corpse lay still in the gutter.

The sniper lay for a long time nursing his wounded arm and planning escape. Morning must not find him wounded on the roof. The enemy on the opposite roof covered his escape. He must kill that·enemy and he could not use his rifle. He had only a revolver to do it. Then he thought of a plan.

Taking off his cap, he placed it over the muzzle of his rifle. Then he pushed the rifle slowly upwards over the parapet, until the cap was visible from the opposite side of the street. Almost immediately there was a report, and a bullet pierced the center of the cap. The sniper slanted the rifle forward. The cap slipped down into the street. Then, catching the rifle in the middle, the sniper dropped his left hand over the roof and let it hang, lifelessly. After a few moments he let the rifle drop to the street. Then he sank·to the roof, dragging his hand with him.

Crawling quickly to the left, he peered up at the corner of the roof. His ruse had succeeded. The other sniper, seeing the cap and rifle fall, thought that he had killed his man. He was now standing before a row of chimney pots, looking across, with his head clearly silhouetted against the western sky.

The Republican sniper smiled and lifted his revolver above the edge of the parapet. The distance was about fifty yards—a hard shot in the dim light, and his right arm was paining him like a thousand devils. He took a steady aim. His hand trembled with eagerness. Pressing his lips together, he took a deep breath through his nostrils and fired. He was almost deafened with the report and his arm shook with the recoil.

Then, when the smoke cleared, he peered across and uttered a cry of joy. His enemy had been hit. He was reeling over the parapet in his death agony. He struggled to keep his feet, but he was slowly falling forward, as if in a dream. The rifle fell from his grasp, hit the parapet, fell over, bounded off the pole of a barber's shop beneath and then clattered on to the pavement.

Then the dying man on the roof crumpled up and fell forward. The body turned over and over in space and hit the ground with a dull thud. Then it lay still.

The sniper looked at his enemy falling and he shuddered. The lust of battle died in him. He became bitten by remorse. The sweat stood out in beads on his forehead. Weakened by his wound and the long summer day of fasting and watching on the roof, he revolted from the sight of the shattered mass of his dead enemy. His teeth chattered. He began to gibber to himself, cursing the war, cursing himself, cursing everybody.

He looked at the smoking revolver in his hand and with an oath he hurled it to the roof at his feet. The revolver went off with the concussion, and the bullet whizzed past the sniper's head. He was frightened back to his senses by the shock. His nerves steadied. The cloud of fear scattered from his mind and he laughed.

Taking the whiskey flask from his pocket, he emptied it at a draught. He felt reckless under the influence of the spirits. He decided to leave the roof and look for his company commander to report. Everywhere around was quiet. There was not much danger in going through the streets. He picked up his revolver and put it in his pocket. Then he crawled down through the skylight to the house underneath.

When the sniper reached the laneway on the street level, he felt a sudden curiosity as to the identity of the enemy sniper whom he had killed. He decided that he was a good shot whoever he was. He wondered if he knew him. Perhaps he had been in his own company before the split in the army. He decided to risk going over to have a look at him. He peered around the corner into O'Connell Street. In the upper part of the street there was heavy firing, but around here all was quiet.

The sniper darted across the street. A machine gun tore up the ground around him with a hail of bullets, but he escaped. He threw himself face downwards beside the corpse. The machine gun stopped.

Then the sniper turned over the dead body and looked into his brother's face.

QUESTIONS FOR DISCUSSION AND WRITING

1. When we first see the Republican sniper, what is he doing? What are his feelings towards his part in the struggle? He is described as a student and a fanatic. How could he be both? How do you know he is used to this war?
2. After his first exchange of shots with the other sniper, how does he show by his actions that he is both cruel and courageous? Do you admire him? Explain.
3. By a ruse (what ruse?) he manages to kill his enemy. Then rather suddenly, how does his attitude change? What changes it?
4. Towards the end of the story what rash acts does the sniper perform? Why?
5. Reread the last sentence of the story. What do you think Liam O'Flaherty ends the story here so suddenly? You are suddenly left thinking about the story and the war. What do you think?

SUGGESTIONS FOR FURTHER WRITING OR DISCUSSION

1. Have you ever seen anything killed? Give an account or write a story of a killing, real or imagined.
2. A problem of our times is violence in the streets, violence in homes, violence on TV, violence in foreign lands. Write an account of some violence you have experienced, or write a story about, or a description of, violence.
3. Perhaps you have some strong feelings about violence and killing. Write them down without worrying about whether you have a "well-organized" paper or not. Do you think violence and killing are ever justified?

THE TEST

by Theodore L. Thomas

A young man is contentedly driving with his mother when suddenly he is hit with a series of shocking surprises. What message does this story convey?

Robert Proctor was a good driver for so young a man. The Turnpike curved gently ahead of him, lightly travelled on this cool morning in May. He felt relaxed and alert. Two hours of driving had not yet produced the twinges of fatigue that appeared first in the muscles in the base of the neck. The sun was bright, but not glaring, and the air smelled fresh and clean. He breathed it deeply, and blew it out noisily. It was a good day for driving.

He glanced quickly at the slim, grey-haired woman sitting in the front seat with him. Her mouth was curved in a quiet smile. She watched the trees and the fields slip by on her side of the pike. Robert Proctor immediately looked back at the road. He said, "Enjoying it, Mom?"

"Yes, Robert." Her voice was as cool as the morning. "It is very pleasant to sit here. I was thinking of the driving I did for you when you were little. I wonder if you enjoyed it as much as I enjoy this."

He smiled, embarrassed. "Sure I did."

She reached over and patted him gently on the arm, and then turned back to the scenery.

He listened to the smooth purr of the engine. Up ahead he saw a great truck, spouting a geyser of smoke as it sped along the Turnpike. Behind it, not passing it, was a long blue convertible, content to drive in the wake of the truck. Robert Proctor noted the arrangement and filed it in the back of his mind. He was slowly overtaking them, but he would not reach them for another minute or two.

He listened to the purr of the engine, and he was pleased with the sound. He had tuned that engine himself over the objections of the mechanic. The engine idled rough now, but it ran smoothly at high speed. You needed a special feel to do good work on engines, and Robert Proctor knew he had it. No one in the world had a feel like his for the tune of an engine.

It was a good morning for driving, and his mind was filled with good thoughts. He pulled nearly abreast of the blue convertible and began to pass it. His speed was a few miles per hour above the Turnpike limit, but his car was under perfect control. The blue convertible suddenly swung out from behind the truck. It swung out without warning and struck his car near the right front fender, knocking his car to the shoulder on the left side of the Turnpike lane.

Robert Proctor was a good driver, too wise to slam on the brakes. He fought the steering wheel to hold the car on a straight path. The left wheels sank into the soft left shoulder, and the car tugged to pull to the left and cross the island and enter the lanes carrying the cars heading in the opposite direction. He held it, then the wheel struck a rock buried in the soft dirt, and the left front tire blew out. The car slewed, and it was then that his mother began to scream.

The car turned sideways and skidded part of the way out into the other lanes. Robert Proctor fought against the steering wheel to straighten the car, but the drag of the blown tire was too much. The scream rang steadily in his ears, and even as he strained at the wheel one part of his mind wondered coolly how a scream could so long be sustained without a breath. An oncoming car struck his radiator from the side and spun him viciously, full into the left-hand lanes.

He was flung into his mother's lap, and she was thrown against the right door. It held. With his left hand he reached for the steering wheel and pulled himself erect against the force of the spin. He turned the wheel to the left, and tried to stop the spin and career out of the lanes of oncoming traffic. His mother was unable to right herself; she lay against the door, her cry rising and falling with the eccentric spin of the car.

The car lost some of its momentum. During one of the spins he twisted the wheel straight, and the car wobblingly stopped spinning and headed down the lane. Before Robert Proctor could turn it off the pike to safety a car loomed ahead of him, bearing down on him. There was a man at the wheel of that other car, sitting rigid, unable to move, eyes wide and staring and filled with fright. Alongside the man was a girl, her head against the back of the seat, soft curls framing a lovely face, her eyes closed in easy sleep. It was not the fear in the man that reached into

Robert Proctor; it was the trusting helplessness in the face of
the sleeping girl. The two cars sped closer to each other, and
Robert Proctor could not change the direction of his car. The
driver of the other car remained frozen at the wheel. At the last
moment Robert Proctor sat motionless staring into the face of.
the onrushing, sleeping girl, his mother's cry still sounding in
his ears. He heard no crash when the two cars collided head-on
at a high rate of speed. He felt something push into his stomach,
and the world began to go grey. Just before he lost consciousness
he heard the scream stop, and he knew then that he had been
hearing a single, short-lived scream that had only seemed to drag
on and on. There came a painless wrench, and then darkness.

Robert Proctor seemed to be at the bottom of a deep black
well. There was a spot of faint light in the far distance, and
he could hear the rumble of a distant voice. He tried to pull
himself toward the light and the sound, but the effort was too
great. He lay still and gathered himself and tried again. The
light grew brighter and the voice louder. He tried harder, again,
and he drew closer. Then he opened his eyes full and looked
at the man sitting in front of him.

"You all right, Son?" asked the man. He wore a blue uniform, and his round, beefy face was familiar.

Robert Proctor tentatively moved his head, and discovered
he was seated in a reclining chair, unharmed, and able to move
his arms and legs with no trouble. He looked around the room,
and he remembered.

The man in the uniform saw the growing intelligence in
his eyes and he said, "No harm done, Son. You just took the
last part of your driver's test."

Robert Proctor focused his eyes on the man. Though he
saw the man clearly, he seemed to see the faint face of the sleeping girl in front of him.

The uniformed man continued to speak. "We put you
through an accident under hypnosis—do it to everybody these
days before they can get their driver's licenses. Makes better
drivers of them, more careful drivers the rest of their lives. Remember it now? Coming in here and all?"

Robert Proctor nodded, thinking of the sleeping girl. She
never would have awakened; she would have passed right from
a sweet, temporary sleep into the dark heavy sleep of death, nothing in between. His mother would have been bad enough; after
all, she was pretty old. The sleeping girl was downright waste.

The uniformed man was still speaking. "So you're all set

now. You pay me the ten dollar fee, and sign this application, and we'll have your license in the mail in a day or two." He did not look up.

Robert Proctor placed a ten dollar bill on the table in front of him, glanced over the application and signed it. He looked up to find two white-uniformed men, standing one on each side of him, and he frowned in annoyance. He started to speak, but the uniformed man spoke first. "Sorry, Son. You failed. You're sick; you need treatment."

The two men lifted Robert Proctor to his feet, and he said, "Take your hands off me. What is this?"

The uniformed man said, "Nobody should want to drive a car after going through what you just went through. It should take months before you can even think of driving again, but you're ready right now. Killing people doesn't bother you. We don't let your kind run around loose in society any more. But don't you worry now, Son. They'll take good care of you, and they'll fix you up." He nodded to the two men, and they began to march Robert Proctor out.

At the door he spoke, and his voice was so urgent the two men paused. Robert Proctor said, "You can't really mean this. I'm still dreaming, aren't I? This is still part of the test, isn't it?"

The uniformed man said, *"How do any of us know?"* And they dragged Robert Proctor out the door, knees stiff, feet dragging, his rubber heels sliding along the two grooves worn into the floor.

QUESTIONS FOR DISCUSSION AND WRITING

1. At the beginning of the story, Robert Proctor is calm and contented. What are the elements of his content? What is his attitude toward driving?
2. Then comes the terrible accident, caused by the action of the blue convertible. What details show you that Robert handled the situation with skill? Could he have avoided the accident? Explain.
3. The accident took only a few seconds to happen and yet it is described as if in slow-motion. Why do you think Theodore Thomas described it this way?

4. Find the sentence that first tells you, and Robert, of the second surprise. Why do the police use hypnosis as a part of the procedure for testing a person's readiness to be granted a license? Would it be a good idea if the police really did this? Explain your view.
5. What is Robert's third surprise? How did he fail the test? Near the end, Robert asks, "I'm still dreaming, aren't I?" What does he mean? Who might be dreaming besides Robert? Who else is sick besides Robert, according to the story? What is the nature of the sickness?
6. "The Interlopers," "The Sniper," and "The Test" all have surprise endings. But now, having read the stories, you will never again be surprised by them. Think about each story. Is it the surprise gimmick ending that is its main appeal? If it isn't, what is it about each story that really appeals?

SUGGESTIONS FOR FURTHER WRITING OR DISCUSSION

1. If you have seen or been in an automobile or other accident, describe it in such detail that the reader will feel that he is a part of your experience. If you prefer, make up a story about an accident.
2. Over 50,000 Americans are killed each year on our roads. Think about this and discuss it with others, and then write a paper suggesting remedies for the tragic situation.

Reason and Risk

A young woman lives in fear of her life.
A skilled hunter relentlessly pursues his prey.

THE ADVENTURE OF THE SPECKLED BAND

by Sir Arthur Conan Doyle

A young girl has died, her sister's life also appears to be threatened, and Sherlock Holmes is again called upon to face a master criminal. Are the clues the author gives you enough to allow you to solve the puzzle along with Holmes?

On glancing over my notes of the seventy odd cases in which I have during the last eight years studied the methods of my friend Sherlock Holmes, I find many tragic, some comic, a large number merely strange, but none commonplace; for, working as he did rather for the love of his art than for the acquirement of wealth, he refused to associate himself with any investigation which did not tend towards the unusual, and even the fantastic. Of all these varied cases, however, I cannot recall any which presented more singular features than that which was associated with the well-known Surrey family of the Roylotts of Stoke Moran. The events in question occurred in the early days of my association with Holmes, when we were sharing rooms as bachelors in Baker Street. It is possible that I might have placed them upon record before, but a promise of secrecy was made at the time, from which I have only been freed during the last month by the untimely death of the lady to whom the pledge was given. It is perhaps as well that the facts should now come to light, for I have reasons to know that there are widespread rumours as to the death of Dr. Grimesby Roylott which tend to make the matter even more terrible than the truth.

It was early in April in the year '83 that I woke one morning to find Sherlock Holmes standing, fully dressed, by the side of my bed. He was a late riser, as a rule, and as the clock on the mantelpiece showed me that it was only a quarter-past seven, I blinked up at him in some surprise, and perhaps just a little resentment, for I was myself regular in my habits.

"Very sorry to knock you up,[1] Watson," said he, "but it's the common lot this morning. Mrs. Hudson has been knocked

---

1. knock . . . up: rouse.

---

up, she retorted upon me, and I on you."

"What is it, then—a fire?"

"No; a client. It seems that a young lady has arrived in a considerable state of excitement, who insists upon seeing me. She is waiting now in the sitting-room. Now, when young ladies wander about the metropolis at this hour of the morning, and knock sleepy people up out of their beds, I presume that it is something very pressing which they have to communicate. Should it prove to be an interesting case, you would, I am sure, wish to follow it from the outset. I thought, at any rate, that I should call you and give you the chance."

"My dear fellow, I would not miss it for anything."

I had no keener pleasure than in following Holmes in his professional investigations, and in admiring the rapid deductions, as swift as intuitions, and yet always founded on a logical basis, with which he unravelled the problems which were submitted to him. I rapidly threw on my clothes and was ready in a few minutes to accompany my friend down to the sitting-room. A lady dressed in black and heavily veiled, who had been sitting in the window, rose as we entered.

"Good-morning, madam," said Holmes cheerily. "My name is Sherlock Holmes. This is my intimate friend and associate, Dr. Watson, before whom you can speak as freely as before myself. Ha! I am glad to see that Mrs. Hudson has had the good sense to light the fire. Pray draw up to it, and I shall order you a cup of hot coffee, for I observe that you are shivering."

"It is not cold which makes me shiver," said the woman in a low voice, changing her seat as requested.

"What, then?"

"It is fear, Mr. Holmes. It is terror." She raised her veil as she spoke, and we could see that she was indeed in a pitiable state of agitation, her face all drawn and gray, with restless, frightened eyes, like those of some hunted animal. Her features and figure were those of a woman of thirty, but her hair was shot with premature gray, and her expression was weary and haggard. Sherlock Holmes ran her over with one of his quick, all-comprehensive glances.

"You must not fear," said he soothingly, bending forward and patting her forearm. "We shall soon set matters right, I have no doubt. You have come in by train this morning, I see."

"You know me, then?"

"No, but I observe the second half of a return ticket in the palm of your left glove. You must have started early, and yet you had a good drive in a dog-cart,[2] along heavy roads, before you reached the station."

The lady gave a violent start and stared in bewilderment at my companion.

"There is no mystery, my dear madam," said he, smiling. "The left arm of your jacket is spattered with mud in no less than seven places. The marks are perfectly fresh. There is no vehicle save a dog-cart which throws up mud in that way, and then only when you sit on the left-hand side of the driver."

"Whatever your reasons may be, you are perfectly correct," said she. "I started from home before six, reached Leatherhead at twenty past, and came in by the first train to Waterloo. Sir, I can stand this strain no longer; I shall go mad if it continues. I have no one to turn to—none, save only one, who cares for me, and he, poor fellow, can be of little aid. I have heard of you, Mr. Holmes; I have heard of you from Mrs. Farintosh, whom you helped in the hour of her sore need. It was from her that I had your address. Oh, sir, do you not think that you could help me, too, and at least throw a little light through the dense darkness which surrounds me? At present it is out of my power to reward you for your services, but in a month or six weeks I shall be married, with the control of my own income, and then at least you shall not find me ungrateful."

Holmes turned to his desk and, unlocking it, drew out a small case-book, which he consulted.

"Farintosh," said he. "Ah yes, I recall the case; it was concerned with an opal tiara. I think it was before your time, Watson. I can only say, madam, that I shall be happy to devote the same care to your case as I did to that of your friend. As to reward, my profession is its own reward; but you are at liberty to defray whatever expenses I may be put to, at the time which suits you best. And now I beg that you will lay before us everything that may help us in forming an opinion upon the matter."

"Alas!" replied our visitor, "the very horror of my situation lies in the fact that my fears are so vague, and my suspicions depend so entirely upon small points, which might seem trivial to another, that even he[3] to whom of all others I have a right to look for help and advice looks upon all that I tell him about it as the fancies of a nervous woman. He does not say so, but

2. dog-cart: a small cart for two people, pulled by one horse.
3. She refers to her fiance.

I can read it from his soothing answers and averted eyes. But I have heard, Mr. Holmes, that you can see deeply into the manifold wickedness of the human heart. You may advise me how to walk amid the dangers which encompass me."

"I am all attention, madam."

"My name is Helen Stoner, and I am living with my stepfather, who is the last survivor of one of the oldest Saxon families in England, the Roylotts of Stoke Moran, on the western border of Surrey."

Holmes nodded his head. "The name is familiar to me," said he.

"The family was at one time among the richest in England, and the estates extended over the borders into Berkshire in the north, and Hampshire in the west. In the last century, however, four successive heirs were of a dissolute and wasteful disposition, and the family ruin was eventually completed by a gambler in the days of the Regency. Nothing was left save a few acres of ground, and the two-hundred-year-old house, which is itself crushed under a heavy mortgage. The last squire dragged out his existence there, living the horrible life of an aristocratic pauper; but his only son, my stepfather, seeing that he must adapt himself to the new conditions, obtained an advance from a relative, which enabled him to take a medical degree and went out to Calcutta, where, by his professional skill and his force of character, he established a large practice. In a fit of anger, however, caused by some robberies which had been perpetrated in the house, he beat his native butler to death and narrowly escaped a capital sentence. As it was, he suffered a long term of imprisonment and afterwards returned to England a morose and disappointed man.

"When Dr. Roylott was in India he married my mother, Mrs. Stoner, the young widow of Major-General Stoner, of the Bengal Artillery. My sister Julia and I were twins, and we were only two years old at the time of my mother's re-marriage. She had a considerable sum of money—not less than 1000 pounds a year—and this she bequeathed to Dr. Roylott entirely while we resided with him, with a provision that a certain annual sum should be allowed to each of us in the event of our marriage. Shortly after our return to England my mother died—she was killed eight years ago in a railway accident near Crewe. Dr. Roylott then abandoned his attempts to establish himself in practice in London and took us to live with him in the old ancestral house at Stoke Moran. The money which my mother had left was enough for all our wants, and there seemed to be no obstacle to our happiness.

"But a terrible change came over our stepfather about this time. Instead of making friends and exchanging visits with our neighbours, who had at first been overjoyed to see a Roylott of Stoke Moran back in the old family seat, he shut himself up in his house and seldom came out save to indulge in ferocious quarrels with whoever might cross his path. Violence of temper approaching to mania has been hereditary in the men of the family, and in my stepfather's case it had, I believe, been intensified by his long residence in the tropics. A series of disgraceful brawls took place, two of which ended in the police-court, until at last he became the terror of the village, and the folks would fly at his approach, for he is a man of immense strength, and absolutely uncontrollable in his anger.

"Last week he hurled the local blacksmith over a parapet into a stream, and it was only by paying over all the money which I could gather together that I was able to avert another public exposure. He had no friends at all save the wandering gypsies, and he would give these vagabonds leave to encamp upon the few acres of bramble-covered land which represent the family estate, and would accept in return the hospitality of their tents, wandering away with them sometimes for weeks on end. He has a passion also for Indian animals, which are sent over to him by a correspondent, and he has at this moment a cheetah and a baboon, which wander freely over his grounds and are feared by the villagers almost as much as their master.

"You can imagine from what I say that my poor sister Julia and I had no great pleasure in our lives. No servant would stay with us, and for a long time we did all the work of the house. She was but thirty at the time of her death, and yet her hair had already begun to whiten, even as mine has."

"Your sister is dead, then?"

"She died just two years ago, and it is of her death that I wish to speak to you. You can understand that, living the life which I have described, we were little likely to see anyone of our own age and position. We had, however, an aunt, my mother's maiden sister, Miss Honoria Westphail, who lives near Harrow, and we were occasionally allowed to pay short visits at this lady's house. Julia went there at Christmas two years ago, and met there a half-pay major of marines, to whom she became engaged. My stepfather learned of the engagement when my sis-

ter returned and offered no objection to the marriage; but within
a fortnight of the day which had been fixed for the wedding,
the terrible event occurred which has deprived me of my only
companion."

Sherlock Holmes had been leaning back in his chair with
his eyes closed and his head sunk in a cushion, but he half
opened his lids now and glanced across at his visitor.

"Pray be precise as to details," said he.

"It is easy for me to be so, for every event of that dreadful
time is seared into my memory. The manor-house is, as I have
already said, very old, and only one wing is now inhabited. The
bedrooms in this wing are on the ground floor, the sitting-rooms
being in the central block of the buildings. Of these bedrooms
the first is Dr. Roylott's, the second my sister's, and the third
my own. There is no communication between them, but they
all open out into the same corridor. Do I make myself plain?"

"Perfectly so."

"The windows of the three rooms open out upon the lawn.
That fatal night Dr. Roylott had gone to his room early, though
we knew that he had not retired to rest, for my sister was
troubled by the smell of the strong Indian cigars which it was
his custom to smoke. She left her room, therefore, and came
into mine, where she sat for some time, chatting about her approaching wedding. At eleven o'clock she rose to leave me, but
she paused at the door and looked back.

" 'Tell me, Helen,' said she, 'have you ever heard anyone
whistle in the dead of the night?' "

" 'Never,' said I.

" 'I suppose that you could not possibly whistle, yourself,
in your sleep?'

" 'Certainly not. But why?'

" 'Because during the last few nights I have always, about
three in the morning, heard a low, clear whistle. I am a light
sleeper, and it has awakened me. I cannot tell where it came
from—perhaps from the next room, perhaps from the lawn. I
thought that I would just ask you whether you had heard it.'

" 'No, I have not. It must be those wretched gypsies in the
plantation.'

" 'Very likely. And yet if it were on the lawn, I wonder that
you did not hear it also.'

" 'Ah, but I sleep more heavily than you.'

" 'Well, it is of no great consequence, at any rate.' She
smiled back at me, closed my door, and a few moments later

I heard her key turn in the lock."

"Indeed," said Holmes. "Was it your custom always to lock yourselves in at night?"

"Always."

"And why?"

"I think that I mentioned to you that the doctor kept a cheetah and a baboon. We had no feeling of security unless our doors were locked."

"Quite so. Pray proceed with your statement."

"I could not sleep that night. A vague feeling of impending misfortune impressed me. My sister and I, you will recollect, were twins, and you know how subtle are the links which bind two souls which are so closely allied. It was a wild night. The wind was howling outside, and the rain was beating and splashing against the windows. Suddenly, amid all the hubbub of the gale, there burst forth the wild scream of a terrified woman. I knew that it was my sister's voice. I sprang from my bed, wrapped a shawl round me, and rushed into the corridor. As I opened my door I seemed to hear a low whistle, such as my sister described, and a few moments later a clanging sound, as if a mass of metal had fallen. As I ran down the passage, my sister's door was unlocked, and revolved slowly upon its hinges. I stared at it horror-stricken, not knowing what was about to issue from it. By the light of the corridor-lamp I saw my sister appear at the opening, her face blanched with terror, her hands groping for help, her whole figure swaying to and fro like that of a drunkard. I ran to her and threw my arms round her, but at that moment her knees seemed to give way and she fell to the ground. She writhed as one who is in terrible pain, and her limbs were dreadfully convulsed. At first I thought that she had not recognized me, but as I bent over her she suddenly shrieked out in a voice which I shall never forget, 'Oh, my God! Helen! It was the band! The speckled band!' There was something else which she would fain have said, and she stabbed with her finger into the air in the direction of the doctor's room, but a fresh convulsion seized her and choked her words. I rushed out, calling loudly for my stepfather, and I met him hastening from his room in his dressing-gown. When he reached my sister's side she was unconscious, and though he poured brandy down her throat and sent for medical aid from the village, all efforts were in vain, for she slowly died without having recovered her consciousness. Such was the dreadful end of my beloved sister."

"One moment," said Holmes; "are you sure about this whistle and metallic sound? Could you swear to it?"

"That was what the county coroner asked me at the inquiry. It is my strong impression that I heard it, and yet, among the crash of the gale and the creaking of an old house, I may possibly have been deceived."

"Was your sister dressed?"

"No, she was in her night-dress. In her right hand was found the charred stump of a match, and in her left a match-box."

"Showing that she had struck a light and looked about her when the alarm took place. That is important. And what conclusions did the coroner come to?"

"He investigated the case with great care, for Dr. Roylott's conduct had long been notorious in the county, but he was unable to find any satisfactory cause of death. My evidence showed that the door had been fastened upon the inner side, and the windows were blocked by old-fashioned shutters with broad iron bars, which were secured every night. The walls were carefully sounded, and were shown to be quite solid all round, and the flooring was also thoroughly examined, with the same result. The chimney is wide, but is barred up by four large staples. It is certain, therefore, that my sister was quite alone when she met her end. Besides, there were no marks of any violence upon her."

"How about poison?"

"The doctors examined her for it, but without success."

"What do you think that this unfortunate lady died of, then?"

"It is my belief that she died of pure fear and nervous shock, though what it was that frightened her I cannot imagine."

"Were there gypsies in the plantation at the time?"

"Yes, there are nearly always some there."

"Ah, and what did you gather from this allusion to a band—a speckled band?"

"Sometimes I have thought that it was merely the wild talk of delirium, sometimes that it may have referred to some band of people, perhaps to these very gypsies in the plantation. I do not know whether the spotted handkerchiefs which so many of them wear over their heads might have suggested the strange adjective which she used."

"These are very deep waters," said he; "pray go on with your narrative."

"Two years have passed since then, and my life has been until lately lonelier than ever. A month ago, however, a dear friend, whom I have known for many years, has done me the

honour to ask my hand in marriage. His name is Armitage—
Percy Armitage—the second son of Mr. Armitage, of Crane Water, near Reading. My stepfather has offered no opposition to
the match, and we are to be married in the course of the spring.
Two days ago some repairs were started in the west wing of
the building, and my bedroom wall has been pierced, so that
I have had to move into the chamber in which my sister died,
and to sleep in the very bed in which she slept. Imagine, then,
my thrill of terror when last night, as I lay awake, thinking over
her terrible fate, I suddenly heard in the silence of the night
the low whistle which had been the herald of her own death.
I sprang up and lit the lamp, but nothing was to be seen in
the room. I was too shaken to go to bed again, however, so I
dressed, and as soon as it was daylight I slipped down, got a
dog-cart at the Crown Inn, which is opposite, and drove to Leatherhead, from whence I have come on this morning with the
one object of seeing you and asking your advice."

"You have done wisely," said my friend. "But have you told
me all?"

"Yes, all."

"Miss Roylott, you have not. You are screening your stepfather."

"Why, what do you mean?"

For answer Holmes pushed back the frill of black lace which
fringed the hand that lay upon our visitor's knee. Five little livid
spots, the marks of four fingers and a thumb, were printed upon
the white wrist.

"You have been cruelly used," said Holmes.

The lady coloured deeply and covered over her injured
wrist. "He is a hard man," she said, "and perhaps he hardly
knows his own strength."

There was a long silence, during which Holmes leaned his
chin upon his hands and stared into the crackling fire.

"This is a very deep business," he said at last. "There are
a thousand details which I should desire to know before I decide
upon our course of action. Yet we have not a moment to lose.
If we were to come to Stoke Moran to-day, would it be possible
for us to see over these rooms without the knowledge of your
stepfather?"

"As it happens, he spoke of coming into town to-day upon
some most important business. It is probable that he will be away
all day, and that there would be nothing to disturb you. We have
a housekeeper now, but she is old and foolish, and I could easily
get her out of the way."

"Excellent. You are not averse to this trip, Watson?"

"By no means."

"Then we shall both come. What are you going to do your-self?"

"I have one or two things which I would wish to do now that I am in town. But I shall return by the twelve o'clock train, so as to be there in time for your coming."

"And you may expect us early in the afternoon. I have my-self some small business matters to attend to. Will you not wait and breakfast?"

"No, I must go. My heart is lightened already since I have confided my trouble to you. I shall look forward to seeing you again this afternoon." She dropped her thick black veil over her face and glided from the room.

"And what do you think of it all, Watson?" asked Sherlock Holmes, leaning back in his chair.

"It seems to me to be a most dark and sinister business."

"Dark enough and sinister enough."

"Yet if the lady is correct in saying that the flooring and walls are sound, and that the door, window, and chimney are impassable, then her sister must have been undoubtedly alone when she met her mysterious end."

"What becomes, then, of these nocturnal whistles, and what of the very peculiar words of the dying woman?"

"I cannot think."

"When you combine the ideas of whistles at night, the presence of a band of gypsies who are on intimate terms with this old doctor, the fact that we have every reason to believe that the doctor has an interest in preventing his stepdaughter's marriage, the dying allusion to a band, and, finally, the fact that Miss Helen Stoner heard a metallic clang, which might have been caused by one of those metal bars that secured the shutters falling back into its place, I think that there is good ground to think that the mystery may be cleared along those lines."

"But what, then, did the gypsies do?"

"I cannot imagine."

"I see many objections to any such theory."

"And so do I. It is precisely for that reason that we are going to Stoke Moran this day. I want to see whether the objections are fatal, or if they may be explained away. But what in the name of the devil!"

The ejaculation had been drawn from my companion by the fact that our door had been suddenly dashed open, and that a huge man had framed himself in the aperture. His costume was a peculiar mixture of the professional and of the agricultural, having a black top-hat, a long frock-coat, and a pair of high gaiters, with a hunting-crop swinging in his hand. So tall was he that his hat actually brushed the cross bar of the doorway, and his breadth seemed to span it across from side to side. A large face, seared with a thousand wrinkles, burned yellow with the sun, and marked with every evil passion, was turned from one to the other of us, while his deep-set, bile-shot eyes, and his high, thin, fleshless nose, gave him somewhat the resemblance to a fierce old bird of prey.

"Which of you is Holmes?" asked this apparition.

"My name, sir; but you have the advantage of me," said my companion quietly.

"I am Dr. Grimesby Roylott, of Stoke Moran."

"Indeed, Doctor," said Holmes blandly. "Pray take a seat."

"I will do nothing of the kind. My stepdaughter has been here. I have traced her. What has she been saying to you?"

"It is a little cold for the time of the year," said Holmes.

"What has she been saying to you?" screamed the old man furiously.

"But I have heard that the crocuses promise well," continued my companion imperturbably.

"Ha! You put me off, do you?" said our new visitor, taking a step forward and shaking his hunting-crop. "I know you, you scoundrel! I have heard of you before. You are Holmes, the meddler."

My friend smiled.

"Holmes, the busybody!"

His smile broadened.

"Holmes, the Scotland Yard[4] Jack-in-office!"

Holmes chuckled heartily. "Your conversation is most entertaining," said he. "When you go out close the door, for there is a decided draught."

"I will go when I have said my say. Don't you dare to meddle with my affairs. I know that Miss Stoner has been here. I traced her! I am a dangerous man to fall foul of! See here." He stepped swiftly forward, seized the poker, and bent it into a curve with his huge brown hands.

"See that you keep yourself out of my grip," he snarled, and hurling the twisted poker into the fireplace he strode out of the room.

4. Scotland Yard; the criminal investigation department of the London Police.

"He seems a very amiable person," said Holmes, laughing. "I am not quite so bulky, but if he had remained I might have shown him that my grip was not much more feeble than his own." As he spoke he picked up the steel poker and, with a sudden effort, straightened it out again.

"Fancy his having the insolence to confound me with the official detective force! This incident gives zest to our investigation, however, and I only trust that our little friend will not suffer from her imprudence in allowing this brute to trace her. And now, Watson, we shall order breakfast, and afterwards I shall walk down to Doctors' Commons, where I hope to get some data which may help us in this matter."

It was nearly one o'clock when Sherlock Holmes returned from his excursion. He held in his hand a sheet of blue paper, scrawled over with notes and figures.

"I have seen the will of the deceased wife," said he. "To determine its exact meaning I have been obliged to work out the present prices of the investments with which it is concerned. The total income, which at the time of the wife's death was little short of 1100 pounds, is now, through the fall in agricultural prices, not more than 750 pounds. Each daughter can claim an income of 250 pounds, in case of marriage. It is evident, therefore, that if both girls had married, this beauty[5] would have had a mere pittance, while even one of them would cripple him to a very serious extent. My morning's work has not been wasted, since it has proved that he has the very strongest motives for standing in the way of anything of the sort. And now, Watson, this is too serious for dawdling, especially as the old man is aware that we are interesting ourselves in his affairs; so if you are ready, we shall call a cab and drive to Waterloo. I should be very much obliged if you would slip your revolver into your pocket. An Eley's No. 2 is an excellent argument with gentlemen who can twist steel pokers into knots. That and a tooth-brush are, I think, all that we need."

At Waterloo we were fortunate in catching a train for Leatherhead, where we hired a trap at the station inn and drove for four or five miles through the lovely Surrey lanes. It was a perfect day, with a bright sun and a few fleecy clouds in the heavens. The trees and wayside hedges were just throwing out their first green shoots, and the air was full of the pleasant smell

5. this beauty: Holmes is referring to Dr. Roylott.

of the moist earth. To me at least there was a strange contrast between the sweet promise of the spring and this sinister quest upon which we were engaged. My companion sat in the front of the trap, his arms folded, his hat pulled down over his eyes, and his chin sunk upon his breast, buried in the deepest thought. Suddenly, however, he started, tapped me on the shoulder, and pointed over the meadows.

"Look there!" said he.

A heavily timbered park stretched up in a gentle slope, thickening into a grove at the highest point. From amid the branches there jutted out the gray gables and high roof-tree of a very old mansion.

"Stoke Moran?" said he.

"Yes, sir, that be the house of Dr. Grimesby Roylott," remarked the driver.

"There is some building going on there," said Holmes; "that is where we are going."

"There's the village," said the driver, pointing to a cluster of roofs some distance to the left; "but if you want to get to the house, you'll find it shorter to get over this stile, and so by the foot-path over the fields. There it is, where the lady is walking."

"And the lady, I fancy, is Miss Stoner," observed Holmes, shading his eyes. "Yes, I think we had better do as you suggest."

We got off, paid our fare, and the trap rattled back on its way to Leatherhead.

"I thought it as well," said Holmes as we climbed the stile, "that this fellow should think we had come here as architects, or on some definite business. It may stop his gossip. Good-afternoon, Miss Stoner. You see that we have been as good as our word."

Our client of the morning had hurried forward to meet us with a face which spoke her joy. "I have been waiting so eagerly for you," she cried, shaking hands with us warmly. "All has turned out splendidly. Dr. Roylott has gone to town, and it is unlikely that he will be back before evening."

"We have had the pleasure of making the doctor's acquaintance," said Holmes, and in a few words he sketched out what had occurred. Miss Stoner turned white to the lips as she listened.

"Good heavens!" she cried, "he has followed me, then."

"So it appears."

"He is so cunning that I never know when I am safe from

him. What will he say when he returns?"

"He must guard himself, for he may find that there is someone more cunning than himself upon his track. You must lock
yourself up from him to-night. If he is violent, we shall take
you away to your aunt's at Harrow. Now, we must make the
best use of our time, so kindly take us at once to the rooms
which we are to examine."

The building was of gray, lichen-blotched stone, with a high
central portion and two curving wings, like the claws of a crab,
thrown out on each side. In one of these wings the windows
were broken and blocked with wooden boards, while the roof
was partly caved in, a picture of ruin. The central portion was
in little better repair, but the right-hand block was comparatively
modern, and the blinds in the windows, with the blue smoke
curling up from the chimneys, showed that this was where the
family resided. Some scaffolding had been erected against the
end wall, and the stone-work had been broken into, but there
were no signs of any workmen at the moment of our visit.
Holmes walked slowly up and down the ill-trimmed lawn and
examined with deep attention the outsides of the windows.

"This, I take it, belongs to the room in which you used to
sleep, the centre one to your sister's, and the one next to the
main building to Dr. Roylott's chamber?"

"Exactly so. But I am now sleeping in the middle one."

"Pending the alterations, as I understand. By the way, there
does not seem to be any very pressing need for repairs at that
end wall."

"There were none. I believe that it was an excuse to move
me from my room."

"Ah! that is suggestive. Now, on the other side of this narrow wing runs the corridor from which these three rooms open.
There are windows in it, of course?"

"Yes, but very small ones. Too narrow for anyone to pass
through."

"As you both locked your doors at night, your rooms were
unapproachable from that side. Now, would you have the kindness to go into your room and bar your shutters?"

Miss Stoner did so, and Holmes, after a careful examination
through the open window, endeavoured in every way to force
the shutter open, but without success. There was no slit through
which a knife could be passed to raise the bar. Then with his
lens he tested the hinges, but they were of solid iron, built firmly
into the massive masonry. "Hum!" said he, scratching his chin

in some perplexity, "my theory certainly presents some difficulties. No one could pass these shutters if they were bolted. Well, we shall see if the inside throws any light upon the matter."

A small side door led into the whitewashed corridor from which the three bedrooms opened. Holmes refused to examine the third chamber, so we passed at once to the second, that in which Miss Stoner was now sleeping, and in which her sister had met with her fate. It was a homely little room, with a low ceiling and a gaping fireplace, after the fashion of old country-houses. A brown chest of drawers stood in one corner, a narrow white-counterpaned bed in another, and a dressing table on the left-hand side of the window. These articles, with two small wickerwork chairs, made up all the furniture in the room save for a square of Wilton carpet in the centre. The boards round and the panelling of the walls were of brown, worm-eaten oak, so old and discoloured that it may have dated from the original building of the house. Holmes drew one of the chairs into a corner and sat silent, while his eyes travelled round and round and up and down, taking in every detail of the apartment.

"Where does that bell communicate with?" he asked at last, pointing to a thick bell-rope which hung down beside the bed, the tassel actually lying upon the pillow.

"It goes to the housekeeper's room."

"It looks newer than the other things?"

"Yes, it was only put there a couple of years ago."

"Your sister asked for it, I suppose?"

"No, I never heard of her using it. We used always to get what we wanted for ourselves."

"Indeed, it seemed unnecessary to put so nice a bell-pull there. You will excuse me for a few minutes while I satisfy myself as to this floor." He threw himself down upon his face with his lens in his hand and crawled swiftly backward and forward, examining minutely the cracks between the boards. Then he did the same with the wood-work with which the chamber was panelled. Finally he walked over to the bed and spent some time in staring at it and in running his eye up and down the wall. Finally he took the bell-rope in his hand and gave it a brisk tug.

"Why, it's a dummy," said he.

"Won't it ring?"

"No, it is not even attached to a wire. This is very interesting. You can see now that it is fastened to a hook just above where the little opening for the ventilator is."

"How very absurd! I never noticed that before."

"Very strange!" muttered Holmes, pulling at the rope. "There are one or two very singular points about this room. For example, what a fool a builder must be to open a ventilator into another room, when, with the same trouble, he might have communicated with the outside air!"

"That is also quite modern," said the lady.

"Done about the same time as the bell-rope?" remarked Holmes.

"Yes, there were several little changes carried out about that time."

"They seem to have been of a most interesting character— dummy bell-ropes, and ventilators which do not ventilate. With your permission, Miss Stoner, we shall now carry our researches into the inner apartment."

Dr. Grimesby Roylott's chamber was larger than that of his step-daughter, but was as plainly furnished. A camp-bed, a small wooden shelf full of books, mostly of a technical character, an armchair beside the bed, a plain wooden chair against the wall, a round table, and a large iron safe were the principal things which met the eye. Holmes walked slowly round and examined each and all of them with the keenest interest.

"What's in here?" he asked, tapping the safe.

"My stepfather's business papers."

"Oh! you have seen inside, then?"

"Only once, some years ago. I remember that it was full of papers."

"There isn't a cat in it, for example?"

"No. What a strange idea!"

"Well, look at this!" He took up a small saucer of milk which stood on the top of it.

"No; we don't keep a cat. But there is a cheetah and a baboon."

"Ah, yes, of course! Well, a cheetah is just a big cat, and yet a saucer of milk does not go very far in satisfying its wants, I daresay. There is one point which I should wish to determine." He squatted down in front of the wooden chair and examined the seat of it with the greatest attention.

"Thank you. That is quite settled," said he, rising and putting his lens in his pocket. "Hallo! Here is something interesting!"

The object which had caught his eye was a small dog lash hung on one corner of the bed. The lash, however, was curled upon itself and tied so as to make a loop of whipcord.

"What do you make of that, Watson?"

"It's a common enough lash. But I don't know why it should be tied."

"That is not quite so common, is it? Ah, me! it's a wicked world, and when a clever man turns his brains to crime it is the worst of all. I think that I have seen enough now, Miss Stoner, and with your permission we shall walk out upon the lawn."

I had never seen my friends's face so grim or his brow so dark as it was when we turned from the scene of this investigation. We had walked several times up and down the lawn, neither Miss Stoner nor myself liking to break in upon his thoughts before he roused himself from his reverie.

"It is very essential, Miss Stoner," said he, "that you should absolutely follow my advice in every respect."

"I shall most certainly do so."

"The matter is too serious for any hesitation. Your life may depend upon your compliance."

"I assure you that I am in your hands."

"In the first place, both my friend and I must spend the night in your room."

Both Miss Stoner and I gazed at him in astonishment.

"Yes, it must be so. Let me explain. I believe that that is the village inn over there?"

"Yes, that is the Crown."

"Very good. Your windows would be visible from there?"

"Certainly."

"You must confine yourself to your room, on pretense of a headache, when your stepfather comes back. Then when you hear him retire for the night, you must open the shutters of your window, undo the hasp, put your lamp there as a signal to us, and then withdraw quietly with everything which you are likely to want into the room which you used to occupy. I have no doubt that, in spite of the repairs, you could manage there for one night."

"Oh, yes, easily."

"The rest you will leave in our hands."

"But what will you do?"

"We shall spend the night in your room, and we shall investigate the case of this noise which has disturbed you."

"I believe, Mr. Holmes, that you have already made up your mind," said Miss Stoner, laying her hand upon my companion's sleeve.

"Perhaps I have."

"Then, for pity's sake, tell me what was the cause of my sister's death."

"I should prefer to have clearer proofs before I speak."

"You can at least tell me whether my own thought is correct, and if she died from some sudden fright."

"No, I do not think so. I think that there was probably some more tangible cause. And now, Miss Stoner, we must leave you, for if Dr. Roylott returned and saw us our journey would be in vain. Good-bye, and be brave, for if you will do what I have told you you may rest assured that we shall soon drive away the dangers that threaten you."

Sherlock Holmes and I had no difficulty in engaging a bedroom and sitting-room at the Crown Inn. They were on the upper floor, and from our window we could command a view of the avenue gate, and of the inhabited wing of Stoke Moran Manor House. At dusk we saw Dr. Grimesby Roylott drive past, his huge form looming up beside the little figure of the lad who drove him. The boy had some slight difficulty in undoing the heavy iron gates, and we heard the hoarse roar of the doctor's voice and saw the fury with which he shook his clenched fists at him. The trap drove on, and a few minutes later we saw a sudden light spring up among the trees as the lamp was lit in one of the sitting-rooms.

"Do you know, Watson," said Holmes as we sat together in the gathering darkness, "I have really some scruples as to taking you tonight. There is a distinct element of danger."

"Can I be of assistance?"

"Your presence might be invaluable."

"Then I shall certainly come."

"It is very kind of you."

"You speak of danger. You have evidently seen more in these rooms than was visible to me."

"No, but I fancy that I may have deduced a little more. I imagine that you saw all that I did."

"I saw nothing remarkable save the bell-rope, and what purpose that could answer I confess is more than I can imagine."

"You saw the ventilator, too?"

"Yes, but I do not think that it is such a very unusual thing to have a small opening between two rooms. It was so small that a rat could hardly pass through."

"I knew that we should find a ventilator before ever we came to Stoke Moran."

"My dear Holmes!"

"Oh yes, I did. You remember in her statement she said that her sister could smell Dr. Roylott's cigar. Now, of course that suggested at once that there must be a communication between the two rooms. It could only be a small one, or it would have been remarked upon at the coroner's inquiry. I deduced a ventilator."

"But what harm can there be in that?"

"Well, there is at least a curious coincidence of dates. A ventilator is made, a cord is hung, and a lady who sleeps in the bed dies. Does not that strike you?"

"I cannot as yet see any connection."

"Did you observe anything very peculiar about that bed?"

"No."

"It was clamped to the floor. Did you ever see a bed fastened like that before?"

"I cannot say that I have."

"The lady could not move her bed. It must always be in the same relative position to the ventilator and to the rope—or so we may call it, since it was clearly never meant for a bell-pull."

"Holmes," I cried, "I seem to see dimly what you are hinting at. We are only just in time to prevent some subtle and horrible crime."

"Subtle enough and horrible enough. When a doctor does go wrong he is the first of criminals. He has nerve and he has knowledge. Palmer and Pritchard were among the heads of their profession. This man strikes even deeper, but I think, Watson, that we shall be able to strike deeper still. But we shall have horrors enough before the night is over; for goodness' sake let us have a quiet pipe and turn our minds for a few hours to something more cheerful."

About nine o'clock the light among the trees was extinguished, and all was dark in the direction of the Manor House. Two hours passed slowly away, and then, suddenly, just at the stroke of eleven, a single bright light shone out right in front of us.

"That is our signal," said Holmes, springing to his feet; "it comes from the middle window."

As we passed out he exchanged a few words with the landlord, explaining that we were going on a late visit to an acquaintance, and that it was possible that we might spend the night there. A moment later we were out on the dark road, a chill wind blowing in our faces, and one yellow light twinkling in front of us through the gloom to guide us on our sombre errand.

There was little difficulty in entering the grounds, for unrepaired breaches gaped in the old park wall. Making our way among the trees, we reached the lawn, crossed it, and were about to enter through the window when out from a clump of laurel bushes there darted what seemed to be a hideous and distorted child, who threw itself upon the grass with writhing limbs and then ran swiftly across the lawn into the darkness.

"My God!" I whispered, "did you see it?"

Holmes was for the moment as startled as I. His hand closed like a vise upon my wrist in his agitation. Then he broke into a low laugh and put his lips to my ear.

"It is a nice household," he murmured. "That is the baboon."

I had forgotten the strange pets which the doctor affected. There was a cheetah, too; perhaps we might find it upon our shoulders at any moment. I confess that I felt easier in my mind when, after following Holmes's example and slipping off my shoes, I found myself inside the bedroom. My companion noiselessly closed the shutters, moved the lamp onto the table, and cast his eyes round the room. All was as we had seen it in the daytime. Then creeping up to me and making a trumpet of his hand, he whispered into my ear again so gently that it was all that I could do to distinguish the words:

"The least sound would be fatal to our plans."

I nodded to show that I had heard.

"We must sit without light. He would see it through the ventilator."

I nodded again.

"Do not go asleep; your very life may depend upon it. Have your pistol ready in case we should need it. I will sit on the side of the bed, and you in that chair."

I took out my revolver and laid it on the corner of the table.

Holmes had brought up a long thin cane, and this he placed upon the bed beside him. By it he laid the box of matches and the stump of a candle. Then he turned down the lamp, and we were left in darkness.

How shall I ever forget that dreadful vigil? I could not hear a sound, not even the drawing of a breath, and yet I knew that my companion sat open-eyed, within a few feet of me, in the same state of nervous tension in which I was myself. The shutters cut off the least ray of light, and we waited in absolute darkness. From outside came the occasional cry of a night-bird, and once at our very window a long drawn catlike whine, which told us that the cheetah was indeed at liberty. Far away we could hear the deep tones of the parish clock, which boomed out every quarter of an hour. How long they seemed, those quarters! Twelve struck, and one and two and three, and still we sat waiting silently for whatever might befall.

Suddenly there was the momentary gleam of a light up in the direction of the ventilator, which vanished immediately, but was succeeded by a strong smell of burning oil and heated metal. Someone in the next room had lit a dark-lantern. I heard a gentle sound of movement, and then all was silent once more, though the smell grew stronger. For half an hour I sat with straining ears. Then suddenly another sound became audible—a very gentle, soothing sound, like that of a small jet of steam escaping continually from a kettle. The instant that we heard it, Holmes sprang from the bed, struck a match, and lashed furiously with his cane at the bell-pull.

"You see it, Watson?" he yelled. "You see it?"

But I saw nothing. At the moment when Holmes struck the light I heard a low, clear whistle, but the sudden glare flashing into my weary eyes made it impossible for me to tell what it was at which my friend lashed so savagely. I could, however, see that his face was deadly pale and filled with horror and loathing.

He had ceased to strike and was gazing up at the ventilator when suddenly there broke from the silence of the night the most horrible cry to which I have ever listened. It swelled up louder and louder, a hoarse yell of pain and fear and anger all mingled in the one dreadful shriek. They say that away down in the village, and even in the distant parsonage, that cry raised the sleepers from their beds. It struck cold to our hearts, and I stood gazing at Holmes, and he at me, until the last echoes of it had died away into the silence from which it rose.

"What can it mean?" I gasped.

"It means that it is all over," Holmes answered. "And perhaps, after all, it is for the best. Take your pistol, and we will enter Dr. Roylott's room."

With a grave face he lit the lamp and led the way down the corridor. Twice he struck at the chamber door without any reply from within. Then he turned the handle and entered, I at his heels, with the cocked pistol in my hand.

It was a singular sight which met our eyes. On the table stood a dark-lantern with the shutter half open, throwing a brilliant beam of light upon the iron safe, the door of which was ajar. Beside this table, on the wodden chair, sat Dr. Grimesby Roylott, clad in a long gray dressing-gown, his bare ankles protruding beneath, and his feet thrust into red heelless Turkish slippers. Across his lap lay the short stock with the long lash which we had noticed during the day. His chin was cocked, upward and his eyes were fixed in a dreadful, rigid stare at the corner of the ceiling. Round his brow he had a peculiar yellow band, with brownish speckles, which seemed to be bound tightly round his head. As we entered he made neither sound nor motion.

"The band! the speckled band!" whispered Holmes.

I took a step forward. In an instant his strange headgear began to move, and there reared itself from among his hair the squat diamond-shaped head and puffed neck of a loathsome serpent.

"It's a swamp adder!" cried Holmes; "the deadliest snake in India. He has died within ten seconds of being bitten. Violence does, in truth, recoil upon the violent, and the schemer falls into the pit which he digs for another. Let us thrust this creature back into its den, and we can then remove Miss Stoner to some place of shelter and let the county police know what has happened."

As he spoke he drew the dog-whip swiftly from the dead man's lap, and throwing the noose round the reptile's neck he drew it from its horrid perch and, carrying it at arm's length, threw it into the iron safe, which he closed upon it.

Such are the true facts of the death of Dr. Grimesby Roylott, of Stoke Moran. It is not necessary that I should prolong a narrative which has already run to too great a length by telling how we broke the sad news to the terrified girl, how we conveyed her by the morning train to the care of her good aunt at Harrow, of how the slow process of official inquiry came to the conclusion that the doctor met his fate while indiscreetly playing with a dangerous pet. The little which I had yet to learn of the case was told me by Sherlock Holmes as we travelled back next day.

"I had," said he, "come to an entirely erroneous conclusion which shows, my dear Watson, how dangerous it always is to reason from insufficient data. The presence of the gypsies, and the use of the word 'band,' which was used by the poor girl, no doubt to explain the appearance which she had caught a hurried glimpse of by the light of her match, were sufficient to put

me upon an entirely wrong scent. I can only claim the merit
that I instantly reconsidered my position when, however, it became clear to me that whatever danger threatened an occupant
of the room could not come either from the window or the door.
My attention was speedily drawn, as I have already remarked
to you, to this ventilator, and to the bell-rope which hung down
to the bed. The discovery that this was a dummy, and that the
bed was clamped to the floor, instantly gave rise to the suspicion
that the rope was there as a bridge for something passing
through the hole and coming to the bed. The idea of a snake
instantly occurred to me, and when I coupled it with my knowledge that the doctor was furnished with a supply of creatures
from India, I felt that I was probably on the right track. The
idea of using a form of poison which could not possibly be discovered by any chemical test was just such a one as would occur
to a clever and ruthless man who had had an Eastern training.
The rapidity with which such a poison would take effect would
also, from his point of view, be an advantage. It would be a
sharp-eyed coroner, indeed, who could distinguish the two little
dark punctures which would show where the poison fangs had
done their work. Then I thought of the whistle. Of course he
must recall the snake before the morning light revealed it to
the victim. He had trained it, probably by the use of the milk
which we saw, to return to him when summoned. He would put
it through this ventilator at the hour that he thought best, with
the certainty that it would crawl down the rope and land on
the bed. It might or might not bite the occupant, perhaps she
might escape every night for a week, but sooner or later she
must fall a victim.

"I had come to these conclusions before ever I had entered
his room. An inspection of his chair showed me that he had
been in the habit of standing on it, which of course would be
necessary in order that he should reach the ventilator. The sight
of the safe, the saucer of milk, and the loop of whipcord were
enough to finally dispel any doubts which may have remained.
The metallic clang heard by Miss Stoner was obviously caused
by her stepfather hastily closing the door of his safe upon its
terrible occupant. Having once made up my mind, you know
the steps which I took in order to put the matter to the proof.
I heard the creature hiss as I have no doubt that you did also,
and I instantly lit the light and attacked it."

"With the result of driving it through the ventilator."

"And also with the result of causing it to turn upon its master at the other side. Some of the blows of my cane came home and roused its snakish temper, so that it flew upon the first person it saw. In this way I am no doubt indirectly responsible for Dr. Grimesby Roylott's death, and I cannot say that it is likely to weigh very heavily upon my conscience."

QUESTIONS FOR DISCUSSION AND WRITING

1. Near the beginning of the story, Dr. Watson expresses his "keen pleasure" in observing Sherlock Holmes "unravel the problems set before him." Find and read again the paragraphs in which Holmes's amazing powers of observation are first revealed to Helen Stoner and to the reader. Why does Conan Doyle put these details here, since they have nothing particular to do with the story?

2. It is interesting to look back over the story after reading it and notice the clues. Here is a list of twelve of them. Can you explain the meaning of each? Which of these clues tend to lead Holmes astray?

   - Helen Stoner expects to be married and to control her own money.
   - Dr. Roylott is hard-up for funds.
   - Dr. Roylott has spent time in India.
   - If his stepdaughters marry, Dr. Roylott loses control of considerable sums of money.
   - Dr. Roylott keeps everyone away from the estate except bands of gypsies. (Why?)
   - He has a passion for Indian animals.
   - Sister Julia died before her wedding.
   - The bedrooms are in a certain order: Roylott's, Julia's, Helen's.
   - Julia could smell cigar smoke in her room. (What is the significance of this?)
   - At about three o'clock in the morning Julia would hear a low, clear whistle, but Helen could not hear it. (What is the significance of this?)
   - The night of Julia's death, Helen heard the scream, the whistle, and a clang of metal. (What was the clang?)
   - Julie dies in agony, shrieking about the "speckled band." She held a charred match in her hand. (What did Holmes think the band might be?)

3. Try making a list of all the rest of the clues up to the point in the story where Holmes explains his theories.
4. In what way in the story is Holmes himself a killer? How does he show that he does not regret it?

SUGGESTIONS FOR FURTHER WRITING OR DISCUSSION.

1. Make up a story of a crime that is solved by a detective using clues. If you know of a real case, use that.
2. Describe or make up a story about a situation where someone wanted to kill someone else for selfish purposes. Be sure his motives become clear to the reader by the time he reaches the end of the story.

THE MOST DANGEROUS GAME

by Richard Connell

*Here is another story in which terror and horror play
a role. How does the game General Zaroff hunts turn
out to be the most dangerous?*

There was no sound in the night as Rainsford sat there
but the muffled throb of the engine that drove the yacht swiftly
through the darkness, and the swish and ripple of the wash of
the propeller. Rainsford, reclining in a steamer chair, indolently
puffed on his favorite brier. "It's so dark," he thought, "that I could
sleep without closing my eyes; the night would be my eyelids—"

An abrupt sound startled him. Off to the right he heard
it, and his ears, expert in such matters, could not be mistaken.
Again he heard the sound, and again. Somewhere, off in the
blackness, someone had fired a gun three times. Rainsford
sprang up and moved quickly to the rail, mystified. He strained
his eyes in the direction from which the reports had come, but
it was like trying to see through a blanket. He leaped upon the
rail and balanced himself there, to get greater elevation; his pipe,
striking a rope, was knocked from his mouth. He lunged for it;
a short, hoarse cry came from his lips as he realized he had
reached too far and had lost his balance. The cry was pinched
off short as the blood-warm waters of the Caribbean Sea closed
over his head.

He struggled up to the surface and tried to cry out, but
the wash from the speeding yacht slapped him in the face and
the salt water in his open mouth made him gag and strangle.
Desperately he struck out with strong strokes after the receding
lights of the yacht, but he stopped before he had swum fifty feet.
A certain coolheadedness had come to him; it was not the first
time he had been in a tight place. There was a chance that his
cries could be heard by someone aboard the yacht, but that
chance was slender, and grew more slender as the yacht raced
on. He wrestled himself out of his clothes, and shouted with all
his power. The lights of the yacht became faint and ever-

vanishing fireflies; then they were blotted out entirely by the night.

Rainsford remembered the shots. They had come from the right, and doggedly he swam in that direction, swimming with slow, deliberate strokes, conserving his strength. For a seemingly endless time he fought the sea. He began to count his strokes; he could do possibly a hundred more, he thought, and then—

Rainsford heard a sound. It came out of the darkness, a high, screaming sound, the sound of an animal in an extremity of anguish and terror. He did not recognize the animal that made the sound; he did not try to; with fresh vitality he swam toward the sound. He heard it again; then it was cut short by another noise, crisp, staccato.

"Pistol shot," muttered Rainsford, swimming on.

Ten minutes of determined effort brought another sound to his ears—the most welcome he had ever heard—the muttering and growling of the sea breaking on a rocky shore. He was almost on the rocks before he saw them; on a night less calm he would have been shattered against them. With his remaining strength he dragged himself from the swirling waters. Gasping, his hands raw, he reached a flat place at the top. Dense jungle came down to the very edge of the cliffs. What perils that tangle of trees and underbrush might hold for him did not concern Rainsford just then. All he knew was that he was safe from his enemy, the sea, and that utter weariness was on him. He flung himself down at the jungle edge and tumbled headlong into the deepest sleep of his life.

When he opened his eyes he knew from the position of the sun that it was late in the afternoon. Sleep had given him new vigor; a sharp hunger was picking at him. He looked about him, almost cheerfully.

"Where there are pistol shots, there are men. Where there are men, there is food," he thought. But what kind of men, he wondered, in so forbidding a place? An unbroken front of snarled and ragged jungle fringed the shore.

He saw no sign of a trail through the closely knit web of weeds and trees; it was easier to go along the shore, and Rainsford floundered along by the water. Not far from where he had landed, he stopped. Some wounded thing, by the evidence a large animal, had thrashed about in the underbrush; the jungle weeds were crushed down and the moss was lacerated; one patch of weeds was stained crimson. A small, glittering object not far away caught Rainsford's eye and he picked it up. It was an empty cartridge.

"A twenty-two," he remarked. "That's odd. It must have been a fairly large animal, too. The hunter had his nerve with him to tackle it with a light gun. It's clear that the brute put up a fight."

He examined the ground closely and found what he had hoped to find—the print of hunting boots. They pointed along the cliff in the direction he had been going. Eagerly he hurried along, now slipping on a rotten log or a loose stone, but making headway; night was beginning to settle down on the island.

Bleak darkness was blacking out the sea and jungle when Rainsford sighted the lights. He came upon them as he turned a crook in the coast line, and his first thought was that he had come upon a village, for there were many lights. But as he forged his way along he saw to his astonishment that all the lights were in one enormous building—a lofty structure with pointed towers plunging upward into the gloom. His eyes made out the shadowy outlines of a palatial chateau;[1] it was set on a high bluff, and on three sides of it cliffs dived down to where the sea licked greedy lips in the shadows.

"Mirage," thought Rainsford. But it was no mirage, he found, when he opened the tall spiked iron gate. The stone steps were real enough; the massive door with a leering gargoyle for a knocker was real enough; yet about it all hung an air of unreality. He lifted the knocker, and it creaked up stiffly as if it had never before been used. He let it fall, and it startled him with its booming loudness. He thought he heard steps within; the door remained closed. Again Rainsford lifted the heavy knocker, and let it fall. The door opened then, opened as suddenly as if it were on a spring, and Rainsford stood blinking in the river of glaring gold light that poured out. The first thing his eyes discerned was the largest man Rainsford had ever seen—a gigantic creature, solidly made and black-bearded to the waist. In his hand the man held a long-barreled revolver, and he was pointing it straight at Rainsford's heart. Out of the snarl of beard two small eyes regarded Rainsford.

"Don't be alarmed," said Rainsford, with a smile which he hoped was disarming. "I'm no robber. I fell off a yacht. My name is Sanger Rainsford of New York City."

1. chateau: castle.

The menacing look in the eyes did not change. The revolver pointed as rigidly as if the giant were a statue. He gave no sign that he understood Rainsford's words, or that he had even heard them. He was dressed in uniform, a black uniform trimmed with gray astrakhan.[2]

"I'm Sanger Rainsford of New York," Rainsford began again. "I fell off a yacht. I am hungry."

The man's only answer was to raise with his thumb the hammer of his revolver. Then Rainsford saw the man's free hand go to his forehead in a military salute, and he saw him click his heels together and stand at attention. Another man was coming down the broad marble steps, an erect, slender man in evening clothes. He advanced to Rainsford and held out his hand. In a cultivated voice marked by a slight accent that gave it added precision and deliberateness, he said: "It is a very great pleasure and honor to welcome Mr. Sanger Rainsford, the celebrated hunter, to my home. I've read your book about hunting snow leopards in Tibet, you see," explained the man. "I am General Zaroff."

Rainsford's first impression was that the man was singularly handsome; his second was that there was an original, almost bizarre quality about the general's face. He was a tall man past middle age, for his hair was a vivid white; but his thick eyebrows and pointed military mustache were as black as the night from which Rainsford had come. His eyes, too, were black and very bright. He had high cheek bones, a sharp-cut nose, a spare, dark face, the face of a man used to giving orders, the face of an aristocrat. Turning to the giant in uniform, the general made a sign. The giant put away his pistol, saluted, withdrew.

"Ivan is an incredibly strong fellow," remarked the general, "but he has the misfortune to be deaf and dumb. A simple fellow, but, I'm afraid, like all his race, a bit of a savage."

"Is he Russian?"

"He is a Cossack," said the general, and his smile showed red lips and pointed teeth. "So am I."

"Come," he said, "we shouldn't be chatting here. We can talk later. Now you want clothes, food, rest. You shall have them. This is a most restful spot. Follow Ivan, if you please, Mr. Rainsford. I was about to have my dinner when you came. I'll wait for you. You'll find that my clothes will fit you, I think."

It was to a huge beam-ceiling bedroom with a canopied bed

2. astrakhan: lamb's fur from Southeast Asia.

big enough for six men that Rainsford followed the silent giant. Ivan laid out an evening suit, and Rainsford, as he put it on, noticed that it came from a London tailor who ordinarily cut and sewed for none below the rank of duke.

The dining room to which Ivan conducted him was in many ways remarkable. It suggested a baronial hall of feudal times with its oaken panels, its high ceiling, its vast refectory table where two score men could sit down to eat. About the hall were the mounted heads of many animals—lions, tigers, elephants, moose, bears; larger or more perfect specimens Rainsford had never seen. The table appointments were of the finest—the linen, the crystal, the silver, the china.

Half apologetically General Zaroff said: "We do our best to preserve the amenities of civilization here. Please forgive any lapses. We are well off the beaten track, you know."

The general seemed a most thoughtful and affable host, a true cosmopolite.[3] But whenever he looked up from his plate Rainsford found the general studying him, appraising him narrowly.

"Perhaps," said General Zaroff, "you were surprised that I recognized your name. You see, I read all books on hunting published in English, French, and Russian. I have but one passion in my life, Mr. Rainsford, and it is the hunt."

"You have some wonderful heads here," said Rainsford. "That Cape buffalo is the largest I ever saw. I've always thought that the Cape buffalo is the most dangerous of all big game."

For a moment the general did not reply; he was smiling his curious red-lipped smile. Then he said slowly: "No. You are wrong, sir. The Cape buffalo is not the most dangerous big game." He sipped his wine. "Here in my preserve on this island," he said, in the same slow tone, "I hunt more dangerous game."

Rainsford expressed his surprise. "Is there big game on this island?"

"Oh, it isn't here naturally, of course, I have to stock the island."

"What have you imported, General?" Rainsford asked. "Tigers?"

The general smiled. "No," he said. "Hunting tigers ceased to interest me some years ago. No thrill left in tigers, no real danger. I live for danger, Mr. Rainsford. We will have some capital hunting, you and I. I shall be most glad to have your society."

---

3. cosmopolite: a person at home in all parts of the world.

"But what game——" began Rainsford.

"I'll tell you," said the general. "You will be amused, I know. I think I may say, in all modesty, that I have done a rare thing. I have invented a new sensation."

The general continued: "God makes some men poets. Some He makes kings, some beggars. Me He made a hunter. My hand was made for the trigger, my father said. When I was only five years old he gave me a little gun, specially made in Moscow for me, to shoot sparrows with. I killed my first bear when I was ten. My whole life has been one prolonged hunt. I went into the army and for a time commanded a division of Cossack cavalry, but my real interest was always the hunt. I have hunted every kind of game in every land. It would be impossible for me to tell you how many animals I have killed.

"After the debacle in Russia[4] I left the country, for it was imprudent for an officer of the Tsar to stay there. Luckily, I had invested heavily in American securities, so I shall never have to open a tea room in Monte Carlo or drive a taxi in Paris. Naturally, I continued to hunt—grizzlies in your Rockies, crocodiles in the Ganges, rhinoceroses in East Africa. I went to the Amazon to hunt jaguars, for I had heard that they were unusually cunning. They weren't." The Cossack sighed. "They were no match at all for a hunter with his wits about him, and a high-powered rifle. I was bitterly disappointed. I was lying in my tent with a splitting headache one night when a terrible thought pushed its way into my mind. Hunting was beginning to bore me! And hunting, remember, had been my life. I asked myself why the hunt no longer fascinated me. You are much younger than I am, Mr. Rainsford, and have not hunted as much, but you perhaps can guess the answer."

"What was it?"

"Simply this: hunting had ceased to be what you call 'a sporting proposition.' It had become too easy. I always got my quarry. Always. There is no greater bore than perfection."

The general lit a fresh cigarette. "No animal had a chance with me any more. That is no boast; it is a mathematical certainty. The animal had nothing but his legs and his instinct. Instinct is no match for reason. When I thought of this it was a tragic moment for me, I tell you."

---

4. debacle in Russia; a debacle is a sudden disaster. Zaroff is referring to the Russian Revolution of 1917.

Rainsford leaned across the table, absorbed in what his host was saying.

"It came to me as an inspiration what I must do," the general went on.

"And that was?"

The general smiled the quiet smile of one who has faced an obstacle and surmounted it with success. "I had to invent a new animal to hunt," he said.

"A new animal? You're joking."

"Not at all," said the general. "I never joke about hunting. I bought this island, built this house, and here I do my hunting. The island is perfect for my purposes—there are jungles with a maze of trails in them, hills, swamps—"

"But the animal, General Zaroff?"

"Oh," said the general, "it supplies me with the most exciting hunting in the world. Every day I hunt, and I never grow bored now, for I have a quarry with which I can match my wits."

Rainsford's bewilderment showed in his face.

"I wanted the ideal animal to hunt," explained the general. "So I said: 'What are the attributes of an ideal quarry?' And the answer was, of course: 'It must have courage, cunning, and, above all, it must be able to reason.' "

"But no animal can reason," objected Rainsford.

"My dear fellow," said the general, "there is one that can."

"But you can't mean—" gasped Rainsford.

"And why not?"

"I can't believe you are serious, General Zaroff. This is a grisly joke."

"Why should I not be serious? I am speaking of hunting."

"Hunting? Good God, General Zaroff, what you speak of is murder."

The general laughed. He regarded Rainsford quizzically. "I refuse to believe that so modern a man harbors romantic ideas about the value of human life. Surely your experiences in the war—"

"Did not make me condone cold-blooded murder," finished Rainsford, stiffly.

Laughter shook the general. "How extraordinarily droll you are!" he said. "One does not expect nowadays to find a young man of the educated class, even in America, with such a naïve, and, if I may say so, mid-Victorian point of view. It's like finding a snuffbox in a limousine. I'll wager you'll forget your notions when you go hunting with me. You've a genuine new thrill in store for you, Mr. Rainsford."

"Thank you, I'm a hunter, not a murderer."

"Dear me," said the general, quite unruffled, "again that unpleasant word. But I think I can show you that your scruples are quite ill-founded."

"Yes?"

"Life is for the strong, to be lived by the strong, and if needs be, taken by the strong. The weak of the world were put here to give the strong pleasure. I am strong. Why should I not use my gift? If I wish to hunt, why should I not? I hunt the scum of the earth—sailors from tramp ships—lascars, blacks, Chinese, whites, mongrels—a thoroughbred horse or hound is worth more than a score of them."

"But where do you get them?"

"This island is called Ship Trap," he answered. "Sometimes an angry god of the high seas sends them to me. Sometimes, when Providence is not so kind, I help Providence a bit. Come to the window with me.

"Watch! Out there!" exclaimed the general, pointing into the night. As the general pressed a button, far out to sea Rainsford saw the flash of lights.

The general chuckled. "They indicate a channel," he said, "where there's none: giant rocks with razor edges crouch like a sea monster with wide-open jaws. They can crush a ship as easily as I crush this nut." He dropped a walnut on the hardwood floor and brought his heel grinding down on it. "Oh, yes," he said, casually, as if in answer to a question, "I have electricity. We try to be civilized here."

"Civilized? And you shoot down men?"

A trace of anger was in the general's black eyes, but it was there for but a second, and he said, in his most pleasant manner: "Dear me, what a righteous young man you are! That would be barbarous. I treat these visitors with every consideration. They get plenty of good food and exercise. They get into splendid physical condition. You shall see for yourself tomorrow."

"What do you mean?"

"We'll visit my training school," smiled the general. "It's in the cellar. I have about a dozen pupils down there now. They're from the Spanish bark *Sanlucar* that had the bad luck to go on the rocks out there. A very inferior lot, I regret to say. Poor specimens and more accustomed to the deck than to the jungle."

He raised his hand, and Ivan brought thick Turkish coffee. Rainsford, with an effort, held his tongue in check.

"It's a game, you see," pursued the general, blandly. "I suggest to one of them that we go hunting. I give him a supply of food and an excellent hunting knife. I give him three hours' start. I am to follow, armed only with a pistol of the smallest caliber and range. If my quarry eludes me for three whole days, he wins the game. If I find him"—the general smiled—"he loses."

"Oh," said the general, "I give him his option, of course. If he does not wish to hunt, I turn him over to Ivan. Ivan once had the honor of serving as official knouter[5] to the Great White Tsar,[6] and he has his own ideas of sport. Invariably, Mr. Rainsford, invariably they choose the hunt."

"And if they win?"

The smile on the general's face widened. "To date I have not lost," he said. Then he added, hastily, "I don't wish you to think me a braggart, Mr. Rainsford. Many of them afford only the most elementary sort of problem. Occasionally I strike a tartar.[7] One almost did win. I eventually had to use the dogs."

The general steered Rainsford to a window. The lights from the windows sent a flickering illumination that made grotesque patterns on the courtyard below, and Rainsford could see moving about there a dozen or so huge black shapes; as they turned toward him, their eyes glittered greenly.

"A rather good lot, I think," observed the general. "They are let out at seven every night. If anyone should try to get into my house—or out of it—something extremely regrettable would occur to him." He hummed a snatch of song.

"And now," said the general, "I want to show you my new collection of heads. Will you come with me to the library?"

"I hope," said Rainsford, "that you will excuse me tonight, General. I'm really not feeling at all well."

"Ah, indeed?" the general inquired, solicitously. "Well, I suppose that's only natural, after your long swim. Tomorrow, you'll feel like a new man, I'll wager. Then we'll hunt, eh? I've one rather promising prospect—"

Rainsford was hurrying from the room.

"Sorry you can't go with me tonight," called the general. "I expect rather fair sport—a big, strong black. He looks re-

5. knouter: one who flogs or whips.
6. Tsar: the emperor of Russia before the Revolution.
7. tartar: an expectedly formidable person.

sourceful— Well, good night, Mr. Rainsford; I hope you have a good night's rest."

The bed was good, and the pajamas of the softest silk, and he was tired in every fiber of his being, but nevertheless Rainsford could not quiet his brain with the opiate of sleep. He lay, eyes wide open. Once he thought he heard stealthy steps in the corridor outside his room. He sought to throw open the door; it would not open. He went to the window and looked out. His room was high up in one of the towers. The lights of the chateau were out now and it was dark and silent, but there was a fragment of sallow moon, and by its light he could see, dimly, the courtyard; there, weaving in and out in the pattern of shadow, were black, noiseless forms; the hounds heard him at the window and looked up expectantly, with their green eyes. Rainsford went back to the bed and lay down. He had achieved a doze when just as morning began to come, he heard, far off in the jungle, the faint report of a pistol.

General Zaroff did not appear until luncheon. He was dressed faultlessly in the tweeds of a country squire. He was solicitous about the state of Rainsford's health.

"As for me," sighed the general, "I do not feel so well. I am worried, Mr. Rainsford. Last night I detected traces of my old complaint. The hunting was not good last night. The fellow lost his head. He made a straight trail that offered no problems at all. That's the trouble with these sailors; they have dull brains to begin with, and they do not know how to get about in the woods. It's most annoying."

"General," said Rainsford, firmly, "I wish to leave this island at once."

The general raised his thickets of eyebrows; he seemed hurt. "But, my dear fellow," the general protested, "you've only just come. You've had no hunting—"

"I wish to go today," said Rainsford. He saw the dead black eyes of the general on him, studying him. General Zaroff's face suddenly brightened.

"Tonight," said the general, "we will hunt—you and I."

Rainsford shook his head. "No, General," he said. "I will not hunt."

The general shrugged his shoulders. "As you wish, my friend," he said. "The choice rests entirely with you. But may I not venture to suggest that you will find my idea of sport more diverting than Ivan's?"

"You don't mean—" cried Rainsford.

"My dear fellow," said the general, "have I not told you I always mean what I say about hunting? This is really an inspiration. I drink to a foeman worthy of my steel—at last."

The general raised his glass, but Rainsford sat staring at him.

"You'll find this game worth playing," the general said, enthusiastically. "Your brain against mine. Your woodcraft against mine. Your strength and stamina against mine. And the stake is not without value, eh?"

"And if I win—" began Rainsford huskily.

"I'll cheerfully acknowledge myself defeated if I do not find you by midnight of the third day," said General Zaroff. "My sloop will place you on the mainland near a town. I will give you my word as a gentleman and a sportsman. Of course, you, in turn, must agree to say nóthing of your visit here."

"I'll agree to nothing of the kind," said Rainsford.

"Oh," said the general, "in that case— But why discuss that now?" Then a business-like air animated him. "Ivan," he said to Rainsford, "will supply you with hunting clothes, food, a knife. I suggest you wear moccasins; they leave a poorer trail. I suggest, too, that you avoid the big swamp in the southeast corner of the island. We call it Death Swamp. There's quicksand there. One foolish fellow tried it. The deplorable part of it was that Lazarus followed him. I loved Lazarus; he was the finest hound in my pack. Well, I must beg you to excuse me now. I always take a siesta after lunch. You'll hardly have time for a nap, I fear. You'll want to start, no doubt. I shall not follow till dusk. Hunting at night is so much more exciting than by day, don't you think? Au revoir, Mr. Rainsford, au revoir."

General Zaroff, with a deep, courtly bow, strolled from the room. From another door came Ivan. Under one arm he carried khaki hunting clothes, a haversack of food, a leather sheath containing a long-bladed hunting knife; his right hand rested on a cocked revolver thrust in the crimson sash about his waist.

Rainsford had fought his way through the bush for two hours. "I must keep my nerve. I must keep my nerve," he said, through tight teeth.

He had not been entirely clear-headed when the chateau gates snapped shut behind him. His whole idea at first was to put distance between himself and General Zaroff, and to this end, he had plunged along, spurred on by panic. Now he had got a grip on himself, had stopped, and was taking stock of himself and the situation.

He saw that straight flight was futile; inevitably it would bring him face to face with the sea. "I'll give him a trail to follow," muttered Rainsford, and he struck off from the rude path he had been following into the trackless wilderness.

He executed a series of intricate loops; he doubled on his trail again and again, recalling all the lore of the fox hunt, and all the dodges of the fox. Night found him legweary with hands and face lashed by the branches, on a thickly wooded ridge. A big tree with a thick trunk and outspread branches was near by, and taking care to leave not the slightest mark, he climbed up into the crotch, and stretching out on one of the broad limbs, after a fashion, rested. Rest brought him new confidence and almost a feeling of security. Even so zealous a hunter as General Zaroff could not trace him there, he told himself; only the devil himself could follow that complicated trail through the jungle after dark.

Toward morning, when a dingy gray was varnishing the sky the cry of some startled bird focused Rainsford's attention. Something was coming by the same winding way Rainsford had come. He flattened himself down on the limb, and through a screen of leaves almost as thick as tapestry, he watched. The thing that was approaching was a man.

It was General Zaroff. He made his way along with his eyes fixed in utmost concentration on the ground before him. He paused almost beneath the tree, dropped to his knees, and studied the ground. Rainsford's impulse was to hurl himself down like a panther, but he saw that the general's right hand held something metallic—a small automatic pistol.

The hunter shook his head several times, as if he were puzzled. Then he straightened up and took from his case one of his black cigarettes; its pungent smoke floated up to Rainsford's nostrils.

Rainsford held his breath. The general's eyes had left the ground and were traveling inch by inch up the tree. Rainsford froze there, every muscle tensed for a spring. But the sharp eyes of the hunter stopped before they reached the limb where Rainsford lay; a smile spread over his face. Very deliberately he blew a smoke ring into the air; then he turned his back on the tree and walked carelessly away, back along the trail he had come.

The swish of the underbrush against his hunting boots grew fainter and fainter.

The pent-up air burst hotly from Rainsford's lungs. His first thought made him feel sick and numb. The general could follow a trail through the woods at night; he could follow an extremely difficult trail; only by the merest chance had the Cossack failed to see his quarry.

Rainsford's second thought was even more terrible. Why had the general smiled? Why had he turned back? Rainsford did not want to believe what his reason told him was true. The general was playing with him! The general was saving him for another day's sport! The Cossack was the cat; he was the mouse. Then it was that Rainsford knew the full meaning of terror.

"I will not lose my nerve. I will not."

He slid down from the tree, and struck off again into the woods. His face was set and he forced the machinery of his mind to function. Three hundred yards from his hiding place he stopped where a huge dead tree leaned precariously on a smaller, living one. Throwing off his sack of food Rainsford took his knife from its sheath and began to work with all his energy.

The job was finished at last, and he threw himself down behind a fallen log a hundred feet away. He did not have to wait long. The cat was coming again to play with the mouse.

Following the trail with the sureness of a bloodhound came General Zaroff. Nothing escaped those searching black eyes, no crushed blade of grass, no bent twig, no mark, no matter how faint, in the moss. So intent was the Cossack on his stalking that he was upon the thing Rainsford had made before he saw it. His foot touched the protruding bough that was the trigger. Even as he touched it, the general sensed his danger and leaped back with the agility of an ape. But he was not quite quick enough; the dead tree struck the general a glancing blow on the shoulder as it fell; he staggered, but he did not fall; nor did he drop his revolver. He stood there, rubbing his injured shoulder, and Rainsford, with fear again gripping his heart, heard the general's mocking laugh ring through the jungle.

"Rainsford," called the general, "if you are within sound of my voice, as I suppose you are, let me congratulate you. Not many men know how to make a Malay man-catcher. Luckily for me, I too have hunted in Malacca. You are proving of interest, Mr. Rainsford. I am going now to have my wound dressed; it's only a slight one. But I shall be back. I shall be back."

When the general, nursing his bruised shoulder, had gone,

Rainsford took up his flight again. It was flight now, a desperate, hopeless flight. Dusk came, then darkness, and still he pressed on. The ground grew softer under his moccasins; the vegetation grew ranker, denser; insects bit him savagely. Then, as he stepped forward, his foot sank into the ooze. He tried to wrench it back, but the muck sucked viciously at his foot. With a violent effort he tore his foot loose. He knew where he was now. Death Swamp and its quicksand. The softness of the earth gave him an idea. He stepped back from the quicksand a dozen feet or so and began to dig. The pit grew deeper; when it was above his shoulders, he climbed out and from some hard saplings cut stakes and sharpened them to a fine point. These stakes he planted in the bottom of the pit with the points sticking up. With flying fingers he wove a rough carpet of weeds and branches and with it he covered the mouth of the pit. Then, wet with sweat and aching with tiredness, he crouched behind the stump of a lightning-charred tree.

He knew his pursuer was coming; he heard the padding sound of feet on the soft earth, and the night breeze brought him the perfume of the general's cigarette. Rainsford, crouching there, lived a year in a minute. Then he felt an impulse to cry aloud with joy, for he heard the sharp crackle of the breaking branches as the cove of the pit gave way; he heard the sharp scream of pain as the pointed stakes found their mark. He leaped up from his place of concealment. Then he cowered back. Three feet from the pit a man was standing, with an electric torch[8] in his hand.

"You've done well, Rainsford," the voice of the general called. "Your Burmese tiger pit has claimed one of my best dogs. Again you score. I think, Mr. Rainsford, I'll see what you can do against my whole pack. I'm going home for a rest now. Thank you for a most amusing evening."

At daybreak Rainsford, lying near the swamp, was awakened by a sound that made him know that he had new things to learn about fear. It was the baying of a pack of hounds. For a moment he stood there, thinking. An idea that held a wild chance came to him, and tightening his belt, he headed away from the swamp.

The baying of the hounds drew nearer, then still nearer, nearer, ever nearer. On a ridge Rainsford climbed a tree. Down a watercourse, not a quarter of a mile away, he could see the

---

8. electric torch: flashlight.

bush moving. Straining his eyes, he saw the lean figure of General Zaroff; just ahead of him, Rainsford made out another figure whose wide shoulders surged through the tall jungle weeds; it was the giant Ivan, holding the pack in leash.

They would be on him any minute now. His mind worked frantically. He thought of a native trick he had learned in Uganda. He slid down the tree. He caught hold of a springy young sapling and to it he fastened his hunting knife, with the blade pointing down the trail; with a bit of wild grapevine he tied back the sapling. Then he ran for his life. The hounds raised their voices as they hit the fresh scent.

He had to stop to get his breath. The baying of the hounds stopped abruptly, and Rainsford's heart stopped, too. They must have reached the knife.

He shinnied excitedly up a tree and looked back, but the hope in his brain died, for he saw in the shallow valley that General Zaroff was still on his feet. Ivan was not. The knife, driven by the recoil of the springing tree, had not wholly failed.

Rainsford had hardly tumbled to the ground when the pack took up the cry again.

"Nerve, nerve, nerve!" he panted, as he dashed along. A blue gap showed between the trees dead ahead. Rainsford forced himself on toward that gap. It was the shore of the sea. Across a cove he could see the gloomy gray stone of the chateau. Twenty feet below him the sea rumbled and hissed. Rainsford hesitated. He heard the hounds. Then he leaped far out into the sea. . . .

When the general and his pack reached the place by the sea, the Cossack stopped. For some minutes he stood regarding the blue-green expanse of water. He shrugged his shoulders. Then he sat down, took a drink of brandy from a silver flask, and hummed a bit from "Madame Butterfly."

General Zaroff had an exceedingly good dinner in his great paneled dining hall that evening. Two slight annoyances kept him from perfect enjoyment. One was the thought that it would be difficult to replace Ivan; the other was that his quarry had escaped him. In his library he read, to soothe himself, from the works of Marcus Aurelius. At ten he went up to his bedroom. He was deliciously tired, he said to himself, as he locked himself in. There was a little moonlight, so before turning on his light he went to the window and looked down at the courtyard. He could see the great hounds, and he called: "Better luck another time," to them. Then he switched on the light.

A man who had been hiding in the curtains of the bed was

standing there.

"Rainsford!" cried the general. "How in God's name did you get here?"

"Swam," said Rainsford. "I found it quicker than walking the jungle."

The general sucked in his breath and smiled. "I congratulate you," he said. "You have won the game."

Rainsford did not smile. "I am still a beast at bay," he said, in a low, hoarse voice. "Get ready, General Zaroff."

The general made one of his deepest bows. "I see," he said. "Splendid! One of us is to furnish a repast for the hounds. The other will sleep in this very excellent bed. On guard, Rainsford...."

He had never slept in a better bed, Rainsford decided.

QUESTIONS FOR DISCUSSION AND WRITING

1. What details right at the beginning of the story let you know that Rainsford is a man of leisure and of action?
2. From the moment Rainsford meets Zaroff, their relationship is formal, polite, elegant. Find details that show this. How does all this elegance and politeness heighten the effect of the rest of the story?
3. What does Zaroff mean when he says on page 212, "Instinct is no match for reason"? Also, what is striking about his use of the verb *stock* on page 211?
4. Find the line that shows that Zaroff's game is *man*. After Rainsford (and the reader) make that discovery, Richard Connell slowly builds up the horror of the situatin for Rainsford. By what details and information does he do it? Find the line where Rainsford at last realizes that he himself is the man now to be hunted.
5. During the hunt, Zaroff and Rainsford meet, or almost meet, five times. Who wins the contest each time? Explain how or why. Explain how one of the meetings shows that Zaroff enjoys the sport of the hunt more than the act of killing.
6. What finally happened to General Zaroff? How do you know?

SUGGESTIONS FOR FURTHER WRITING OR DISCUSSION

1. Tell about a person whose life is dominated by a single passion or desire, as General Zaroff's was dominated by his passion for the hunt.
2. Zaroff and Rainsford are engaged in a contest of wits and cleverness, and a contest of physical skill. Tell about an experience you have had involving a contest of brain or of body, or make up a story about such a contest.
3. "The Most Dangerous Game" is really a "tall story," one in which the characters and happenings are so exaggerated that they never could be real, real though they might seem while you are caught up in the story. Some movies and TV programs are also tall stories as are the Paul Bunyan stories which you may have read. Write a tall story of your own, in which you don't worry about its seeming true but in which it is the very lack of reality that gives the reader his pleasure.

Who Needs Help?

A British nurse in India faces a stubborn, dying man.
Three housewives help a poor old man.

SISTER MALONE AND THE OBSTINATE MAN

by Rumer Godden

Sister Malone, a British nurse in India, needs all her faith and character to face the horrors of accident and disease that passed under her hands each day. She criticizes her patients for their lack of faith, but upon meeting a man whose faith really sustains him, how does she react?

Sister Malone had an extraordinary capacity for faith. She was in charge of the Out-patients in the Elizabeth Scott Memorial Hospital for Women and Children which was run in this suburb of Calcutta[1] by the Order to which she belonged. She needed her faith. Terrible things passed under her hands.

All sorts of patients came in all sorts of vehicles: rickshaws, curtained or uncurtained, hired carriages that had shutters to close them into boxes, a taxi with an accident case lying on the floor so that its blood should not soil the cushions, perhaps a case that the taxi itself had run over—it was astonishing how often taxis did run over patients. A few came pillion[2] on a bicycle; some could walk and some were carried; there were fathers carrying children, mothers carrying children, small children carrying smaller children. Sometimes whole families brought one patient; servants of the rich brought their charges, or their mistress, or brought themselves. There were Hindu women in *purdah*;[3] Mohammedan women in *burkas*, white coverings like a tent that hid them from their heads to the ground; and hill women walking free as did the beggar women; there were high-caste, low-caste, untouchables,[4] and all colours of skin, dark,

1. Calcutta: largest city in India.
2. pillion: sitting behind the rider.
3. in purdah: screened from the world; veiled.
4. untouchables: members of a lower caste (class) whose touch was believed by the Hindus to defile (make spiritually unclean) members of a higher caste.

brown, pale, and all sorts of flesh, soft, pampered, thin, withered, sweet, ill-treated.

There were diseased women, diseased children, burnt children, very, very often burnt children; even more often there were tubercular children: deep and dreadful tubercular abscesses on breasts and groins and armpits were common. There was a great deal of ophthalmia and rickets and scabies, cases of leprosy and poisoning and fevers, and broken bones made septic[5] by neglect or wounds treated with dung, and oozing pus. There were bites from rabid dogs and sometimes bites from human beings, and, like a repeating chorus, always burns and tuberculosis. This was not the result of famine nor of war, this was everyday, an everyday average in one of the departments of one of the hospitals in the city; an everyday sample of its pain and poverty and indifference and the misuse of its human beings. Sister Malone certainly needed that extraordinary faith.

The Sisters who were detailed to help her always asked to be transferred after a few months; they became haunted and could not sleep, but Sister Malone had worked here for seven years. '*Sister*, how *can* you? I . . . You . . . I . . . I cannot bear it, Sister.'

'You must have faith,' said Sister Malone, and she quoted, as she had quoted a hundred, hundred times, ' "And now abideth these three, faith, hope and charity." ' She paused, looking through the thick lenses of her glasses that had the effect of making her look a little blind. 'God forgive me for differing,' said Sister Malone, 'but you know, dear, the greatest to me is faith.' Then a question, a little, persistent question sometimes reared its head: was Sister Malone, then, lacking a little in charity, a little unsympathetic? Surely not. She was so splendid with the patients, though there was one small sign that no one noticed; the patients called her '*Didi*,' 'Sister'; she spoke of them as 'they' a race apart. 'If only,' she said, and she said this continually, 'if only they could have a little faith for themselves!'

She tried to give it to them. In the corner of the treatment-room there was a shelf on which lay paper-covered gospels translated into Hindi, Bengali, Urdu, and Ghurkali. Sister Malone gave one to every patient. She walked sincerely in what she believed to be the footsteps of Christ. 'It is seeing so much eye-trou-

---

5. septic: rotten.

ble and lepers,' said Sister Malone, 'that makes it so very vivid. Of course Our Lord knew that lepers are not nearly as infectious as is commonly thought. People are *so* mistaken about lepers,' said Sister Malone earnestly, 'I have always thought it a pity to use the word "unclean." I have known some quite clean lepers. Think of it, dear,' she said wistfully. 'He put out His hand and touched them and made them whole. So quick, and here it is such a slow, slow business. But of course,' she said and sighed, 'they need to have faith.'

Sister Malone herself was a small, firm, flat woman. Her hands probably knew more of actual India, had probed it more deeply, than any politician's brain. These implements—yes, implements, because the dictionary definition of 'implement' is 'whatever may fill up or supply a want' and that was a good description of Sister Malone's hands—these implements were small and flat and firm; they needed to be firm.

At eight o'clock one blinding white-hot morning in June, just before the break of the rains, Sister Malone, Sister Shelley and Sister Latch walked into the treatment-room. Over their white habits, black girdles and the ebony crucifixes on their breasts, they put on aprons; the crosses showed through the bibs. They turned up their sleeves and went across to the sink, where the tap ran perpetually, to scrub their hands, nails, wrists and forearms, afterwards immersing them in a basin of water and disinfectant.

Sister Shelley and Sister Latch were the two nuns detailed to help in the treatment-room at that time. Sister Shelley was pale, her face drawn and sensitive between the bands of her coif; her eyes looked as if she had a headache. Sister Latch was newly out from home. Her steps were firm and certain, her pink face was made pinker by the heat, her body, well fed, solid, was already sweating through her clothes. She was cheerful and observant and sensible and interested. It was her first morning with the Out-patients.

Through the window, as she scrubbed her hands, she noticed two little green parakeets tumbling into a golmohur tree. She would have liked to have drawn the other Sisters' attention to them but she did not dare.

The Out-patients was divided into the doctor's rooms, the waiting-hall, the dispensary and the treatment-room, which had a small examination-room leading off it. The patients waited in the hall that was furnished only by pictures; they sat in rows on the floor. They went to the doctor in turn and then, with their tickets in their hands, were admitted to the dispensary for free medicine, or to the treatment-room for dressings, examination, slight operations or emergency treatment. 'You let no one in without a ticket,' said Sister Malone to Sister Latch, 'and you treat no one unless the ticket bears today's date and the doctor's signature. You can let the first two in.'

Sister Latch went eagerly to the door. There was already a crowd and it pressed round the door, a collection of dark faces, clothes and rags and nakedness and smells. Sister Latch held up two fingers and cried 'Two,' in her new Bengali, but seven edged past her into the room. 'It's all right,' said Sister Shelley in her even, toneless voice, 'there are only two. The others are relations,' and she set to work.

The first case was nothing remarkable, a septic ear; a woman of the sweeper caste sat herself down on a stool and, clasping her ankles until she was bent almost double, inclined her head to her shoulder so that Sister Shelley could conveniently clean her ear. Sister Malone was poulticing,[6] in a woman's armpit, an abscess which had been opened the day before.

The next two patients came and then another, an old woman. 'You can attend to her,' said Sister Shelley to Sister Latch. 'She is an old case and knows what to do.' Sister Latch went slowly up to the old woman. She was an old, under-dressed crone,[7] wound in a meagre grey-white cotton sari that showed her naked waist and withered, filthy breasts; her head was shaved and her feet were bare. She sat down on a stool and began to unwind an enormous, dirty bandage on her thumb.

'Don't do that,' said Sister Latch. 'Let me.'

'*Nahin, baba,*' said the old woman, unwinding steadily, 'you fetch the bowl for it to soak in.'

Sister Latch had not been called 'child' before. A little piqued she looked round. 'That is the bowl,' said the old woman, pointing to a kidney-dish on the table. 'The hot water is there, and there is the medicine.' She had come to the last of the bandage and she shut her eyes. 'You can pull it off,' she said. 'It makes me sick.'

Sister Latch pulled, and a tremor shook her that seemed to open a fissure, a crevasse from her knees through her stomach to her heart. The thumb was a stump, swollen, gangrened. 'It—it makes me sick, too,' said poor Sister Latch, and ran out.

---

6. poulticing: putting on a wet, hot dressing to draw out infection.
7. crone: wrinkled old woman; hag.

When she came back the thumb was soaking and Sister Shelley was preparing the dressing. 'She is a maidservant in a rich house,' said Sister Shelley without emotion, 'and they make her go on working, scouring cooking-pots and washing-up; with the thumb continually in water of course it cannot heal.'

Sister Latch was dumb with indignation and pity.

At that moment Sister Malone came bustling back. 'Ah, Tarala!' she said to the old woman in Bengali. 'Well, how's your disgraceful thumb?' She took it gently from the bath. 'Ah, it's better!' she examined it. 'It *is* better. It actually is. Look, Sister, do you see how its beginning to slough off here? Isn't that wonderful? Give me the scissors. Now the dressing, Sister, quickly.' Her fingers wound on the bandage swiftly and steadily. She finished and lifted the hand and put it in the bosom of the *sari*. 'There, that's beautiful,' she said, and the old woman crept out, still seared with pain but comforted.

'But *how* can it heal?' asked Sister Latch, with tears in her sympathetic eyes. 'What is the use?'

'We must hope for the best,' said Sister Malone.

Sister Shelley was silent.

'We must temper our work with faith,' said Sister Malone, emptying the kidney-dish. Through being steeped in ritual and reality Sister Malone's words were often accidentally beautiful. 'We must have faith for them, Sister Latch dear. Sister Shelley, this child is for operation.' She put a piece of brown paper under the child's dusty feet as he lay on the table. He began to scream as Sister Shelley cleaned his face.

The abscess on his forehead was like a rhinoceros horn; he was a dark little boy, and the skin round the abscess was stretched and strained with colours of olive green and fig purple. His eyes rolled with fright, showing the whites, and the muscles of his stomach were drawn in, and tensed into the shape of a cave under his ribs. He screamed continually in short, shrill screams as the doctor came.

Suddenly Sister Shelley began to scream as well. She was holding the boy's hands out of the way while Sister Malone cleaned his forehead, and now she beat them on the table. 'Stop that noise!' she screamed. 'Stop that! Stop! Stop! Stop that noise!' Sister Malone knocked her hands away, spun her round by the shoulders and marched her outside, then came in quickly and shut the doors. 'Take her place, Sister Latch,' she said curtly. 'The doctor is here.'

'But—no anaesthetic?' asked Sister Latch.

'There's no money for anaesthetics for a small thing like this.' said Sister Malone sadly. 'Never mind,' she added firmly, 'it is over in a minute.'

The morning went on growing steadily hotter, the smells steadily stronger, the light more blind and white. The heat in the treatment-room was intense, and both Sisters were wet, their hands clammy. In half an hour Sister Shelley, made curiously empty and blank by her tears, came back. Sister Malone said nothing. The patients came in until Sister Latch lost count of them, the wounds and the sores and disease and shame were shown and the room echoed with cries, screams and tears . . . rivers of tears, thought Sister Latch.

Then in the middle of the hubbub quiet descended.

A car had driven up, a large car, and from it two young men had jumped down, calling for a stretcher. They were two well-dressed young Hindus in white, and between them they lifted from the car something small and fragile and very still, wrapped in vivid violet and green. Sister Latch saw a fall of long black hair.

The stretcher was brought straight into the treatment-room and the girl was lifted from it to the table. She lay inert, with the brilliant colours heaped round her. Her face was a pale oval turned up to the ceiling, her mouth white brown, her nostrils wide as if they were stamped with fright, and her eyes open, glazed, the pupils enormous. Her hair hung to the floor and she was very young. 'Seventeen?' asked Sister Latch aloud. 'Or sixteen? How beautiful she is.' She looked again and cried, 'Sister, she is dead.'

'She is breathing,' said Sister Malone. Her flat little hand was spread on the girl's breast.

One of the young men was terribly unnerved. Sister Latch wondered if he were the husband. He shivered as he stood waiting by the table. 'She t-took her l-life,' he said involuntarily.

The other man, darker, stronger, said sternly, 'Be quiet.'

'And why? Why?' said Sister Malone's glasses, but her lips said evenly, 'Well, she didn't succeed. She is breathing.'

'You th-think th-there is—hope?'

'There is always hope,' said Sister Malone, 'while there is breath.'

Then the doctor and orderlies came in with pails and the stomach-pump and the young men were sent out of the room. Sister Shelley went to the window and stood there with her back to everyone; Sister Malone, after a glance at her, let her stand.

'You will have to help me,' said Sister Malone to Sister Latch. 'Be strong.'

'But—only tell me what it is *about*. I don't understand,' cried Sister Latch, quite out of herself. 'I don't understand.'

'She has poisoned herself,' said Sister Malone. 'Opium poisoning. Look at her eyes.'

'But why?' cried Sister Latch again. 'Why? She is so young. So beautiful. Why should she?'

''It—is best not to be too curious.'

'Yes,' said Sister Shelley suddenly, still with her back to them. 'Don't ask. Don't understand. Only try and drag her back— for more.'

After a time the doctor paused; waited; bent; waited another minute; stood up and slowly, still carefully, began to withdraw the tube.

'No?' cried Sister Malone, her hands suddenly still.

'Yes,' said the doctor, and the last of the hideous tube came from the girl's mouth. He wiped her chin and gently closed her mouth and drew down her lids, but the mouth would not stay closed; it dropped open in an O that looked childish and dismayed, inadequate to the sternness of the oval of the face and sealed lids. 'Snuffed out,' said Sister Malone, as she stood up and gently put the draperies back and looked down on the girl's shut face. 'They have nothing to sustain them,' said Sister Malone, 'nothing at all.'

Sister Latch began to cry quietly. The young men came in and carried the girl away and, from the window, Sister Shelley and Sister Latch saw the car drive away, with a last sight of violet and green on the back seat. A tear slid down Sister Latch's cheek. 'Forgive me,' said Sister Latch, but no one answered; her tears slid unnoticed into that great river. 'Forgive me,' said Sister Latch 'she wore . . . exactly the same green . . . as those little parrots.'

She stood in tears, Sister Shelley seemed chiselled in stone, but Sister Malone was tidying up the room for the next patients. 'Nothing to sustain them,' said Sister Malone, and sighed.

At the very end of the morning, when they had finished and taken off their aprons, an old man came into the waiting-hall from the doctor's room. He moved very slowly and led a small girl by the hand; he held his ticket uncertainly between his finger and thumb as if he did not know what to do with it.

'Another!' said Sister Shelley. 'It is too late.'

'No,' said Sister Malone with her faithful exactness. 'It wants one minute to one o'clock when we should stop.' And she took the paper. 'It is nothing,' she said, 'only stitches to be taken out of a cut on the child's lip. I remember her now. You may go, Sisters. It won't take me five minutes.'

Sister was left with the man and the child.

As she lifted the scissors from the steriliser with the forceps she caught his gaze fixed on her and she saw that he was not old, only emaciated until his flesh had sunken in. His skin was a curious dead grey-brown.

'You are ill,' said Sister Malone.

'I am ill,' the man agreed, his voice calm.

Sister Malone turned the little girl to the light. The child began to whimper and the man to plead with her in a voice quite different from the one he had used when he had spoken of himself. 'She will not hurt you. *Nahin. Nahin. Nahin.*'

'Of course I will not hurt you if you stand still," said Sister Malone to the child. 'Hold her shoulders.'

The child gave two cries as the stitches came out but she did not move, though the tears ran out of her eyes and the sweat ran off the man. When it was over and he could release his hands, he staggered. Sister Malone thought he would have fallen if she had not caught him and helped him to a stool. His arm was burning.

'You have fever,' said Sister Malone.

'I continually have fever,' said the man.

'What is it you have?' asked Sister Malone.

'God knows,' he answered, but as if he were satisfied, not wondering.

'You don't know? But you are very ill. Haven't you seen the doctor?'

'No.'

'Then you must come with me at once,' said Sister Malone energetically. 'I will take you to the doctor.'

'I do not need a doctor.'

'But—how can we know what to do for you? How can you know?'

'I do not need to know.'

'But you should have medicine . . . treatment.'

He smiled. 'I have my medicine.'

His smile was so peculiarly calm that it made Sister Malone pause. She looked at him silently, searchingly. He smiled again and opened the front of his shirt and showed her where round his neck, hung a silver charm on a red thread of the sort she saw every day and all day long round the necks of men and women and children. He held it and turned his face upwards and his eyes. 'My medicine,' he said, 'God.'

Sister Malone suddenly flushed. 'That's absurd,' she said. 'You will die.'

'If I die I am happy.'

'But, man!' cried Sister Malone. 'You mean you will give yourself up without a struggle?'

'Why should I struggle?'

'Come with me to the doctor.'

'No.'

'That's sheer senseless obstinacy,' cried Sister Malone. 'If you won't come, let me fetch him to you.'

'No.'

'Obstinate! Obstinate!' Her eyes behind her glasses looked bewildered and more than ever blind. Then they fell on the child. 'You came for her,' she said, 'then why not for yourself?'

'She is too young to choose her path. I have chosen.' There was a silence. 'Come, Joya,' he said gently, 'greet the Sister Sahib and we shall go.'

'Wait. Wait one minute. If you won't listen to me, let the doctor talk to you. He is wise and good. Let him talk to you.'

She had barred his way and the old man seemed to grow more dignified and a little stern. 'Let me go,' he said. 'I have told you. I need nothing. I have everything. I have God.'

Sister Malone, left alone, was furious as she washed her hands; her face was red and her glasses glittered. 'Mumbo-jumbo!'[8] she said furiously as she turned the tap off. 'Mumbo-jumbo! Heavens! What an obstinate man!'

8. mumbo-jumbo: confusing, meaningless superstition (from the supposedly meaningless words of tribal witch doctors).

QUESTIONS FOR DISCUSSION AND WRITING

1. After Rumer Godden describes the horrible things that Sister Malone has to face daily, she has Sister Malone quote the Bible: "And now abideth . . . faith, hope and charity." Re-read the passage and then explain how it shows Sister Malone to have not only great strength, but also a weakness. What was her weakness?

2. Sister Malone was coolly competent. Why does Miss Godden use the word *implements* to refer to her hands?
3. When the old crone with the infected thumb comes in, how do the different sisters react: Sister Latch, Sister Shelley, and Sister Malone? Who reacts most realistically? Most helpfully? Explain. What does Sister Latch mean when she asks, "What is the use?"
4. How do the sisters react to the failure to save the life of the girl who attempted suicide? Think of the various crises Sister Malone meets. How do you explain her reaction to each of them?
5. The old man, near the end, says (on page 233), "I have my medicine;...Why should I struggle?...I have chosen;" and "I have God." What does he mean by each of these statements?
6. Why was Sister Malone furious at the old man? Why did her eyes look bewildered? Why does she call the old man's faith "mumbo-jumbo"?
7. Throughout the story Sister Malone has been complaining that the people she treats have no faith to sustain them. Then she meets a man who has absolute faith, and it defeats and angers her. This is *irony*. Explain. (Look up the word in the dictionary if you need to.)

SUGGESTIONS FOR FURTHER WRITING OR DISCUSSION

1. Describe an experience you have had in a hospital or an injury or disease you had; or write a story about such an experience.
2. What is faith? Explain something, or some things, you have faith in. Try to make your reader understand your faith and why you hold it.

COME DANCE WITH ME IN IRELAND

by Shirley Jackson

Three women are gossiping in young Mrs. Archer's apartment when a poor old man collapses at the door. Why does the old man react as he does at the end? Who needs help?

Young Mrs. Archer was sitting on the bed with Kathy Valentine and Mrs. Corn, playing with the baby and gossiping, when the door bell rang. Mrs. Archer, saying, "Oh, dear!" went to push the buzzer that released the outside door of the apartment building. "We *had* to live on the ground floor," she called to Kathy and Mrs. Corn. "Everybody rings our bell for everything."

When the inner doorbell rang she opened the door of the apartment and saw an old man standing in the outer hall. He was wearing a long, shabby black overcoat and had a square white beard. He held out a handful of shoelaces.

"Oh," Mrs. Archer said. "Oh, I'm terribly sorry, but—"

"Madam," the old man said, "if you would be so kind. A nickel apiece."

Mrs. Archer shook her head and backed away. "I'm afraid not," she said.

"Thank you anyway, Madam," he said, "for speaking courteously. The first person on this block who has been decently polite to a poor old man."

Mrs. Archer turned the doorknob back and forth nervously. "I'm awfully sorry," she said. Then, as he turned to go, she said, "Wait a minute," and hurried into the bedroom. "Old man selling shoelaces," she whispered. She pulled open the top dresser drawer, took out her pocketbook, and fumbled in the change purse. "'Quarter," she said. "Think it's all right?"

"Sure," Kathy said. "Probably more than he's gotten all day." She was Mrs. Archer's age, and unmarried. Mrs. Corn was a stout woman in her middle fifties. They both lived in the building and spent a good deal of time at Mrs. Archer's, on account of the baby.

Mrs. Archer returned to the front door. "Here," she said, holding out the quarter. "I think it's a shame everyone was so rude."

The old man started to offer her some shoelaces, but his hand shook and the shoelaces dropped to the floor. He leaned heavily against the wall. Mrs. Archer watched, horrified. "Good Lord," she said, and put out her hand. As her fingers touched the dirty old overcoat she hesitated and then, tightening her lips, she put her arm firmly through his and tried to help him through the doorway. "Girls," she called, "come help me, quick!"

Kathy came running out of the bedroom, saying, "Did you call, Jean?" and then stopped dead, staring.

"What'll I do!" Mrs. Archer said, standing with her arm through the old man's. His eyes were closed and he seemed barely able, with her help, to stand on his feet. "For heaven's sake, grab him on the other side."

"Get him to a chair or something," Kathy said. The hall was too narrow for all three of them to go down side by side, so Kathy took the old man's other arm and half-led Mrs. Archer and him into the living-room. "Not in the good chair," Mrs. Archer exclaimed. "In the old leather one." They dropped the old man into the leather chair and stood back. "What on earth do we do now?" Mrs. Archer said.

"Do you have any whiskey?" Kathy asked.

Mrs. Archer shook her head. "A little wine," she said doubtfully.

Mrs. Corn came into the living-room, holding the baby. "Gracious!" she said. "He's drunk!"

"Nonsense," Kathy said. "I wouldn't have let Jean bring him in if he were."

"Watch out for the baby, Blanche," Mrs. Archer said.

"Naturally," Mrs. Corn said. "We're going back into the bedroom, honey," she said to the baby, "and then we're going to get into our lovely crib and go beddy-bye."

The old man stirred and opened his eyes. He tried to get up.

"Now you stay right where you are," Kathy ordered, "and Mrs. Archer here is going to bring you a little bit of wine. You'd like that, wouldn't you?"

The old man raised his eyes to Kathy. "Thank you," he said.

Mrs. Archer went into the kitchen. After a moment's thought she took the glass from over the sink, rinsed it out, and poured some sherry into it. She took the glass of sherry back into the living-room and handed it to Kathy.

"Shall I hold it for you or can you drink by yourself?" Kathy asked the old man.

"You are much too kind," he said, and reached for the glass. Kathy steadied it for him as he sipped from it, and then he pushed it away.

"That's enough, thank you," he said. "Enough to revive me." He tried to rise. "Thank you," he said to Mrs. Archer, "and thank *you*," to Kathy. "I had better be going along."

"Not until you're quite firm on your feet," Kathy said. "Can't afford to take chances, you know."

The old man smiled. "*I* can afford to take chances," he said.

Mrs. Corn came back into the living-room. "Baby's in his crib," she said, "and just about asleep already. Does *he* feel better now? I'll bet he was just drunk or hungry or something."

"Of course he was," Kathy said, fired by the idea. "He was hungry. That's what was wrong all the time, Jean. How silly we were. Poor old gentleman!" she said to the old man. "Mrs. Archer is certainly not going to let you leave here without a full meal inside of you."

Mrs. Archer looked doubtful. "I have some eggs," she said.

"Fine!" Kathy said. "Just the thing. They're easily digested," she said to the old man, "and especially good if you haven't eaten for"—she hesitated—"for a while."

"Black coffee," Mrs. Corn said, "if you ask me. Look at his hands shake."

"Nervous exhaustion," Kathy said firmly. "A nice hot cup of bouillon is all he needs to be good as ever, and he has to drink it very slowly until his stomach gets used to food again. The stomach," she told Mrs. Archer and Mrs. Corn, "shrinks when it remains empty for any great period of time."

"I would rather not trouble you," the old man said to Mrs. Archer.

"Nonsense," Kathy said. "We've got to see that you get a good hot meal to go on with." She took Mrs. Archer's arm and began to walk her out to the kitchen. "Just some eggs," she said. "Fry four or five. I'll get you half a dozen later. I don't suppose you have any bacon. I'll tell you, fry up a few potatoes too. He won't care if they're half-raw. These people eat things like heaps of fried potatoes and eggs and—"

"There's some canned figs left over from lunch," Mrs. Archer said. "I was wondering what to do with them."

"I've got to run back and keep an eye on him," Kathy said. "He might faint again or something. You just fry up those eggs and potatoes. I'll send Blanche out if she'll come."

Mrs. Archer measured out enough coffee for two cups and set the pot on the stove. Then she took out her frying pan. "Kathy," she said, "I'm just a little worried. If he really is drunk, I mean, and if Jim should hear about it, with the baby here and everything. . . ."

"Why, Jean!" Kathy said. "You should live in the country for a while, I guess. Women always give out meals to starving men. And you don't need to *tell* Jim. Blanche and I certainly won't say anything."

"Well," said Mrs. Archer, "you're sure he isn't drunk?"

"I know a starving man when I see one," Kathy said. "When an old man like that can't stand up and his hands shake and he looks so funny, that means he's starving to death. Literally starving."

"Oh, my!" said Mrs. Archer. She hurried to the cupboard under the sink and took out two potatoes. "Two enough, do you think? I guess we're really doing a good deed."

Kathy giggled. "Just a bunch of Girl Scouts," she said. She started out of the kitchen, and then she stopped and turned around. "You have any pie? They always eat pie."

"It was for dinner, though," Mrs. Archer said.

"Oh, give it to him," Kathy said. "We can run out and get some more after he goes."

While the potatoes were frying, Mrs. Archer put a plate, a cup and saucer, and a knife and fork and spoon on the dinette table. Then, as an afterthought, she picked up the dishes and, taking a paper bag out of a cupboard, tore it in half and spread it smoothly on the table and put the dishes back. She got a glass and filled it with water from the bottle in the refrigerator, cut three slices of bread and put them on a plate, and then cut a small square of butter and put it on the plate with the bread. Then she got a paper napkin from the box in the cupboard and put it beside the plate, took it up after a minute to fold it into a triangular shape, and put it back. Finally she put the pepper and salt shakers on the table and got out a box of eggs. She went to the door and called, "Kathy! Ask him how does he want his eggs fried?"

There was a murmur of conversation in the living-room and Kathy called back, "Sunny side up!"

Mrs. Archer took out four eggs and then another and broke them one by one into the frying-pan. When they were done she called out,

"All right, girls! Bring him in!"

Mrs. Corn came into the kitchen, inspected the plate of potatoes and eggs, and looked at Mrs. Archer without speaking. Then Kathy came, leading the old man by the arm. She escorted him to the table and sat him down in a chair. "There," she said. "Now, Mrs. Archer's fixed you a lovely hot meal."

The old man looked at Mrs. Archer. "I'm very grateful," he said.

"Isn't that nice!" Kathy said. She nodded approvingly at Mrs. Archer. The old man regarded the plate of eggs and potatoes. "Now pitch right in," Kathy said. "Sit down, girls, I'll get a chair from the bedroom."

The old man picked up the salt and shook it gently over the eggs. "This looks delicious," he said finally.

"You just go right ahead and eat," Kathy said, reappearing with a chair. "We want to see you get filled up. Pour him some coffee, Jean."

Mrs. Archer went to the stove and took up the coffee-pot.

"Please don't bother," he said.

"That's all right," Mrs. Archer said, filling the old man's cup. She sat down at the table. The old man picked up the fork and then put it down again to take up the paper napkin and spread it carefully over his knees.

"What's your name?" Kathy asked.

"O'Flaherty, Madam. John O'Flaherty."

"Well, John," Kathy said, "I am Miss Valentine and this lady is Mrs. Archer and the other one is Mrs. Corn."

"How do you do?" the old man said.

"I gather you're from the old country," Kathy said.

"I beg your pardon?"

"Irish, aren't you?" Kathy said.

"I am, Madam." The old man plunged the fork into one of the eggs and watched the yolk run out onto the plate. "I knew Yeats,"[1] he said suddenly.

"Really?" Kathy said, leaning forward. "Let me see—he was the writer, wasn't he?"

" 'Come out of charity, come dance with me in Ireland,' "[2] the old man said. He rose and, holding on to the chair back,

---

1. William Butler Yeats: famous Irish poet and playwright.
2. Lines from a poem of Yeats, "I Am of Ireland." The first stanza goes:
   "I am of Ireland,
   And the Holy Land of Ireland,
   And time runs on," cried she.
   "Come out of charity,
   Come dance with me in Ireland."

bowed solemnly to Mrs. Archer, "Thank you again, Madam, for your generosity." He turned and started for the front door. The three women got up and followed him.

"But you didn't finish," Mrs. Corn said.

"The stomach," the old man said, "as this lady has pointed out, shrinks. Yes, indeed," he went on eminiscently, "I knew Yeats."

At the front door he turned and said to Mrs. Archer, "Your kindness should not go unrewarded." He gestured to the shoe-laces lying on the floor. "These," he said, "are for you. For your kindness. Divide them with the other ladies."

"But I wouldn't dream—" Mrs. Archer began.

"I insist," the old man said, opening the door. "A small re-turn, but all that I have to offer. Pick them up yourself," he added abruptly. Then he turned and thumbed his nose at Mrs. Corn. "I hate old women," he said.

"Well!" said Mrs. Corn faintly.

"I may have imbibed[3] somewhat freely," the old man said to Mrs. Archer, "but I never served bad sherry to my guest. We are of two different worlds, Madam."

"Didn't I tell you?" Mrs. Corn was saying. "Haven't I kept telling you all along?"

Mrs. Archer, her eyes on Kathy, made a tentative motion of pushing the old man through the door, but he forestalled her.

" 'Come dance with me in Ireland.' " he said. Supporting himself against the wall, he reached the outer door and opened it. " 'And time runs on.' " he said.

3. imbibed: a slightly elegant word for "drunk."

QUESTIONS FOR DISCUSSION AND WRITING

1. How do the ladies react when the old man collapses? What is shown by these remarks?: *Mrs. Corn:* "He's drunk." *Mrs. Archer:* "Watch out for the baby."
2. How do the ladies react after they have the old man seated in the chair? Why does the old man say (Page 238), "*I can afford to take chances,*" and on the same page "*I would rather not trouble you*"? What remarks of the ladies show that they are feeling very self-satisfied and superior?

3. What does it show when Mrs. Archer spread the paper bag on the table? Why did Miss Valentine call the old man *John*?
4. What actions does the old man perform that show that he thoroughly despises the helpful ladies? Why does he quote the poet Yeats? What does he mean when he says, "We are of two different worlds, Madam"? What is his attitude toward himself? Why is this surprising to the ladies?
5. What effect has the experience had on the three ladies, do you think? What would you say is the theme, or main idea, of the story?

SUGGESTION FOR FURTHER WRITING OR DISCUSSION

Two of the most difficult things in the world to do are to give help so that it is acceptable, or to receive help without resentment. Tell an experience, or write a story, about giving or receiving help, trying to show the feelings of the helpers and the helped.

Author and Title Index